Phil … tiæ

philosophie

Studien zur Wissenschaftsgeschichte und Philosophie

Studies in History of Sciences and Philosophy

Archives Henri-Poincaré –
Philosophie et Recherches sur les Sciences et les Technologies
Université de Lorraine – Université de Strasbourg
UMR 7117 CNRS

L'analyse dans les mathématiques grecques

Édité par Gianluca Longa &
Sébastien Gandon

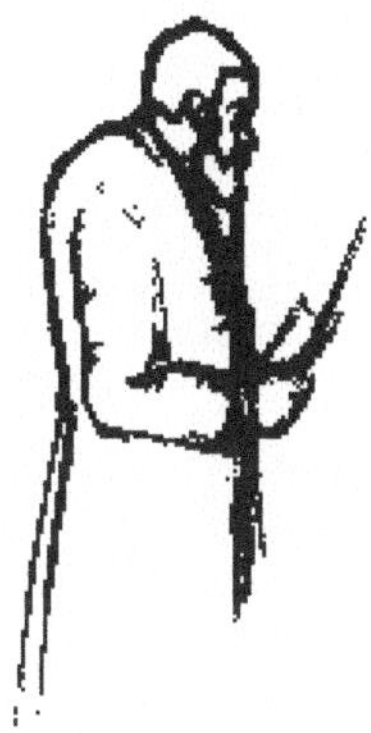

2021
Vol. 25 Cahier 3
Revue soutenue par l'Université de Lorraine,
l'Institut des Sciences Humaines et Sociales du CNRS,
le FNSO et le Centre National du Livre

Philosophia Scientiæ

Travaux d'histoire des sciences et de philosophie
Studien zur Wissenschaftsgeschichte und Philosophie
Studies in History of Sciences and Philosophy

Adresse de la rédaction
Archives H.-Poincaré -- PReST
Université de Lorraine
91, avenue de la Libération - BP 454
54001 NANCY Cedex
Tél : 33/3 72 74 15 75
phscientiae-redac@univ-lorraine.fr

Philosophia Scientiæ est une revue scientifique à comité de lecture qui publie des travaux originaux en épistémologie, en histoire et en philosophie des sciences, en philosophie analytique. Ouverte aux travaux portant sur l'ensemble des disciplines scientifiques, elle accueille notamment des études traitant de la logique, des mathématiques et de la physique. L'un des thèmes forts de la revue porte sur les contributions allemandes ou franco-allemandes à l'épistémologie et à l'histoire des sciences. Il paraît trois numéros par an, consacrés à des travaux de recherche ou à l'oeuvre d'auteurs passés ou contemporains. Des dossiers thématiques sont également publiés, sous la responsabilité d'éditeurs invités, à la suite d'appels à contribution.
Philosophia Scientiæ est disponible en libre accès intégral et immédiat sur les plateformes OpenEdition et Cairn. Ses archives sont disponibles sur Numdam. Ce projet est financé avec le soutien du Fonds National pour la Science Ouverte (projet PhSc-SO-2020).
La revue est référencée par plusieurs bases de données internationales (Philosopher's Index, Scopus, Zentralblatt MATH, MathSciNet, le Répertoire International de la Philosophie et l'ERIH).
Site web de la revue : https://journals.openedition.org/philosophiascientiae/

ISSN 1281-2463

L'analyse dans les mathématiques grecques

Préface

Gianluca Longa
PHIER, Université Clermont Auvergne (France)

Sébastien Gandon
PHIER, Université Clermont Auvergne (France)

Plutarque nous raconte [*VP* I.1, 12.4.4–5] que le grand Varron s'adressa un jour à un certain Tarutius, connu pour ses talents de mathématicien et d'astrologue, pour déterminer le jour et l'heure de la naissance de Romulus « de la même manière que l'on tire l'analyse des problèmes géométriques » [ὥσπερ αἱ τῶν γεωμετρικῶν ὑφηγοῦνται προβλημάτων ἀναλύσεις]. Or, puisque dans la science astrologique ancienne on pouvait prédire, en prenant le jour et l'heure de la naissance d'un homme, ce que lui réserverait sa vie, et, inversement, en prenant les événements de sa vie, en déduire le jour et l'heure de sa naissance, Tarutius put, en rassemblant les événements de la vie de Romulus, comment il mourut, etc., déterminer avec certitude, par voie d'analyse, non seulement le jour et l'heure de sa naissance (« le 21 du mois Thoth, vers le lever du soleil »), mais aussi la date et l'heure exactes de sa conception (à l'évidence, « le 23 du mois égyptien Chœac, à la troisième heure du jour, pendant une éclipse totale de soleil »). À l'époque à laquelle Plutarque écrit, Clément d'Alexandrie, théologien, apologète et père de l'Église (mais hélas pas un grand mathématicien), chercha à expliciter en quoi consistait la méthode de division et de définition dans le domaine de la dialectique en la mettant en rapport de similitude avec la méthode géométrique d'analyse et synthèse [*Strom.* VIII, 6.18.4]. Quelques siècles plus tôt, chez Platon, nous retrouvons la même attitude : bien qu'il n'utilise jamais explicitement le mot « analyse », il tente d'expliquer en quoi consiste sa dialectique en se référant à la procédure d'analyse et de synthèse pratiquée par les géomètres [*Resp.* 509d–511e]. De même, Aristote [*EN* III, 1112b11-24] nous apprend ce qu'il faut entendre par « délibération » en établissant une analogie entre l'activité de la personne qui délibère et l'activité de recherche par analyse propre aux géomètres [ὁ γὰρ βουλευόμενος ἔοικε ζητεῖν καὶ ἀναλύειν τὸν εἰρημένον τρόπον ὥσπερ διάγραμμα].

Ces références rapidement esquissées nous montrent que, pendant une certaine période de l'Antiquité, l'analyse géométrique était une notion considérée comme connue, au moins vaguement, dans divers domaines du savoir et sur laquelle il était possible de prendre appui. Cet usage s'est ensuite perdu et, au moins depuis Pappus d'Alexandrie (IVe siècle après J.C.) et sa célèbre description de la méthode d'analyse et de synthèse [*Coll.* VII.1–3], un questionnement sur le sens et la portée de l'analyse géométrique ancienne a alors émergé, qui refait périodiquement surface dans l'histoire de la pensée occidentale.

On trouve ainsi chez les mathématiciens arabes de nombreux efforts pour comprendre la nature de l'analyse ancienne. Ibn al-Haytham, par exemple, consacre deux de ses plus importants ouvrages (*L'Analyse et la Synthèse* et *Les Connus*) à l'analyse géométrique. Quelques siècles plus tard, en Occident, dans la longue tradition qui va de Viète à Leibniz, en passant par Descartes, Galilée et Newton, nous trouvons un effort important pour comprendre ce qu'était l'analyse géométrique ancienne et pour en faire un des piliers fondamentaux de la nouvelle pensée scientifique naissante.

Avec le développement des mathématiques dites modernes, le problème de l'analyse a progressivement perdu de son intérêt auprès des mathématiciens et est devenu un domaine d'investigation historique et philosophique. Montucla [1758] d'abord et Hankel [1874] ensuite, ont jeté les bases de ce que l'on pourrait appeler l'interprétation traditionnelle de l'analyse géométrique ancienne. Elle a été critiquée et révisée, au cours du vingtième siècle, sous divers aspects (historique, philologique, philosophique) et plusieurs nouvelles interprétations ont été proposées. Les résultats de ces recherches n'ont toutefois pas permis de dégager une vision unifiée. Ainsi, aujourd'hui encore, on ne peut pas dire qu'il existe une interprétation commune de l'analyse géométrique ancienne, de son fonctionnement et de sa signification : quel est le but de l'application de la méthode analytique ? L'analyse géométrique a-t-elle un caractère heuristique ou apodictique ? Quel est le rapport entre analyse géométrique et démonstration par l'absurde ? Quelle est la relation entre la forme ancienne de l'analyse et son aboutissement moderne (son emploi, par exemple, chez Viète et Descartes) ?

Ce dossier a pour ambition de faire un bilan de l'état actuel de certaines de ces questions. On y trouvera une partie des contributions au colloque *Greek Geometrical Analysis. Problems and Prospects* qui s'est tenu à Clermont-Ferrand du 4 au 6 mars 2020 et auquel ont participé certains des plus importants spécialistes de l'histoire des mathématiques grecques anciennes.

Nous tenons à remercier toutes les personnes qui ont aidé à la réalisation de ce dossier, parmi lesquelles Alain Bernard, Leo Corry, Micheline Decorps-Foulquier, Olivier Dubouclez, Vincent Gérard, David Rabouin, Benoît Timmermans et Roy Wagner. Nous remercions tout particulièrement Nathan Sidoli et Marco Panza pour leur aide précieuse.

Bibliographie

HANKEL, Hermann [1874], *Zur Geschichte der Mathematik in Alterthum und Mittelalter*, Leipzig : Teubner.

MONTUCLA, Jean-Étienne [1758], *Histoire des mathématiques, dans laquelle on rend compte de leurs progrès depuis leur origine jusqu'à nos jours [...]*, Paris : Jombert, 4 vol., rééd. citée de la seconde édition (Paris, H. Agasse, 1799) : Paris, A. Blanchard, 1968.

Aristotle and Greek Geometrical Analysis

Enrico Berti
University of Padua

Translated by Gianluca Longa[1]

Résumé : Cet article vise à montrer dans quelle mesure l'examen de certains passages de l'œuvre d'Aristote peut contribuer à la résolution d'importants problèmes liés à l'interprétation de l'analyse géométrique ancienne. Nous nous concentrons notamment sur le célèbre passage des *Seconds Analytiques* dans lequel Aristote se réfère de manière apparemment cryptique à l'analyse pratiquée par les géomètres (*Seconds Analytiques*, livre I, chapitre 12) et nous montrons l'importance fondamentale de ce passage pour une compréhension correcte de l'analyse géométrique ancienne.

Abstract: This paper aims to show that an examination of some passages in Aristotle's work can contribute to the resolution of crucial problems related to the interpretation of ancient geometrical analysis. In this context, we will focus in particular on the famous passage of the *Posterior Analytics* in which Aristotle cryptically refers to the analysis practised by the geometers (*Posterior Analytics*, book I, chapter 12) and we will show the fundamental importance of this passage for a correct understanding of ancient geometrical analysis.

In an appendix of the Book XIII of Euclid's *Elements*, before some alternative demonstrations of propositions 1–5 of the same book [*EE* IV,

1. This article was originally published in Italian as "Aristotele e l'analisi matematica greca", in A. Repola Boatto (ed.), *Filosofia, logica, matematica dal periodo classico al nostro secolo*, Quaderni di "Innovazione scuola", 1994, pp. 41–53 (reprinted in E. Berti, *Nuovi studi aristotelici*, vol. 1 : Epistemologia, logica e dialettica, Morcelliana, Brescia, pp. 113–125). We would like to thank both the author and the publisher for the permission to publish the translation of the article in this volume.

364.18–376.22], we find the oldest surviving description of the mathematical procedures of analysis and synthesis:

> ἀνάλυσις μὲν οὖν ἐστι λῆψις τοῦ ζητουμένου ὡς ὁμολογουμένου διὰ τῶν ἀκολούθων ἐπί τι ἀληθὲς ὁμολογούμενον. σύνθεσις δὲ λῆψις τοῦ ὁμολογουμένου διὰ τῶν ἀκολούθων ἐπί τὴν τοῦ ζητουμένου κατάληξιν ἤτοι κατάληψιν.
>
> Analysis is the assumption of what is sought, as if admitted, through the consequences, up to something admitted as true. And synthesis is the assumption of what is admitted, through the consequences, up to the ending up or apprehension of what is sought.[1]

This description has raised at least four problems, the first of which involves its text. The version reported here, being the most intelligible, is in fact transcribed only in some medieval manuscripts—the *Bodleianus scr.* 888 (siglum **B**), the *Vindobonensis XXXI* 13 (siglum **V**), the *Bononiensis* (siglum **b**) and the *Parisinius Gr.* 2344 (siglum **q**). Though the English translator of the *Elements*, Th. L. Heath, considered it as authentic [Heath 1908, III, 442], there exists a variant, in a 9th century manuscript—the *Vaticanus Gr.* 190 (siglum **P**)—in which the definition of the analysis is the same, whereas the one of the synthesis is different:

> σύνθεσις δὲ λῆψις τοῦ ὁμολογουμένου διὰ τῶν ἀκολούθων ἐπί τι ἀληθὲς ὁμολογούμενον.
>
> And synthesis is the assumption of what is admitted, through the consequences, *up to something admitted as true.*

This variant was preferred by the first modern editor of the *Elements*, J. L. Heiberg [*EE* IV, 366.2]. Therein, the final part of the definition of the synthesis is identical with the final part of that of the analysis, which is seemingly inexplicable. As known, we dispose of two versions of Euclid's *Elements*, one edited by Theon of Alexandria in the 4th century AD, and an older one. **P** reports the latter, while **B**, **V**, **b**, and **q** reproduce the Theonine version [Heiberg 1903, 46]. The variant in **P**, which indeed raises difficulties, is therefore the oldest, while the text presented in **B** and **V** seems to be more like a revision done to make sense of the definition of the synthesis; it reflects, probably, a rewriting of Theon himself. According to Heiberg, however, the whole appendix in question—the two definitions and the alternative proofs of the first five propositions of Book XIII—represents an interpolation, being completely extraneous to the way of exposition of the *Elements.*[2] According to him, the appendix might have been initially in the margin, in the

1. Classical quotations are directly translated from Greek into English. [Translator's note]

2. "Nam hoc totum interpolatum esse, certissimum est, quippe quod toto genere a ratione institutoque Elementorum abhorreat" [*EE* V, LXXXIV].

form of a scholium, as allegedly confirmed by the fact that, even in **V**, only its first part is placed in the main text, while the remaining is transcribed in the margin [*EE* V, LXXXIV].

The second problem concerns the origins of the two definitions. Bretschneider [1870, 167–169], by relying on Proclus's passage stating that Eudoxus "multiplied the number of propositions concerning the 'section' [περὶ τὴν τομὴν] which had their origin in Plato, employing the method of analysis for their solution" [*iEE*, 67.6–8], argued that they date back to Eudoxus of Cnidus, a contemporary and collaborator of Plato, author of many of the doctrines contained in the *Elements*. At first, Heiberg endorsed this thesis, indicating as possible authors of the definitions, either Eudoxus or Theaetetus, the mathematician contemporary of Plato after whom the homonymous dialogue is named. He then modified this view, after the publication of the commentary by al-Nairīzī (who lived around AD 900) on the first ten books of the *Elements* in the Medieval Latin translation by Gerard of Cremona. In this text, we find several quotations from the lost commentary of Heron of Alexandria (1st century AD) on the *Elements*, one of which reports two definitions of analysis and synthesis:

> Dissolutio autem est, <ut>, qualibet questione proposita, primo ponamus illud in ordine rei quesite, que est inventa, deinde reducemus <ad illam)>, cuius probatio iam precessit. Tunc ergo manifestum dicimus, quod iam inventa est res quesita secundum dissolutionem. Compositio vero est, ut incipiamus a re nota, deinde conponemus, donec res quesita inveniantur. Ergo tunc res quesita iam erit manifesta secundum compositionem.
>
> Now analysis is when, to any question proposed, we first set it in the order of the thing sought, which has been found, then we reduce it to something whose proof has already preceded. Then it is manifest that the thing sought was found according to the analysis.
>
> And synthesis is, when we begin from a thing known, then we compose, until the thing sought is found. Thus the thing sought is manifest by synthesis.[3] [al-Nairīzī 1899, 89.6–20]

Heiberg deemed this text very similar to that of the *Elements* [Heiberg 1903, 58–59] and concluded, followed then by several other scholars,[4] that both definitions were to be ascribed to Heron. As shown in [Berti 1984, 93–127], the similarities detected by Heiberg are not so striking to induce to consider

3. This text should be compared with the scholium n. 82 of book XIII of Euclid's *Elements* [*EE* V, 675.12–18]: "τί ἐστι τὸ κατὰ ἀνάλυσιν; ὅταν προβλήματος δοθέντος λάβῃ τις τὸ ὡς εὑρημένον καὶ ἀναλύσῃ ἐπί τι γνώριμον τῶν ζητούμενον προαποδεδειγμένων, καὶ ἤδη, λελύσθαι λέγεται τότε εὕρῃ πρόβλημα ἀνάλυσιν: Τί ἐστι τὸ κατὰ σύνθεσιν; ὅταν τις ἀπὸ τῶν γνωρίμων ἀρξάμενος καὶ συνθεὶς εὕρηται τὸ ζητούμενον." [*T. N.*]

4. [Heath 1908, III, 442], [Mugler 1948, 297], [Hintikka & Remes 1974, 30, n. 4].

Heron as the author of the two definitions. After all, the teaching of analysis in Antiquity was commonly attributed to Plato, as witnessed by the *Index of Academic Philosophers* [Mekler 1902, 17], Diogenes Laertius [*VP* III, 24], and Proclus [*iEE*, 211.21–22].[5] However, the problem of establishing whether the definitions of analysis and synthesis are pre-Euclidean or post-Euclidean remains unsolved.

The third problem, related to that of the origin of the two definitions, is about the "direction" of analysis. It was first raised by F. M. Cornford [Cornford 1932, 37–52 and 173–190], who claimed that analysis and synthesis should be identified with the two procedures described by Plato in the Books VI and VII of the *Republic*, one that goes up from the "hypotheses" to the "unhypothetical principle", called "upward movement", and the one that goes down from the unhypothetical principle, i.e., from the idea of good, to the other ideas, called "downward movement". Against this argument, R. Robinson observed that the "upward movement" described in the *Republic* is presented by Plato as a dialectical procedure, not as a mathematical one, and that analysis, in all the extant definitions, is always described as a procedure passing through "consequences" (ἀκόλουθα in Greek), that is, as a "downward movement" [Robinson 1936, 464–473]. According to Robinson, the difference between analysis and synthesis, is not in the direction, which is always the same, i.e., "downward", but in the fact that analysis starts from a sought proposition, taken as a hypothesis, and deduces a *known* proposition as a consequence, whereas synthesis starts from known propositions and deduces a *sought* proposition as a consequence. The problem is complicated by the fact that, in the definitions of analysis and synthesis proposed by Pappus of Alexandria [*PAC* II, 634–636]—who greatly influenced some of the most important early-modern philosophers like, for instance, Galilei and Descartes—there are some clues in favour of the "downward" interpretation and others in favour of the "upward" interpretation. This has led some scholars to suppose that Pappus description is contradictory [Gulley 1958, 1–14], and others to condemn as spurious the passage in favour of the "upward" interpretation [Mahoney 1968, 319-348]. Others again[6] have denied that the Greek term ἀκόλουθα means "consequences" and stated that it'd rather mean "concomitants", so it can denote both an "upward" and a "downward" reasoning.

The last problem, raised by Hintikka & Remes [1974, 31–40], concerns the question of whether analysis applies to propositions or figures. In geometry, the "constructive" meaning of analysis—that concerning figures and, more specifically, the finding of auxiliary constructions—is in fact the most important. Nevertheless, the expression "something admitted as true"

5. Heath [1921, 290–291], moreover, like others before and after him, like [Tannery 1915, 162–169], [Milhaud 1934, 175–176], and [Cambiano 1967, 115–149], endorsed the thesis that geometrical analysis was already practised, before Plato, by the Pythagoreans and by Hippocrates of Chios (5th century BC).

6. [Hintikka & Remes 1974, 7–21], [Szabó 1974, 118–130].

[τι ἀληθὲς ὁμολογούμενον], used in the Euclidean definition to indicate the point of completion of the analysis, seems to refer more to a proposition than to a figure.

1 Aristotle's clarifications on analysis

A decisive contribution to the solution of the four problems outlined above might be gained from a passage devoted to geometrical analysis contained in Aristotle's *Posterior Analytics* [78a6–12]:

> εἰ δ' ἦν ἀδύνατον ἐκ ψεύδους ἀληθὲς δεῖξαι, ῥᾴδιον ἂν ἦν τὸ ἀναλύειν· ἀντέστρεφε γὰρ ἂν ἐξ ἀνάγκης. ἔστω γὰρ τὸ *A* ὄν· τούτου δ' ὄντος ταδὶ ἔστιν, ἃ οἶδα ὅτι ἔστιν, οἷον τὸ *B*. ἐκ τούτων ἄρα δείξω ὅτι ἔστιν ἐκεῖνο. ἀντιστρέφει δὲ μᾶλλον τὰ ἐν τοῖς μαθήμασιν, ὅτι οὐδὲν συμβεβηκὸς λαμβάνουσιν (ἀλλὰ καὶ τούτῳ διαφέρουσι τῶν ἐν τοῖς διαλόγοις) ἀλλ' ὁρισμούς.
>
> If it were impossible to prove truth from falsehood, then analysis would be easy; for [propositions] would necessarily convert. Let *A* be true: if this is true, then these things, for instance *B*, are true—things which, in fact, I know to be true. From the latter, then, I will prove that the former is true. Now, mathematical [propositions] convert more often, because they do not assume accidents—even in this they differ from those in the discussions—but definitions.

The sentence opening this passage is clearly an unreal conditional: according to Aristotle, it is possible to demonstrate the truth from the false, just as it is possible to prove the truth from the truth and the false from the false. The only impossibility is that of proving the false from the truth [*An. Pr.* I, 2-4]. Hence, analysis is generally "difficult". But let us follow Aristotle's reasoning and sketch what would happen if—an unreal hypothesis—it were impossible to prove the truth from the false, that is, if the truth could only be proved from the truth. In this case, analysis would be easy because "[propositions] would necessarily convert" [ἀντέστρεφε γὰρ ἂν ἐξ ἀνάχς]. Indeed, the convertibility of a proposition consists in the possibility of exchanging the subject and the predicate, without affecting the truth-value of the proposition itself. When this happens, Aristotle observes that it is not only possible, starting from a proposition *A* to prove a proposition *B*, but also to prove *A* starting from *B*. In other words, the convertibility ensures the reversibility of the passage from premises to the conclusion and from the conclusion to premises, as it would happen if it were impossible to prove the truth from the false, i.e., if the truth could only be proved from the truth.

To illustrate this point, we can imagine the following syllogism:

"A is B"

"B is C"

$\therefore$ "A is C"

If the proposition "B is C" is true and convertible, then we can plainly say that "C is B" is also a true proposition. This allows us to set a syllogism in the opposite direction, by taking "A is C" as a premise and obtaining "A is B" as a conclusion:

"A is C"

"C is B"

$\therefore$ "A is B"

In such a case, we are not only able to prove the conclusion from the premises, but we can also prove one of the premises from the conclusion and the other premise, once converted. In this way, we obtain a situation in which, according to Aristotle, analysis is easy.

If we apply this observation to the Euclidean definitions of analysis and synthesis, we can readily see that the propositions denoted by A and B in Aristotle's text correspond respectively to the expressions "that which is sought" and "something admitted as true" in the Euclidean definition of analysis. Thus, the sense of Aristotle's remark is the following: if it were impossible to prove the true from the false, the propositions could necessarily be converted. This means that, once proved B from A by analysis, one's can straightforwardly prove A from B by the synthesis. In such a situation, analysis is easy insofar as it permits to achieve those true propositions that, by synthesis, prove what is being sought. Aristotle remarks then that "propositions in mathematics convert more often because they do not assume accidents [...] but definitions" [ἀντιστρέφει δὲ μᾶλλον τὰ ἐν τοῖς μαθήμασιν, ὅτι οὐδὲν συμβεβηκὸς λαμβάνουσιν [...] ἀλλ᾽ὁρισμούς]. With these words, he indicates in which cases propositions are convertible and in which they are not. Definitions are always convertible because there is a perfect identity between the subject and the predicate in them, which can therefore be exchanged without any alteration of the truth-value of the proposition obtained by conversion. On the other hand, propositions consisting in the assumption of an accident are not convertible because in them, there is no identity between the subject and the predicate and their conjunction is entirely contingent. Propositions used in mathematics are usually definitions, in which there is an identity between subject and predicate, or equations, and in fact mathematicians use the algebraic sign of equality (=) instead of the copula "is", or propositions which indicate a property of the subject, a predicate which necessarily belongs to it, and not an accident. Therefore, mathematical propositions are usually convertible. But this is not always the case. Even in mathematics, there may be propositions that cannot be converted, and for this reason analysis may be difficult [*Soph. El.* 175a 25–27]:

> συμβαίνει δέ ποτε καθάπερ ἐν τοῖς διαγράμμασιν· καὶ γὰρ ἐκεῖ ἀναλύσαντες ἐνίοτε συνθεῖναι πάλιν ἀδυνατοῦμεν·
>
> At times, it happens in geometrical propositions: there too, after doing the analysis, we are sometimes unable to synthesise back.

Since, in mathematics, propositions are not always convertible, analysis may fail in its purpose. It is nevertheless clear that propositions are convertible "especially" in mathematics, and that analysis is therefore especially easy in this discipline.

In the passage from the *Posterior Analytics* quoted above, Aristotle makes a further observation: the fact of assuming definitions and not accidents is one of the differences between mathematics and "discussions" [διάλογοι]. With the latter expression, Aristotle indicates the whole field of the non-mathematical discussions, governed by the technique he calls "dialectics", which is sometimes used by him also in particular non-mathematical disciplines, such as physics and ethics. Analysis can also be used in these fields, but it is not equally easy to handle, since it is not as reliable as it is in mathematics. Aristotle provides two examples of the use of analysis in non-mathematical fields. The first concerns physics and, in particular, the notion of "hypothetical necessity" existing in the natural world, once this is conceived as a finalistic order. In this realm, as Aristotle states there is only a hypothetical necessity: if an end happens, the means must also happen, but on the contrary, if a means happens, the end does not necessarily happen. For example, if the house is the end and the bricks are the means, we can say that, if there is a house, bricks must also be there. On the other hand, we cannot say that if there are bricks, there *must* be a house [*Phys.* II.9, 200a 5–30]. Here we are dealing with a relation that is necessary only in one direction that which goes from the end to a means, exactly as it happens in analysis, when it takes place between non-convertible propositions. Therefore, we may say that once the end is known, the search for the means is a procedure of analysis. This is not necessarily followed by a synthesis, i.e., by a demonstration of the end based on the means. Aristotle does not explicitly mention analysis here, but the process he describes, as noted by various scholars[7], corresponds perfectly to it.

The second example deals again with the relationship between the end and the means in the domain of ethics, and more precisely in the analysis of human action. It is exposed in the comparison made between "deliberation" [βούλευσις] and geometrical analysis in the *Nicomachean Ethics* [III.3, 1112a 18–28]:

> ὁ γάρ βουλευόμενος ἔοικε ζητεῖν καὶ ἀναλύειν τὸν εἰρημένον τρόπον ὥσπερ διάγραμμα.

7. [Mugler 1948, 331–351], [Gulley 1958, 8], [Heath 1949, 100–101].

> [The person] who deliberates seems to inquire and analyse in the way described, as though with a geometrical proposition.

For Aristotle, deliberation is not about ends, but about the means necessary to achieve them: in deliberation the end is presupposed, just as "what is sought" is presupposed in geometrical analysis. Means make possible to realise the end, just as in analysis the "consequences" are what enable to demonstrate what is sought. The mean found at the end is the first cause as in analysis the true principle reached at the end is the premise from which it is possible to prove the consequences up to what is sought. Here the procedure of analysis is explicitly mentioned, always in connection with a relation necessary only in one direction.

In physics and ethics, therefore, it is possible to use analysis. Nevertheless, here analysis is not always reliable. Both deal in fact with connections that are not necessarily in both directions, but, in the case of the natural world, apply only "for the most part" and, in the case of ethics, concern "things that can also be otherwise", i.e., that depend on human freedom. In mathematics, on the other hand, the consequences of a premise "always" occur when connections are necessarily in both directions. Therefore, in this context, analysis is usually reliable.

2 Aristotle's observations and the Euclidean definitions

In the aforementioned passages, as we have seen, Aristotle reveals a keen awareness of the *modus operandi* and import of geometrical analysis, partially disproving the common saying, dating back to Galileo [Galileo Galilei 1842, I, 302], whereby Aristotle was *parum in geometria [...] versatus* [little versed in geometry]. As T. L. Heath has argued[8] although Aristotle did not make any personal contribution to the development of mathematics, he had a broad knowledge of the mathematics of his time, viz. the mathematics practised in Plato's Academy and later systematised in Euclid's *Elements.* It might be added that Aristotle regarded mathematics as a discipline already brought to excellence within the Academy—where he himself lived for twenty years—to

8. "Aristotle was evidently not a mathematician by profession, but he was abreast of the knowledge of his day [...] He was aware of the important discoveries of Eudoxus which affected profoundly the exposition of the *Elements* by Euclid. One allusion clearly shows that Aristotle knew of Eudoxus' great Theory of Proportion which was expanded by Euclid in his Book V, and recognized the importance of it. Another passage recalls the fundamental assumption on which Eudoxus based his "method of exhaustion" for measuring areas and volumes; and, of course, Aristotle was familiar with the system of concentric spheres by which Eudoxus and Callippus accounted theoretically for the independent motions of the sun, moon, and planets" [Heath 1949, 1–2].

the extent of taking it as a model, especially in the *Posterior Analytics.* But the passages examined above also represent a major contribution to the solution of the issues raised by the Euclidean definitions of analysis and synthesis.

They provide an immediate answer to the two—so to speak—less interesting problems, that of establishing whether the two definitions are pre- or post-Euclidean, and that of determining if they involve propositions or figures. There is no doubt, in fact, that Aristotle speaks of geometrical analysis as a known procedure, fitting perfectly with the Euclidean definitions. Trying to date the latter becomes, therefore, completely uninteresting. However, I would not go so far as Arpád Szábo [Szabó 1953, 378–389] and [Szabó 1974] and attribute the discovery of analysis to the Eleates, claiming its derivation from Zeno's *reductio ad absurdum.* It is certainly true that analysis, when it deduces a false consequence from a certain hypothesis, falsifies that hypothesis, but it is not equally true that the Eleatic's arguments, especially Zeno's famous paradoxes, are *reductio ad absurdum.* They are indeed dialectical demonstrations, as noted by Plato, who presents Zeno as a dialectician in the *Parmenides*, and by Aristotle, who referred to Zeno as the "inventor" of dialectics in his lost dialogue entitled the *Sophist.* In geometry, the derivation of the absurdity of a conclusion results from its contradiction with other premises, so that, in this context, *reductio ad absurdum* are always convertible to direct demonstrations. In dialectical demonstrations, as those attributed to Zeno, the absurdity of a conclusion results, instead, from its contradiction with itself and it does not need to refer to other premises [Berti 1987]. There is no doubt, moreover, that the procedure of analysis described by Aristotle in the *Posterior Analytics* concerns propositions, not figures. Only with regard to the formers, it is meaningful to speak of convertibility. This does not affect the fact that an analysis by means of figures also existed, consisting in the search for the solution of a problem by means of the construction of appropriate figures. This was also well known to Aristotle, as it is evident from two passages quoted above.

However, the problem of the "direction" of analysis is more interesting, i.e., whether it is a "way up" or a "way down". A fundamental contribution to the solution of this question is given by the *Posterior Analytics*, which probably also helps to solve the first problem raised by the Euclidean definitions, that of the text.

The example given by Aristotle—in which it is impossible to prove the truth from the false and in which, consequently, all propositions are necessarily convertible—shows how the procedure followed by analysis is exactly the same to that followed by synthesis, which consists in the passage from premises to conclusions that follow necessarily from them (and it is generally called "deduction"). This is why analysis is reliable in mathematics and not in "discussions": exactly because it performs the same kind of deduction performed by the synthesis. When the propositions employed are convertible, it is possible to provide the same reasoning in both directions, without the risk of failing the proof. When, on the other hand, the propositions are not convertible, analysis can fail—it may take a course that cannot be provided in the opposite direction by the synthesis. Therefore, it may fail in its objective of finding the proof of a certain hypothesis.

At this point, it is no longer important to establish whether analysis is a "way up" or a "way down", since it is identical in its process to synthesis. We may say that it is a "way up"—as its very name indicates[9]—because it looks for principles, and principles are generally supposed to be higher than what comes from them.

On the other hand, the procedure applied by analysis is a deduction, which is a "way down", in the same way as synthetic reasoning. Hence, analysis and synthesis are simply two opposite directions along which the same process can be followed. Yet, the legitimacy of analysis, i.e., the certainty that it follows a process that can also be followed in the opposite direction, is conditioned by the fact that the propositions of which it is composed must be convertible.

This condition occurs above all in mathematics because there, most often, there is no difference regarding the type of process, between analysis and synthesis, in the sense that both are deductions of necessary consequences, i.e., "ways down". In other fields, however, like the discussions concerning everyday life, or the disciplines not reducible to mathematics, like physics (as understood by Aristotle) and ethics, the above-mentioned condition does not exist. Analysis, in these contexts, is not entirely reliable since it does not have the character of necessity that is required by synthesis and, thus, it can be considered as a "way up". This reasoning may also explain the discrepancy between the two definitions of analysis in manuscript tradition. The older text, reported in **P**, makes no distinction between the procedure of analysis and that of synthesis, probably because, belonging to a mathematical context, it refers to the use of analysis and synthesis between convertible propositions, which is frequent especially in mathematics, as we have seen. The more recent text reported by the other manuscripts makes instead a distinction between the two procedures, and it is due, probably, to a correction suggested by the possibility of using analysis between non-convertible propositions as well.

A further confirmation of the different meanings of analysis, depending on whether it is applied to convertible or non-convertible propositions, can be found in Pappus's description of analysis [*PAC* II, 634.11–636.14]. In the first part he says that in the analysis, once the sought-after is posited as granted, one looks for "that from which it derives" and "then again for the antecedent of that", until one arrives at something which "in order is a principle" [ἢ τάξιν ἀρχῆς]. This clearly alludes to analysis conceived as a "way up", not to geometrical analysis in particular.

In the second part of Pappus's description, however, there is an account of analysis that is more specifically mathematical, or geometrical. It distinguishes between analysis of a theorematic type, consisting in the search for the

9. For ἀνά means "up" and λύσις means "solution".

principles from which a theorem can be proved, and analysis of a problematic type, consisting in the search for the solution of a problem. Here Pappus refers to analysis that takes place in conditions of convertibility,[10] that is, analysis conceived as a "way down", which is the one actually practised in the rest of his work. With regard to the first part of Pappus's illustration of analysis, it is worth noting a detail that may have had some importance for the history of philosophy. The Renaissance Latin translation of Pappus's work, carried out by Federico Comandino in 1589, at the very point where the Greek text says that analysis, once the sought-after is posited as granted, seeks "that from which it derives", renders this expression as *quid ex hoc contingat*, which means "what derives from this". While the Greek text speaks of the search for antecedents, and therefore understands analysis as "the way up", the Renaissance translation speaks of the search for consequents, and therefore understands analysis as "the way down".

It is impossible to determine whether the translator had a different text from the one at our disposal, or whether he corrected the text on his own initiative. At any rate, it is safe to say that modern philosophers, from Galilei to Descartes, who read Pappus's text in Latin translation, were forced to understand it as the way down, that is, as a procedure applicable to convertible propositions. This may have contributed, for example, to lead Descartes, who considered analysis as the philosophical procedure *par excellence*, to conceive the creation as ordered in a deterministic way, i.e., based on necessary connections in both senses, and to expose Galilei, who considered analysis (which he called the "resolutive method") as *the* procedure of physical sciences [Berti 1983a], to some serious misunderstandings of his worldview.

The lack of distinction between the two types of analysis, one between convertible propositions and one between non-convertible propositions, may in fact have contributed to Galilei's condemnation. His demonstration of the motion of the earth (true conclusion) from the tides phenomenon (false premise or explanation) gave to Urban VIII the impression of limiting divine omnipotence, attributing to the cosmic order a character of absolute necessity, such as is found only in mathematical processes, where it is impossible to demonstrate the true from the false [Berti 1983b]. If this is true, it will be a further confirmation of the importance of Aristotle's clarifications.

Abbreviations

EE: *Euclidis Elementa.* 5 vol. Leipzig: B. G. Teubner, 1969-1977.

iEE: *Procli Diadochi in primum Euclidis Elementorum librum commentarii.* Leipzig: B. G. Teubner 1873.

10. And, in fact, Pappus [*PAC* II, 636.5] use the expression "and proof is the converse of the analysis" [καὶ ἡ ἀπόδειξις ἀντίστροφος τῇ ἀναλύσει].

PAC: *Pappi Alexandrini Collectionis quae supersunt, e libris manu scriptis edidit latina interpretatione et commentariis instruxit F. Hultsch.* 3 vol. Berlin: Weidmann 1876–1878.

Bibliography

AL-NAIRĪZĪ [1899], *Anaritii in decem libros priores Elementorum Euclidis commentarii. Ex interpretatione Gherardi Cremonensis in codice Cracoviensi 569 servata*, Leipzig: B. G. Teubner, edidit M. Curtze; supplementum ad *Euclidis Opera Omnia*, ediderunt I. L. Heiberg et H. Menge. Leipzig, B. G. Teubner 1883-1916.

BERTI, Enrico [1983a], Differenza tra il metodo risolutivo degli aristotelici e la "resolutio" dei matematici, in: *Aristotelismo veneto e scienza moderna*, edited by L. Olivieri, Padova: Antenore, vol. 1, 435–457.

—— [1983b], Implicazioni filosofiche della condanna di Galilei, *Giornale di metafisica*, 5, 239–261.

—— [1984], L'analisi geometrica della tradizione euclidea e l'analitica di Aristotele, in: *La scienza ellenistica*, edited by G. Giannantoni & M. Vegetti, Naples: Bibliopolis, 93–127.

—— [1987], *Contraddizione e dialettica negli antichi e nei moderni*, Palermo: L'epos.

BRETSCHNEIDER, Carl Anton [1870], *Die Geometrie und die Geometer vor Eukleides. Ein historischer Versuch*, Leipzig: B. G. Teubner.

CAMBIANO, Giuseppe [1967], Il metodo ipotetico e le origini della sistemazione Euclidea della geometria, *Rivista di filosofia*, 58, 115–149.

CORNFORD, Francis M. [1932], Mathematics and Dialectic in the Republic VI.-VII.(I.), *Mind*, XLI(161), 37–52, doi: 10.1093/mind/XLI.161.37.

GALILEO GALILEI [1842], *Le Opere di Galileo Galilei, prima edizione completa condotta sugli autentici manoscritti palatini e dedicata a S. A. I. e R. Leopoldo II Granduca di Toscana*, Florence: Societaà editrice fiorentina, 15 vols., ed. by E. Alberi.

GULLEY, Norman [1958], Greek geometrical analysis, *Phronesis*, 3(1), 1–14, doi: 10.1163/156852858X00011.

HEATH, Thomas L. [1908], *The Thirteen Books of the Euclid's Elements*, Cambridge: Cambridge University Press, 2nd ed. reprinted by Dover, New York, 1956.

—— [1921], *A History of Greek Mathematics*, vol. I: From Thales to Euclid, Oxford: Clarendon Press, 2nd edn.

—— [1949], *Mathematics in Aristotle*, Oxford: Clarendon Press.

HEIBERG, J. L. [1903], Paralipomena zu Euklid, *Hermes*, 38(1), 46–74, doi: 10.2307/4472878.

HINTIKKA, Jaakko & REMES, Unto (eds.) [1974], *The Method of Analysis: Its Geometrical Origins and Its General Significance*, *Boston Studies in the Philosophy of Science*, vol. XXV, Dordrecht; Boston: Reidel.

MAHONEY, Michael S. [1968], Another look at Greek geometrical analysis, *Archive for History of Exact Sciences*, 5(3), 318–348, doi: 10.1007/BF00411631.

MEKLER, Siegfried [1902], *Academicorum Philosophorum Index Herculanensis*, Berlin: Weidmann.

MILHAUD, Gaston [1934], *Les Philosophes géomètres de la Grèce*, Paris: Vrin.

MUGLER, Charles [1948], *Platon et la recherche mathématique de son époque*, Strasbourg; Zurich: Éditions P. H Heitz.

ROBINSON, Richard [1936], Analysis in Greek geometry, *Mind*, 45(180), 464–473, doi: 10.1093/mind/XLV.180.464.

SZABÓ, Arpád [1953], Towards a history of greek dialectics (zurgeschichte der griechischen dialektik), *Acta Antiqua Academiae Scientiarum Hungaricae I*, 377–410.

—— [1974], Working backward and proving by synthesis, in: *The Method of Analysis: Its Geometrical Origins and Its General Significance*, edited by J. Hintikka & U. Remes, Dordrecht; Boston: Reidel, *Boston Studies in the Philosophy of Science*, vol. XXV, 118–130.

TANNERY, Paul [1915], Du sens des mots analyse et synthèse chez les Grecs et de leur algèbre géométrique, *Mémoires scientifiques*, III, 162–169.

Analysis, si uti scias, potens est Reappraisal of Heuristic Power of Greek Geometrical Analysis

Ken Saito
Osaka Prefecture University. Professor emeritus (Japan)

Résumé : Dans cet article, nous évaluons la puissance heuristique de l'analyse géométrique grecque en essayant de reconstruire l'analyse de certaines propositions dont la démonstration (synthèse) est encore existante. Nous reconstruisons notamment l'analyse de (1) la trisection de l'angle (exposée par Pappus dans le Livre IV de sa *Collection*), (2) la propriété de la tangente à la parabole, (3) à l'hyperbole/ellipse (Apollonius, *Coniques* Livre I) et (4) à la spirale (Archimède, *Sur les spirales*). Dans tous ces cas, les résultats et les démonstrations peuvent être trouvés par l'analyse seule, sans arguments par analogie avec d'autres figures, et sans considérations cinématiques. Dans ces cas, l'analyse se révèle être un outil beaucoup plus puissant qu'on ne le suppose habituellement. Nous examinons également une partie du rapport *Section selon le rapport* d'Apollonius, pour montrer que le nombre de possibles cas à distinguer dans l'analyse tendait à augmenter, puisque les objets géométriques et les magnitudes qui y sont liées étaient toujours pris en compte dans la disposition géométrique dans laquelle ils apparaissent. En effet, l'absence d'une approche algébrique, qui aurait détaché les magnitudes de leur contexte géométrique, a été l'un des principaux obstacles au développement de la géométrie grecque.

Abstract: In this article, we assess the heuristic power of Greek geometrical analysis by trying to reconstruct some analyses of extant propositions of which only the demonstration (synthesis) is found in the text. We have reconstructed the analysis of (1) the trisection of an angle (Pappus' *Collection*, Book IV), (2) the property of the tangent to the parabola, (3) to the hyperbola/ellipse (Apollonius' *Conics*, Book I), and (4) to the spiral line (Archimedes' *On Spirals*). In all of these cases, the results and the demonstrations can be found by the analysis alone, without arguments by analogy with other figures or kinematic considerations. We have thus concluded that analysis is a much more powerful tool than is usually assumed to be. We have also examined a

Philosophia Scientiæ, 25(3), 2021, 23–54.

part of Apollonius' *Cutting off of a ratio* and confirmed that the number of possible cases to be distinguished in analysis tended to increase because the geometric objects and the magnitudes related to them were always considered in the geometric arrangement in which they appear. We suggest that the absence of an algebraic approach that would have detached the magnitudes from their geometrical context may have been one of the major obstacles to further development of Greek geometry.

1 Introduction

This article examines how Greek geometrical analysis was used, and tries to evaluate to what extent it was useful as a tool for investigations in geometry.[1] As its title suggests, the conclusion is that the analysis was a much more

1. For the readers who are not specialists of Greek mathematics, we briefly explain Greek geometrical analysis, and a much debated issue concerning it, which however we do not treat in this article.

Analysis in ancient Greek mathematics is a research approach which consists in assuming the required result as if it were obtained. This is a simple trick that everyone who learns elementary geometry uses to solve a problem even without being taught to do so. The particular style and terminology of the ancient Greek analysis, with a typical example, is best illustrated in [Behboud 1994].

The central issue, since the fundamental study [Hintikka & Remes 1974], is the "direction" of the analysis. However, we consider that this was a problem invented by modern scholarship, and had little to do with Greek geometry itself. The problem arose from Pappus' rather vague and inconsistent presentation of analysis at the very beginning of Book VII of the *Collection*. In this book, Pappus enumerates the works which he thought were useful to learn analysis, and collects about 150 propositions which would serve to understand the propositions in those works.

Pappus' definition of analysis begins as follows:

> Now, analysis is the path from what one is seeking, as if it were established, by way of its consequences, to something that is established by synthesis. That is to say, in analysis we assume what is sought as if it has been achieved, and look for the thing from which it follows, and again what comes before that, until by regressing in this way we come upon some one of the things that are already known, [...].
> (Translation in [Jones 1986, 1:82])

The interest of the historians is concentrated on the direction of the reasoning in analysis. Let us assume that the figure to be constructed has been obtained, or the property to be demonstrated is true (let us call it assumption A). Then, one finds B logically related to it. But is B one of the logical consequence that follows from A, or is it one of the properties from which A can be derived? That is, which did Pappus mean, (1) or (2)?

(1) $A \leftarrow B \leftarrow C \cdots$
(2) $A \rightarrow B \rightarrow C \cdots$

powerful tool than usually supposed. We also argue that analysis can also find new theorems. If the power of the analysis is not duly evaluated, this is mainly due to the inexpertness in Greek geometry on the part of modern historians. There are a number of reasons for this inexpertness. We know more advanced mathematics which can resolve all the problems that the Greeks solved, and even many they could not solve, so we are not motivated to dedicate as much effort to learn Greek analysis as ancient mathematicians. We can add that today there are no teachers who can teach us Greek geometry and show how to use their analysis.

In this article, we try to teach ourselves the method of analysis by reconstructing possible analyses from the demonstrations of complicated theorems.[2] We start with a solution to the problem of trisecting an angle in Pappus' Book IV, and reconstruct its analysis. This rather simple exercise shows that geometrical objects were not like quantities in algebraic expression. Each object was particular, in the sense that it has its own position and spatial relation to other objects, and particular techniques or "tips" were necessary to treat such objects.

More complicated propositions are then examined: determination of tangents to the conic sections (in Apollonius' *Conics*) and to the spiral line (in Archimedes' *On Spirals*). In the demonstrations of these propositions, the authors give no suggestion about how they have found the result they prove. A reconstructed analysis is proposed for each of them, which (hopefully) will appear to be possible to find even without knowing the result beforehand. The tangent to the parabola (*Conics* I.33) is treated in the main text of the present article, while more complicated propositions are examined in the appendix: tangent to the ellipse/hyperbola (*Conics* I.34), and to the spiral

Pappus' words cited above seem to suggest (1), but some of his words after the quoted passage can be interpreted to mean (2).

However, this is not as important a difference as it seems, for most of the deductions in mathematics are reversible: for example, in isosceles triangles the angles at the base are equal (*Elements* I.5), and if two angles in a triangle are equal, the two sides subtending the equal angles are equal, so that the triangle is isosceles (*Elements* I.6). Indeed, before [Hintikka & Remes 1974], Mahoney had already pointed out this reversibility of mathematical deduction, making much less important the question about the direction of deduction in analysis [Mahoney 1968]. More recently, Acerbi, by careful examination of each term used by Pappus, convincingly argued that the alleged inconsistency of Pappus' presentation does not really exist [Euclide 2007, 442–445].

The real problem in constructing synthesis (ordinary demonstration) by inversion of the accomplished analysis, is the existence of the solution. Some problems do not always have solution, and it is necessary to determine the initial conditions which allow one or more solutions. Such arguments are called diorism, which occupies not a small part of analysis [see Saito & Sidoli 2012].

2. The approach of this article was pursued in [Knorr 1986] which is still one of the most important and illuminating works in the history of Greek mathematics. We try to show the power of analysis more clearly, by careful examination of limited number of complicated propositions in extant works.

(*On Spirals*, prop. 18, and its lemmata prop. 7 and 8). The readers are invited to examine the appendix as well, in order to appreciate the power of Greek geometrical analysis.

Before the conclusion, the limitations of Greek geometric analysis are discussed. It is true that the reach of geometric analysis was quite limited. The limitation is mainly due to the nature of the objects of Greek geometry. They were figures, and were treated where they are and as they are, and no abstract operation was possible. Quantities, which we treat in algebra, have no position, and we apply algebraic formulas and transformations to such quantities, which are objects abstracted from geometrical figures, depriving them of their geometrical particularity such as position and positional relationships to other objects. This is a process alien to Greek geometry. The objects of Greek geometry were always accompanied by their position and configuration, and this entailed frequent and tedious division of cases according to the arrangement of the figure. We will show an example of explosive multiplication of cases in Apollonius' *Sectio rationis* (*Cutting off of a ratio*).

2 Reconstructed analyses

2.1 Angle trisection in Pappus IV.32

This proposition treats the trisection of an angle, and the problem is reduced to another one, that of *neusis* (inclination), which we will explain in the course of the presentation of the analysis.[3]

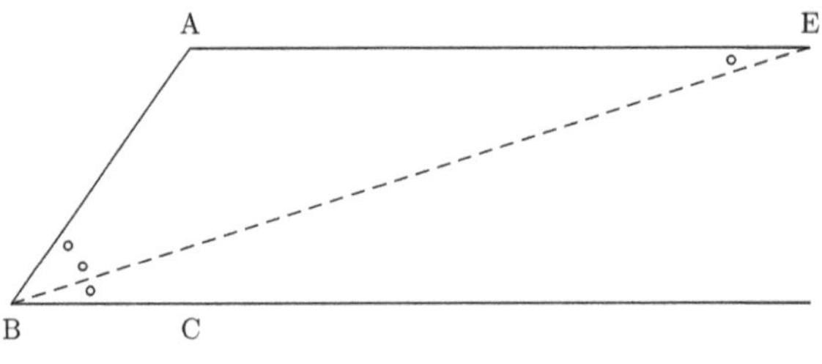

Figure 1: Angle trisection, reconstructed analysis (1) [Pappus 1876-1878, 1:274*ff.*]

Let an angle ABC be given (Fig. 1). And it is proposed to divide it into three equal parts. Let it be done (a typical beginning of an analysis), and let

3. In the preceding proposition IV.31, Pappus resolves this *neusis* problem using an hyperbola. So Pappus did not consider the solution by *neusis* as a legitimate means of construction, and it had to be further reduced to another solution. We here concentrate on the discovery of the solution by *neusis*.

the straight line BE be the trisection of the angle ABC. And let the line AE be drawn parallel to BC. Then the line AE is given, and we show it by solid line, while the line BE by a dashed line, for this line is not yet given, i.e., we don't know where it is. So the angle AEB is equal to the angle EBC, so that the angle ABE is double the angle AEB. This means, although we don't know either of the angles, we know that the former is twice the latter.

Now, let the line AH be drawn, which makes the angle EAH equal to the angle AEH (Fig. 2). Why can we suppose that a Greek mathematician could have the idea of drawing AH? With this line one would have an isosceles triangle AEH, and its exterior angle AHB is double of the angle AEB, that is, equal to the angle ABH. Therefore, the triangle ABH is isosceles, so AB is equal to AH, which is also equal to HE. As AB is given in position and in magnitude, both AH and HE are given in magnitude (but not yet in position).[4]

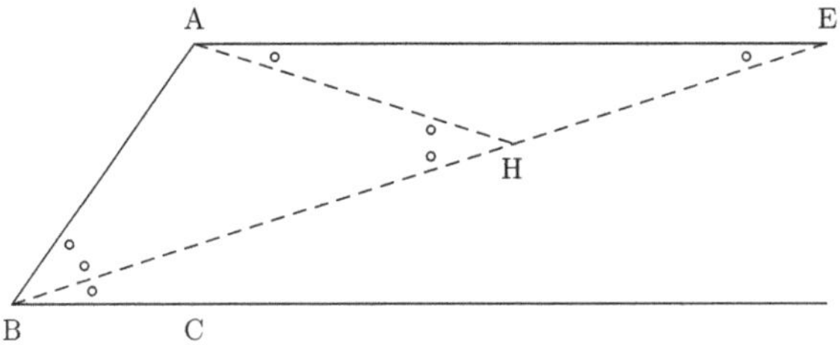

Figure 2: Angle trisection, reconstructed analysis (2)

This is significant progress. Now, draw AC, perpendicular to BC (so AC is given), and let AC, BE meet at point D (Fig. 3). Then AHD is another isosceles triangle, for both the angles HAD and HDA are one right angle less the angle AED. Therefore, DH is equal to AH, and since AH is given in magnitude, so is DH. Therefore, DE (= DH + HE = 2DH) is also given in magnitude. And the lines AE and AC are given in position.

So the problem is reduced to another one, to set a line DE, equal to double of AB, between two lines AE and AC, verging toward the point B. This sort of configuration is called a *neusis* (inclination) in Greek. We restate it more faithfully to Pappus' text.

> Between the given lines CAE, let a line ED be put (κείσθω) inflected (νεύουσα) toward (ἐπὶ τὸ) B, equal to twice AB. [Pappus 1876-1878, 1:276]

4. To be able to go ahead, it is required to "see" the triangle AHB which is not yet drawn in the diagram. To be able to "see" it, one has to know, not only that the angles at the base of an isosceles triangle are equal to each other (*Elements* I.5), but also that the exterior angle at the vertex of an isosceles triangle is double of the angle at the base. The latter is an obvious corollary of *Elements* I.5, but one has to keep it in memory in its explicit form. We will come back to this argument later in §2.2.

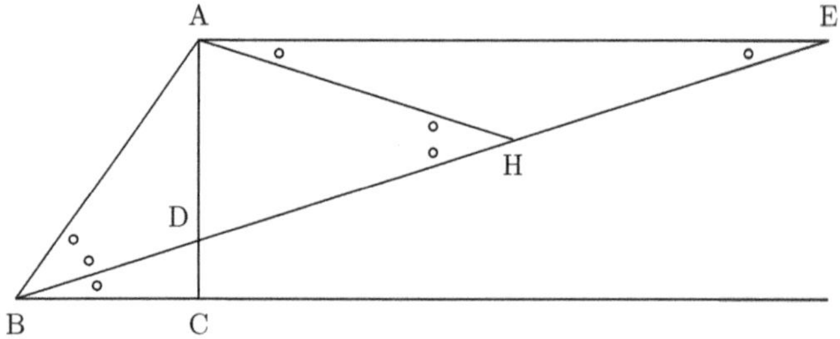

Figure 3: Angle trisection, reonstructed analysis (3)

2.2 Tool-box

This example shows us not only how the analysis works, but also why it is not easy to use analysis. The key step is to draw the line AH, which makes two isosceles triangles AEH and ABH. Without this step the analysis gets nowhere. Then, how could a Greek mathematician find this construction?

Let us go back to the figure before drawing the auxiliary line AH (Fig. 1). We have the angles EBC and AEB, one-third of the given angle, and the angle ABE, which is double of the angle AEB. Then, the task at this stage is to somehow relate the angle AEB with its double, the angle ABE.

For us, to double something we call x is to take $2x$. But this makes no sense in geometry. Instead, there were several ways to double a given geometrical object, depending on what that object is, and on the kind of configuration in which it is found. For example, if it is an angle on the circumference of a circle, one can get its double by constructing the angle at the center on the same arc or an equal arc. In this case, we have to remember another property. Namely, the exterior angle at the vertex of an isosceles triangle is double the angle at the base. So it is natural to try constructing the isosceles triangle AEH.

An ancient geometer knew various specific ways of doubling a geometrical object, and when it comes to an angle, one could at once think of the angles in a circle, or the exterior angle of an isosceles triangle. Put in another way, there were several different tools to double a geometric object, according to whether it was an angle, a line, or a surface. The process was not something like writing $2x$ instead of x. For us the expression $2x$ makes sense, for we have all the algebraic formulas, theorems and functions—for example, trigonometric functions help us to get algebraic expression for various geometric configurations. The construction of the regular pentagon is reduced to the calculation of the value of sine or cosine of 72 degrees. In Antiquity, in the absence of such a set of tools, the situation was completely different. The expression like $2x$ did not make sense. Thus, it was not enough to know that the exterior angle of a triangle is equal to the sum of the opposite internal angles (*Elements* I.32), but one also had to know that this property could be used to double an angle by constructing an isosceles triangle.[5]

If the demonstrations in Greek mathematical texts look like an aggregate of nice but inexplicable inspirations, and if we cannot but suspect that Greek mathematicians hid their true techniques as Descartes believed, it is because we have not learned Greek geometry in the way that the ancients did. One has to know how to use tools. If one has never seen a screw, one may take it for a nail, and perhaps use a hammer, not a screwdriver, to drive it into a hole. Various techniques for doubling an angle in Greek mathematics can be compared to screwdrivers. They had cross head (Phillips) screwdrivers and slotted head screwdrivers, and used them according to the screw they came across. We moderns have the golden hammer called algebra, which we can use everywhere. So the moral we should remember when we read Greek mathematics is: when all you have is a hammer, everything looks like a nail (Maslow's law).

2.3 Tangent to the parabola (*Conics* I.33)

Let us turn again to an ancient source and see another example which shows the power of analysis: the determination of the tangent to a parabola (*Conics* I.33).[6] In Fig. 4, the curve ΓE is a parabola, whose diameter is AB. Γ is a point on parabola, and ΓΔ is the ordinate drawn from Γ. Apollonius shows that if AE is equal to EΔ, then ΓA is tangent to the parabola, without explaining how he got the idea of making AE equal to EΔ.

To reconstruct the analysis, let us start from Apollonius' conclusion, that the line ΓA is tangent. Then, any point Z on ΓA falls outside of the parabola.[7] Following Apollonius' proof in reverse order, one should arrive at the relation that AE is equal to EΔ.

5. The set of useful propositions (or tools) in the investigation of Greek mathematicians is expressed by the term "tool-box" [Netz 1999*b*, 216*ff.*], [Chemla 2012, 30].

6. We use [Apollonius 2008*b*] for the text of the *Conics*. Since all the extant manuscripts of the *Conics* derive from Vat. Gr. 206, the recent critical edition [Apollonius 2008*b*] (with French translation) does not present significant differences. The diagrams in the latter are very different from those in the manuscripts (especially in I.34 which is treated in appendix of this article) but metrically correct, while those in Heiberg's edition [Apollonius 1891-1893] are a little bit closer to the manuscript diagrams.

A critical edition (with French translation) of the Arabic version of the *Conics* is also available [Apollonius 2008*a*].

7. Apollonius formulates his argument as a proof by contradiction, and assumes that a point Z on AE falls inside the parabola and proves that this is impossible. In the diagram also, the point Z is inside the parabola. However, the mathematical arguments do not essentially change if we reconstruct an analysis departing from the premise that Z is outside the parabola as we do here. We have also changed the diagram.

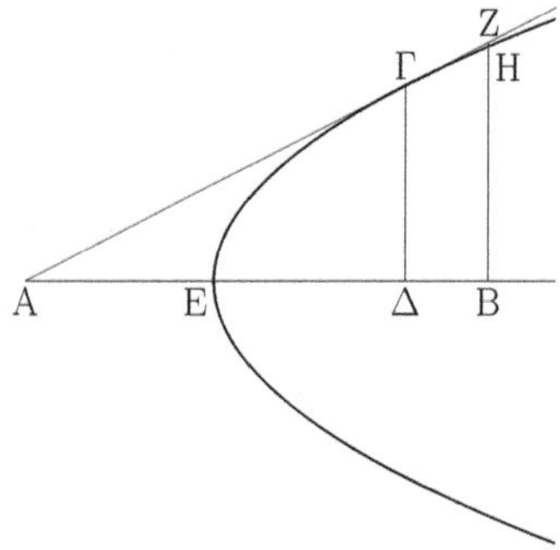

Figure 4: *Conics* I.33. Tangent to a parabola.

On the tangent ΓA, let a point Z be taken, and let ZHB be drawn, parallel to the ordinate ΓΔ. Since ΓA is tangent to the curve, Z must fall outside the parabola (Z can also be between A and Γ), that is

$$\mathrm{ZB} > \mathrm{HB}. \tag{1}$$

Since ΓΔ and HB are ordinates, the squares on them are as the abscissas, that is

$$q(\Gamma\Delta) : q(\mathrm{HB}) = \mathrm{E}\Delta : \mathrm{EB}. \tag{2}$$

And since ΓΔ and ZB are parallel, triangles AΓΔ and AZB are similar, so

$$q(\Gamma\Delta) : q(\mathrm{ZB}) = q(\mathrm{A}\Delta) : q(\mathrm{AB}). \tag{3}$$

From (1), (2) and (3),

$$\mathrm{E}\Delta : \mathrm{EB} > q(\mathrm{A}\Delta) : q(\mathrm{AB}). \tag{4}$$

This relation is not easy to handle, for the left side is a ratio of lines while the right side is that of areas. So let us add some line to the left side, and convert the ratio on the left side to a ratio between rectangles.

Since a ratio is easier to handle if its terms contain more common lines and common points, it is a good idea to choose AE as the side of the rectangle. Thus we have

$$r(\mathrm{AE}, \mathrm{E}\Delta) : r(\mathrm{AE}, \mathrm{EB}) > q(\mathrm{A}\Delta) : q(\mathrm{AB}). \tag{5}$$

Exchanging the inner terms, we have

$$r(\mathrm{AE}, \mathrm{E}\Delta) : q(\mathrm{A}\Delta) > r(\mathrm{AE}, \mathrm{EB}) : q(\mathrm{AB}). \tag{6}$$

Why is one motivated to exchange the inner terms? Because only three points appear in each of the ratios of both sides after exchanging the inner terms. It is easier to handle.

Now, the ratios on the left and right sides are those of the rectangles contained by two segments of a line to the square of the whole line. Every Greek mathematician knew that such a rectangle is largest when the lines are divided into two equal parts, making a square on the half of the whole line. This is a straightforward result of *Elements* II.5.

Therefore, on either side, four times the antecedent (four times the rectangle) is equal to or less than the consequent. So the relation is more directly visible if one takes four times the antecedents:

$$4r(\mathrm{AE}, \mathrm{E}\Delta) : q(\mathrm{A}\Delta) > 4r(\mathrm{AE}, \mathrm{EB}) : q(\mathrm{AB}). \tag{7}$$

Then, on both sides of (7), the antecedent is equal to the consequent only when E is the midpoint of the line AΔ (left side), or of AB (right side).

So, if E is *not* the midpoint of AΔ, taking the point B so that AE is equal to EB, one can make the ratio on the right side bigger than that of the left side, which is a contradiction. Therefore, E must be the midpoint of AΔ.

Modern scholars wonder how Apollonius found this proposition. However, the transition from (4) to (5) is not so mysterious as it may seem to us moderns. Greek mathematicians must have tacitly learned the tip: when you treat a proportion between two ratios whose terms are not homogeneous, try to make them homogeneous. And they also knew how to use *Elements* II.5 as a tool to determine the maximum of a rectangle contained by two segments of a line. Here again, it is not enough to know a proposition, but one has to know how to use it as a tool.

2.4 Determination of the tangent of more complex curves

The power of analysis as a tool for investigation in geometry is best appreciated in more complicated problems. In the appendix, we have also reconstructed analyses for the determination of the tangent to a hyperbola/ellipse (*Conics* I.34), and to a spiral (Archimedes *On Spirals*, 18).

The conclusions (the properties of the tangents) are simple and elegant and it seems possible to guess them beforehand—by analogy with the tangent of circle for the ellipse/hyperbola, and by kinematic consideration for the spiral. However, the property of the tangent appears in the premise of each proposition, from which the demonstration begins, and, as is usually the case in Greek mathematical works, the author does not explain how that property has been found. The demonstrations are of course correct, but very difficult to follow, for they depend on unexpected auxiliary constructions which look like *deus ex machina*. So the readers are left with the question "how could the author find this demonstration?"

Our reconstruction of the analysis starts from the simple assumption that the tangent is drawn and it falls always outside the curve except the point of contact, and from this the property of the tangent is found. So both the conclusion and the demonstration of these complicated propositions concerning the tangents can be found by analysis. Though we have no documents discussing how these properties were discovered, we can at least say that we do not have to suppose any other method besides analysis.

3 Limitation of geometric analysis

Now we turn to the defects or limitations of geometric analysis, pointing out two of them. First, as it treats the geometrical objects as they are, in the configuration where they appear, the number of possible cases of a proposition tends to be multiplied. It is not rare that in a proposition dozens of possible cases are hidden. If one tries to make an exhaustive argument, it tends to be intolerably long, and this, indeed, happens in one of Apollonius' work, which we will examine.

The second point is that the problems which could be invented and investigated were limited. This limitation also comes from the geometry itself, but there is another factor. The only mathematical language for handling geometrical magnitudes was ratio and proportion. This entails difficulties in making and resolving problems which correspond to our equations of third and higher degrees.

3.1 Apollonius' *Sectio rationis*

Pappus reports some works of Apollonius concerning analysis. Most of them are lost, but one work, *Sectio rationis* (*Cutting off of a ratio*), is extant in Arabic, and has long been known to us through Edmund Halley's Latin translation [Apollonius 1706]. Recently, the Arabic text with a French translation was published [Apollonius 2010]. English translation [Apollonius 1987] is also available.

This work treats only one problem, divided into many cases. The problem is: given two infinite straight lines on a plane, and a point on each of them, and given a ratio, and besides, given a point not lying on the given lines; to draw a straight line from the given point outside the given lines, so that the segments which are cut off on each line from the given point on it, have the given ratio between them.

Apollonius divides the problem according to the arrangement of given lines and given points, and call each possible arrangement a "locus", then, each locus is divided into cases, according to the possible ways of cutting given lines. In each case, Apollonius gives an analysis which may be accompanied by a diorism (examination of the condition for the solution to exist: see the final part of the note 1 above), then the synthesis follows. We are going to examine only the analysis part of one of the cases.

We take the first case of the sixth locus. In this locus, the given straight lines AB and CD meet at point E (Fig. 5), and the given point on AB is the intersection point E itself, while the given point on CD is G. And H is the given point from which the cutting line JL is drawn. And HK, parallel line to AB through H is supposed to meet CD at point K, which is in the prolongation of EG. Then point K is given, so that HK is also given in position and magnitude.[8]

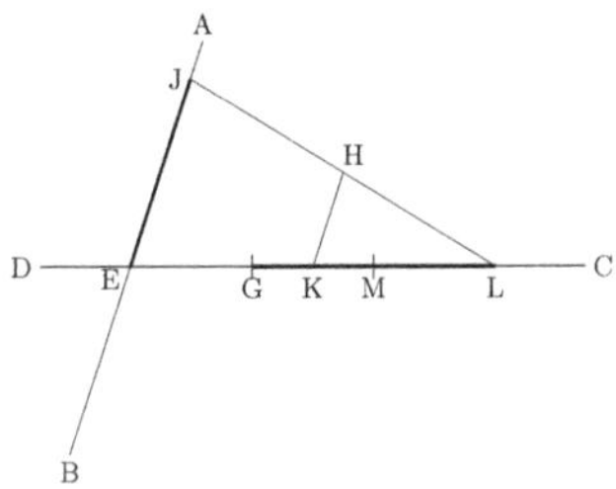

Figure 5: *Sectio rationis*, Book 1, locus 6, case 1. The segments EJ and GL, which will be shown to have the given ratio to each other, are drawn in thick lines.

In the first case of this sixth locus (see Fig. 5), the segment EJ on AB is cut off on the side of the point H, and the segment GL on CD is cut off in the prolongation of EK. Let the line JL be drawn, so that the ratio of the segments EJ:GL is given, i.e.,

$$\mathrm{EJ} : \mathrm{GL} = \text{the given ratio}. \tag{8}$$

To be able to investigate this problem, there are two things to be done. Firstly, one has to express the given ratio as a ratio of two given lines in the diagram. Although we can express a ratio as an abstract value, say r, this was not the case in Greek mathematics, and a given ratio had to be expressed as a ratio of two lines in the diagram. Secondly, since there are two undetermined (i.e., not given) points J and L on the two different straight lines AB and CD, one has to "move" one of the points to the other line, so that the required condition can be argued on one straight line. Apollonius takes a point M on

8. Because the point H is given and HK is drawn parallel to the given line AB, the line HK is given in position. And the line CD is also given in position, so that the point K is also given. Then, because points H and K are given, HK is given in position and in magnitude.

AC, which satisfies the condition

$$\mathrm{HK} : \mathrm{GM} = \text{the given ratio}. \tag{9}$$

Since HK is given in magnitude, and the ratio HK : GM is given, GM is also given in magnitude. And the point G is given, so GM is given in position and in magnitude, so that M is given. Thus, the given ratio is expressed as a ratio of two given line segments HK and GM. This relation is also used to eliminate the point J, one of the undetermined points.

Then, since the ratio JE:GL is the given ratio (hereafter we underline the undetermined points J and L),

$$\underline{\mathrm{J}}\mathrm{E} : \mathrm{G}\underline{\mathrm{L}} = \mathrm{HK} : \mathrm{GM}. \tag{10}$$

Alternately (*Elements*, V.16),

$$\underline{\mathrm{J}}\mathrm{E} : \mathrm{HK} = \mathrm{G}\underline{\mathrm{L}} : \mathrm{GM}. \tag{11}$$

Because JE is parallel to HK,

$$\underline{\mathrm{J}}\mathrm{E} : \mathrm{HK} = \mathrm{E}\underline{\mathrm{L}} : \underline{\mathrm{L}}\mathrm{K} \tag{12}$$

From (11), (12), we have

$$\mathrm{E}\underline{\mathrm{L}} : \underline{\mathrm{L}}\mathrm{K} = \underline{\mathrm{L}}\mathrm{G} : \mathrm{GM}. \tag{13}$$

Thus the point J has been eliminated, and all the terms of the proportion (13) are found on the line CD. This is a significant advance toward the solution. In the proportion (13), E, G, M are given points, and L is the only point which is not given. But this point L appears in three of the four terms. Apollonius proceeds by reducing the number of the terms in which L appears. By separation of ratio (*Elements* V.17; to take the difference of the antecedent and consequent instead of the antecedent itself), we get

$$\mathrm{EK} : \underline{\mathrm{L}}\mathrm{K} = \underline{\mathrm{L}}\mathrm{M} : \mathrm{GM}. \tag{14}$$

Now we have the undetermined point L in two terms only. Transforming the proportion into the equality of rectangles, we will have the point L on only one side of an equality:

$$r(\mathrm{K}\underline{\mathrm{L}}, \underline{\mathrm{L}}\mathrm{M}) = r(\mathrm{EK}, \mathrm{GM}). \tag{15}$$

The right side $r(\mathrm{EK}, \mathrm{GM})$ is given, for EK and GM are given. Therefore, the left side $r(\mathrm{KL}, \mathrm{LM})$ is also given in magnitude. And K and M are given points. This is a well-known problem of application of areas with square excess.[9]

9. Our examination suggests the reason why application of areas with excess or defect was one of the fundamental techniques in Greek geometry. If a problem is

3.2 Multiplication of cases

We skip the diorism (examination of the existence and the number of the solution) and synthesis (demonstration) which follow the analysis, and we turn to the analyses of other cases.

In case 2, the point L is between G and K, so that the point J is on the other side of the line CD (Fig. 6). In the third case, the point L falls between E and G (Fig. 7), and consequently the point J is on the other side of the line CD. Then, in the fourth and last case, L is supposed to be on the other side of the line AB (Fig. 8),

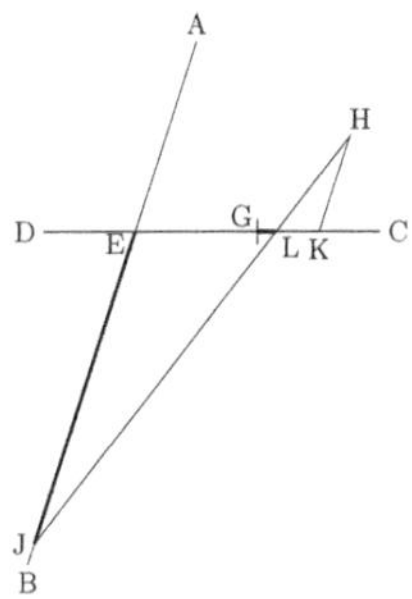

Figure 6: *Sectio rationis*, Book 1, locus 6, case 2.

---

reduced to one proportion in which there is only one undetermined point X, and all the terms of the proportion are line segments on one straight line—this is the case of the present problem we examine—then the problem is solved by transforming the ratio so that not more than two terms contain the undetermined point. If the two terms containing the undetermined point X are the antecedent and the consequent of a ratio, i.e., the condition is reduced to the form

$$\mathrm{AX} : \mathrm{XB} = \mathrm{CD} : \mathrm{EF},$$

then the problem is reduced to cutting the given line AB into given ratio CD : EF at point X. This is a division of a line into a given ratio (internally or externally).

If, on the other hand, the two terms containing the undetermined point X are both inner terms or both outer terms of a proportion, then, transforming the proportion to an equality of rectangles, the problem has the form

$$r(\mathrm{AX}, \mathrm{XB}) = r(\mathrm{CD}, \mathrm{EF}).$$

Since the rectangle on the right side of the equality is given, the problem is reduced to that of application of areas with defect (if X is between A and B), or with excess (if X is in the prolongation of AB).

Therefore, the solution of a problem expressed by a proportion leads either to the division of a line in a given ratio, or to the application of areas with excess or defect.

This consideration suggests that we don't have to assume the concept of quadratic equation to explain the origin of the application of areas with excess or defect in Greek geometry.

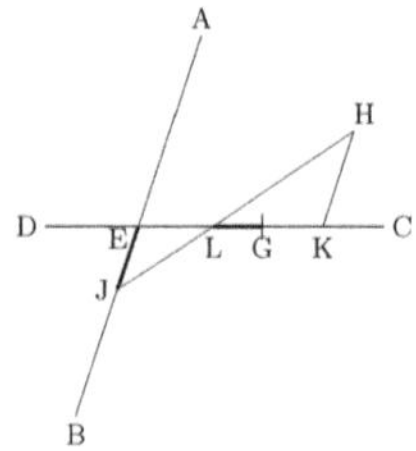

Figure 7: *Sectio rationis*, Book 1, locus 6, case 3.

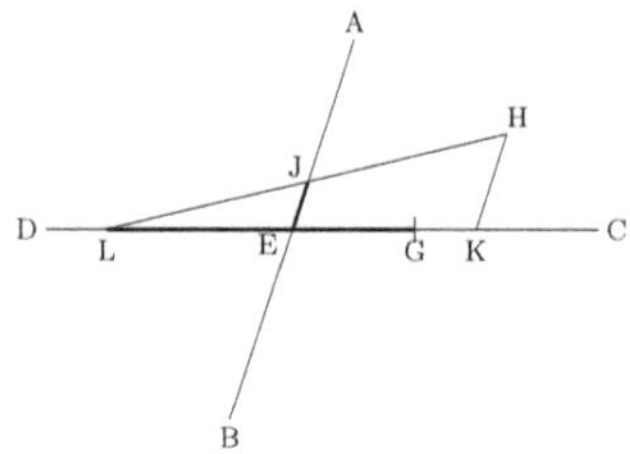

Figure 8: *Sectio rationis*, Book 1, locus 6, case 4.

The cases 2 and 4 are quite complicated, because the ratio EJ:KL, which must be the same as the given ratio, cannot be as big as you please, and there is a restriction to the given ratio in order for the problem to have a solution. Indeed, the analysis of these cases ends up with the application of areas with a defect, that is, a rectangle contained by two segments of a given line is equal to a given area (see also the note 9 above). The rectangle has a maximum, as we saw in our examination of the tangent to the parabola in §2.3. Here Apollonius embarks on a extremely complicated investigation of the limiting value of the given ratio.[10] This is a series of really tedious arguments.

But another, no less serious problem is that one has to divide the problem into several cases according to the configuration of the geometrical objects and to repeat an argument that is essentially the same. Such multiplication of cases can be seen on many occasions. This was inevitable as long as Greek geometry was concerned with geometric objects—figures and their magnitudes—without extracting abstract "quantities" which are independent of the positions and configurations of the original objects.

However, ancient mathematicians do not seem to have thought of this as a serious problem. Euctocius, in his commentary to Apollonius' *Conics*, meticulously counts the number of possible cases in several propositions. For example, in his comment to proposition I.43, which is concerned with

10. For an examination of locus 6, case 4, see [Saito & Sidoli 2012, 610*ff.*].

the hyperbola, ellipse and circle, Eutocius says that there are 12 cases for hyperbola, and 42 cases for ellipse and circle—we would regard a circle as a special ellipse, and would not count its cases separately—so that the total number of the cases is 12+42+42=96. It seems as if Eutocius were quite content to be able to count the number of cases accurately. For us, this is not very productive work for a mathematician.

4 Concluding remarks: slash-and-burn mathematics

Another particularity with Greek geometry was that the problems that could be conceived and posed were limited. Since ratios and proportions were the main means to express the relations between geometrical objects, it was not easy to formulate a problem beyond those corresponding to quadratic equations. A proportion such as "a is to b so c is to d" is reduced, in algebraic terms, to the equality $ad = bc$, so if all the terms a, b, c, d are lines, the relation is equivalent to a quadratic equation. If, for example, a, b are areas while c, d are lines, the relation can be equivalent to a cubic equation. This is indeed the case of the problem of dividing a sphere into a given ratio, treated by Archimedes.[11] However, we find but few examples of such problems ("of higher degree" in modern terms) in Greek geometry. They were less often posed, and rarely solved.

Many of the problems in Greek geometry were those which we moderns can reduce to quadratic equations, and these were the problems that Apollonius treated in exhaustive manner in his lost works on analysis reported by Pappus, of which the only extant one is the *Sectio rationis*, which we have examined.

Thus, "why did the analysis of geometric problems decline after Archimedes and Apollonius?" seems to be a bad question. The limitation was set by the mathematical language and available techniques. And the limitation existed not only in the techniques for solution, but also in the range of the problems the mathematicians could think of.

When a theory or a technique for solution was invented in Greek mathematics (we can imagine the conic section, or the exhaustion method, for example), it was exploited as far as possible, and the problems which could be posed and resolved within that theory and technique were investigated. When most of the possible problems were resolved (or left unresolved), there was little room left for further development. In this view, the history of Greek mathematics was a series of invention/ exploitation/ consumption of theories, techniques, and problems. It looks like slash-and-burn agriculture.

11. *Sphere and Cylinder* II.4, and Eutocius' commentary to this proposition. For detailed examination, see [Netz 1999*a*, 2004].

To conclude, we repeat that analysis is much more powerful than we usually think, if one knows several "tips" in geometry to enhance its potential power. The limitation to geometrical analysis comes largely from the simple fact that it was geometry. It always treated geometrical objects where they are and as they are. There was no notion of abstract quantity. However, Greek mathematicians probably were not even aware of this limitation. Though they may have lamented the lack of nice problems when they had exploited and consumed them, but did not lament the lack of powerful methods or theory. Analytical geometry was lacking for Archimedes and Apollonius no more than a radio telescope for Galileo.

5 Appendix: Reconstructed analyses of problems

5.1 Tangent to the hyperbola and the ellipse in Apollonius' *Conics*

Apollonius establishes the property of the tangent to the hyperbola and the ellipse in *Conics* I.34. We propose an analysis reconstructed from Apollonius' demonstration. Our point is that an analysis could certainly find the property of the tangent, without knowing it beforehand through some other considerations such as by analogy with the circle.

Let AB be the diameter of a hyperbola/ellipse (Fig. 9), E the intersection of the tangent at Γ and the diameter AB, and let ΓΔ be the ordinate drawn from Γ. Apollonius begins with the assertion that

$$\mathrm{A\Delta : \Delta B = AE : EB}, \tag{1}$$

without explaining how he has decided on this starting point. Then, from this assumption, he proves that ΓE is, indeed, tangent to the section. As in the case of parabola (§2.3 of the present article), the proof assumes that a point Z on the straight line EΓ falls inside the section (it is depicted as such in the diagram, which we have changed), and obtains a contradiction. This is, practically, the same as proving that any point Z on the straight line EΓ (except Γ itself) is outside the section.

In the proof, from both extremities of diameter AB, straight lines AOΞ and BMK are drawn parallel to EΓ, but the intention of this construction is not explained. Then, from (1), Apollonius derives (after several complicated steps)

$$\mathrm{AN = N\Xi}, \tag{2}$$

then, from this equality, he deduces the inequality

$$\mathrm{ZH > \Theta H}. \tag{3}$$

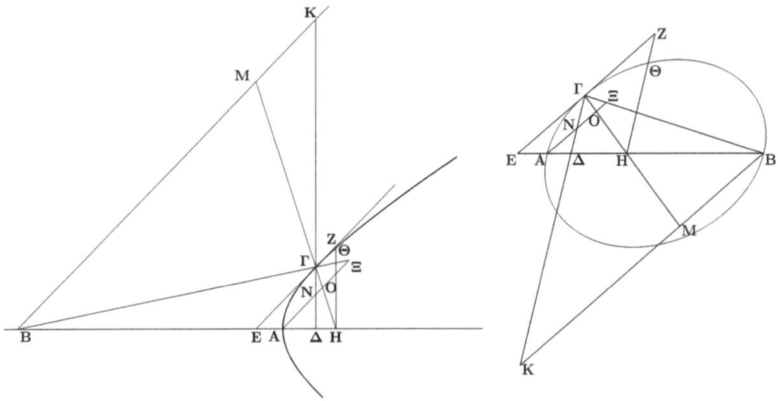

Figure 9: *Conics* I.34 (hyperbola/ellipse)

This shows that the line EΓZ is the tangent at the point Γ (in the context of Apollonius' proof by contradiction, this is the desired contradiction).

The readers of the *Conics* are at a loss partly because they cannot understand how Apollonius has found the relation (1), but mainly because of the desperately long and complicated argument. As for (1), a possible conjecture is that it was obtained by analogy with the tangent of a circle, but throughout the *Conics*, an ellipse is not treated as a prolonged or compressed circle. Even if one accepted this conjecture, how the demonstration has been found would remain a riddle.

We show how an analysis can find (1), using only the property of tangent, i.e., the inequality (3). What we propose is a reconstruction of an analysis, which is practically Apollonius' demonstration of I.34 put in reverse order. We have added our comments to some key inferences, explaining how they are "natural" and can be found without being aided by any mysterious revelations. We hope to show, again, that analysis is quite powerful if you know some "tips", especially those concerning the use of theory of proportion in geometry. In the following, the labels such as (2.11) are numbered in the order of the synthetic proof in the text of the *Conics* I.34. So the reader will encounter them roughly in reverse order in this reconstruction.

Let us start, following the method of analysis, by assuming that the tangent ΓE has been drawn (although the position of E is not yet known). Then, any point Z on the tangent (except Γ) is outside the conic section, i.e.,

$$\mathrm{ZH} > \Theta\mathrm{H}. \tag{3}$$

This can be transformed into:

$$q(\Gamma\Delta) : q(\Theta\mathrm{H}) > q(\Gamma\Delta) : q(\mathrm{ZH}). \tag{2.13}$$

This transformation is motivated by the following proportions which come from the property of hyperbola/ellipse and similar triangles:

$$r(\mathrm{A}\Delta, \Delta\mathrm{B}) : r(\mathrm{AH}, \mathrm{HB}) = q(\Gamma\Delta) : q(\Theta\mathrm{H}), \tag{2.11}$$

$$q(\Delta\mathrm{E}) : q(\mathrm{EH}) = q(\Gamma\Delta) : q(\mathrm{ZH}). \tag{2.12}$$

Replacing the ratios on each side of (2.13) with the right sides of (2.11) and (2.12), we have

$$r(\mathrm{B}\Delta, \Delta\mathrm{A}) : r(\mathrm{AH}, \mathrm{HB}) > q(\Delta\mathrm{E}) : q(\mathrm{EH}). \tag{2.10}$$

In this proportion, there are two rectangles and two squares, and it is easier to treat them if the inner terms are exchanged so that we have one ratio formed by lines ending at Δ, and another ratio formed by lines ending at H. We have thus

$$r(\mathrm{B}\Delta, \Delta\mathrm{A}) : q(\Delta\mathrm{E}) > r(\mathrm{BH}, \mathrm{HA}) : q(\mathrm{HE}). \tag{2.9}$$

We have come to a deadlock. The difficulty lies in the fact that the consequents of two ratios, $q(\Delta\mathrm{E})$ and $q(\mathrm{HE})$, have different endpoints (Δ and H). Let us transform the proportion so that the both ratio have the same consequents. Making use of the proportion produced by parallel lines, we can change both consequents to $q(\Gamma\mathrm{E})$. This explains why Apollonius draws lines AΞ and BK.

The details of the argument are as follows. First, let us consider the left side of (2.9). To change ΔE into ΓE, the lines AΔ and ΔB should also be changed proportionally. To this purpose, the lines AN and BK should be drawn from A and B respectively, parallel to the tangent ΓE. Thus we have

$$r(\mathrm{KB}, \mathrm{AN}) : q(\Gamma\mathrm{E}) = r(\mathrm{B}\Delta, \Delta\mathrm{A}) : q(\Delta\mathrm{E}). \tag{2.7}$$

To obtain a similar transformation of the right side of the proportion, we only have to join ΓH and prolong it to the point M. Then,

$$r(\mathrm{MB}, \mathrm{AO}) : q(\Gamma\mathrm{E}) = r(\mathrm{BH}, \mathrm{HA}) : q(\mathrm{HE}). \tag{2.8}$$

From (2.9), (2.7), and (2.8) we get

$$r(\mathrm{KB}, \mathrm{AN}) : q(\Gamma\mathrm{E}) > r(\mathrm{MB}, \mathrm{AO}) : q(\Gamma\mathrm{E}). \tag{2.6}$$

That is,

$$r(\mathrm{KB}, \mathrm{AN}) > r(\mathrm{MB}, \mathrm{AO}). \tag{2.5}$$

This inequality of areas can be better handled if it is transformed to an inequality of ratios, whose antecedent and consequent have common extremities on the left side, A on the right:

$$\mathrm{KB} : \mathrm{BM} > \mathrm{OA} : \mathrm{AN}. \tag{2.4}$$

The ratio on the left side can be carried onto the line AO, since

$$\mathrm{N\Xi : \Xi O = KB : BM}. \tag{2.3}$$

From (2.4) and (2.3), we have

$$\mathrm{N\Xi : \Xi O > OA : AN}. \tag{2.2}$$

In this relation, we have only four points N, Ξ, O, A, all situated on the straight line AO. Of these points N, Ξ and A are given (fixed) in the sense that they do not depend on the position of the point Z arbitrarily taken on the tangent ΓE, and O is the only non-fixed point. So it is natural to bring the lines having the point O to one side of the relation:[12]

$$r(\mathrm{AN : N\Xi}) > r(\mathrm{AO, O\Xi}). \tag{2.1}$$

Both terms are rectangles, contained by two segments of line AΞ divided at a point (O or N). Such a rectangle is the greatest when divided at the midpoint of AΞ (*Elements* II.5). (We have seen this already in our reconstructed analysis of the tangents to the parabola in §2.3.)

Thus, we see that the inequality (2.1) holds regardless of the position O (which depends on the position of Z), if and only if N is the midpoint of AΞ. That is,

$$\mathrm{AN = N\Xi}. \tag{2}$$

Thus we have arrived at (2) starting from (3).

Now we only have to transform the relation (2) so that the position of the point E is determined. This is relatively easy. Considering the ratio of BK to each of AN and NΞ, from (2), we have

$$\mathrm{BK : AN = BK : N\Xi}. \tag{1.3}$$

Because of similar triangles,

$$\mathrm{BK : AN = B\Delta : \Delta A}, \tag{1.2}$$

$$\mathrm{BK : N\Xi = B\Gamma : \Gamma\Xi = BE : EA}. \tag{1.1}$$

From (1.3), (1.2), and (1.1), we have

$$\mathrm{B\Delta : \Delta A = BE : EA}. \tag{1}$$

This is the relation which determines the point E. So we have shown that the tangent of the hyperbola/ellipse can be found by using analysis alone.

12. This manipulation and the transformation from (2.4) to (2.2) are quite similar to that used by Apollonius in *Sectio rationis* which we have examined in §3.1.

5.2 Archimedes' determination of the tangent to spiral

5.2.1 Proposition 18 (first half)

Archimedes, in *On Spirals*, determines the tangent of the spiral. We examine proposition 18 which determines the tangent at the point Θ (Figs. 10, 11), the endpoint of the first rotation of the spiral.[13] In Figs. 10, 11, the line AΘ is the start of the rotation, and the point on the spiral reaches Θ after one whole rotation. The straight line AZ is drawn from A at right angles to ΘA.

In this proposition, Archimedes establishes that if ΘZ is tangent at Θ, AZ is equal to the circumference of the first circle, i.e., the circle having the center A and passing through Θ.[14] Hereafter, we denote this circumference by c, and the radius of this circle by r (= AΘ). The proof is divided into two parts.

1. The first part treats the "forward" case, where Archimedes demonstrates that if

$$\mathrm{AZ} > c, \tag{1}$$

then the line AZ falls inside the spiral, somewhere in the "forward" part, i.e., after the spiral has completed the first rotation at Θ.

2. The second part treats the "backward" case which is much more complicated. If

$$\mathrm{AZ} < c, \tag{2}$$

then the line AZ falls inside the spiral, before it completes the first rotation.

How Archimedes found the equality of the subtangent AZ to the circumference c of the first circle, has been a persistent question. Conjectures of a hidden process aided by kinematic approach or approximating consideration (i.e., with the concept of limit) have been proposed.[15] Here we will argue that

---

13. We use the critical edition [Archimedes 1910-1915], accepting the proposal in [Archimedes 2017, 61], where Netz rejects an emendation of Commandino followed by Heiberg, restoring the manuscript reading. The diagrams in the present article are not reproductions of the manuscript diagrams, for we have drawn those which we believe serve best for understanding the complicated mathematical arguments.

14. Usually a proposition concerning the tangent to a curve is stated in the manner "such and such a line is the tangent to the curve". Archimedes states its converse. He proves that ΘZ (with AZ = c) is the only possible candidate of the tangent at Θ, but he does not really prove that this line is the tangent. This seems to come from the technical difficulty of the spiral which is a very particular curve.

15. Dijksterhuis proposes an approximating process [Dijksterhuis 1987, 271*ff.*]. See the next note.

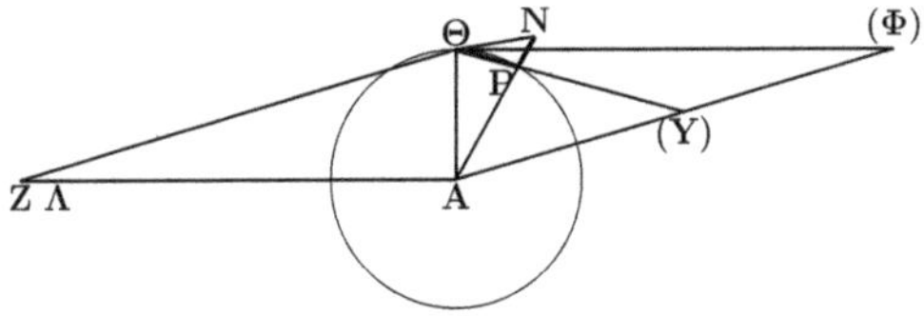

Figure 10: Prop. 18 first half (the Figures in its lemma prop. 7 included)

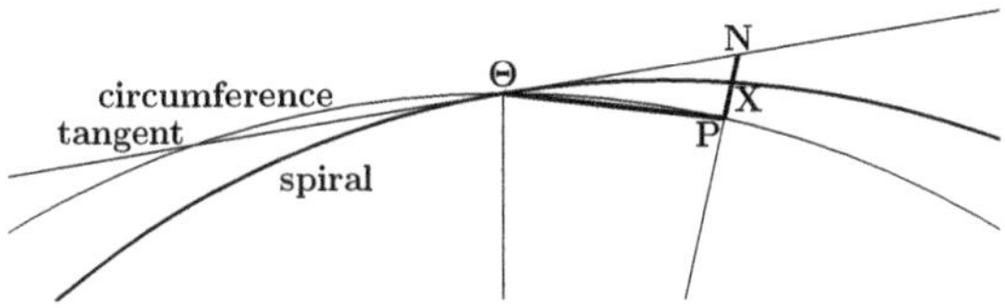

Figure 11: Prop. 18 "forward" case: enlarged

one can find the tangent and provide its proof by means of analysis alone, without any other alleged heuristic methods.[16]

Now, it is intuitively obvious that if AZ is too long, ΘZ (candidate for the tangent at Θ) must fall inside the spiral in the "forward" part of the point Θ, and if AZ is too short, ΘZ must fall inside in the "backward" part.

First, let us assume that AZ is too long, and that a point N in the "forward" part of the point Θ falls inside the spiral. That is, contrary to the diagram, we assume that (Fig. 11)

$$\mathrm{NP} < \mathrm{XP}, \tag{3}$$

and we look for the minimum length of AZ for a point N satisfying (3) to exist.

The difficulty is that there is no direct way to compare NP and XP. As for the point X, the only available relation is the following, which comes from the fact that X is a point on the spiral:[17]

$$\mathrm{XP} : \overset{\frown}{\Theta\mathrm{P}} = r : c. \tag{4}$$

16. As for the analyses proposed by previous scholars, see [Heath 1921, 2:556–561], [Dijksterhuis 1987, 268–274] and [Knorr 1986, 163–166]. Knorr, referring to his predecessors [Knorr 1986, 200, note 51], states that his "own version is not far different from Dijksterhuis', although less closely wedded to modern differential considerations". In our reconstructed analysis, we avoid any concept of convergence or limiting value.

17. This relation is derived from

$$\mathrm{XA} : r = \overset{\frown}{\Theta\mathrm{P}} + c : c,$$

which in turn results from the definition of the spiral, through proposition 15.

So we have to find a relation between NP and $\overset{\frown}{\Theta \mathrm{P}}$, but we have no method to treat the ratio of NP : $\overset{\frown}{\Theta \mathrm{P}}$.

Instead, we may consider the ratio NP : ΘP, to obtain a sufficient condition for (3) to be true. The reason for this is as follows. If a point N is found such that

$$\mathrm{NP} : \Theta\mathrm{P} < r : c \; (= \mathrm{XP} : \overset{\frown}{\Theta \mathrm{P}}), \tag{5}$$

then, since

$$\mathrm{NP} : \overset{\frown}{\Theta \mathrm{P}} < \mathrm{NP} : \Theta\mathrm{P}, \tag{6}$$

we have

$$\mathrm{NP} : \overset{\frown}{\Theta \mathrm{P}} < \mathrm{XP} : \overset{\frown}{\Theta \mathrm{P}} . \tag{7}$$

This means that NP is smaller than XP, i.e., (3) is true.

So let us look for the condition for AZ which makes (5) true. To compare both sides of (5), it is convenient to make the antecedent of the left side equal to the antecedent of the right side r.

This is easy. In Figure 10, draw the tangent ΘΦ of the circle (parallel to AZ) and the line AΦ parallel to ZΘ through A, and prolong ΘP to AΦ, and let Y the point of intersection.[18] Then, since

$$\mathrm{NP} : \mathrm{P}\Theta = \mathrm{AP} : \mathrm{PY}, \tag{8}$$

and AP is the radius r of the first circle,

$$\mathrm{NP} : \mathrm{P}\Theta = r : \mathrm{PY}. \tag{9}$$

So (5) is true if

$$\mathrm{PY} > c. \tag{10}$$

And PY is smaller than ΘΦ (= AZ), but as Y approaches Φ, the difference becomes as small as one wishes. Therefore, if AZ is greater than c, (10) is true for a certain straight line AN.

Archimedes expresses this fact in a different manner. For any point Λ on AZ such that

$$\mathrm{AZ} > \mathrm{A}\Lambda > c, \tag{11}$$

he affirms that it is possible to find a line ΘPY such that

$$\mathrm{PY} = \mathrm{A}\Lambda. \tag{12}$$

18. The labels Φ and Y do not exist in the Archimedean text of proposition 18, but the points corresponding to them are found in proposition 7, which serves as a lemma. See also the following note.

This is a *neusis* construction: find PY equal to AΛ verging toward Θ. The line ΘY being taken in this manner[19] the point P is determined as the intersection of ΘY and the circle, then the line APN satisfies (5), so that the point N on the straight line ZΘ falls inside the spiral in the "forward" part of Θ (against our figure).

Archimedes' demonstration in proposition 18 (and in proposition 7) for the "forward" case of the tangent to the spiral, can thus be found by way of the analysis we have reconstructed above, without any assumed kinematic considerations.

5.2.2 Second half of the proposition 18: backward part

The first half of proposition 18 we have just examined establishes that if AZ is greater than c, the line ΘZ is not the tangent of the spiral at the point Θ, for it falls inside the spiral somewhere after Θ (in the "forward" part of the spiral).

Now, Archimedes demonstrates that if point Z is too near to A for line ZΘ to be tangent to the curve at Θ, namely

$$\mathrm{AZ} < c, \tag{13}$$

(that is, the point Z is too near to the point A), then the line ΘZ falls inside the spiral somewhere in the "backward" part of the curve, before point Θ. This is proved by showing that a line ANΠ can be drawn from the center A so that AN is smaller than AX (Figs. 12, 13).

---

19. Archimedes separates this part of the demonstration as proposition 7 and locates it among preparatory lemmata before the definitions concerning the spiral which appear between propositions 11 and 12. So the labels of the points and his way of stating the proposition is different from what we present here, but the nucleus of the argument is the same: it is possible to make PY (verging towards Θ) equal to any given line smaller than AZ.

The possibility of constructing PY verging towards Θ is intuitively obvious. However, this is a *neusis* (inclination) which tended to be excluded from legitimate methods of construction in the development of Greek mathematics. According to Pappus, Apollonius wrote a work in which certain *neusis* problems were resolved by constructions using straight lines and circles (however not all *neusis* problems can be solved by straight lines and circles).

Modern scholars argue about Archimedes' intention in admitting *neusis* in *On Spirals* ([Knorr 1978] and comments to proposition 7 in [Archimedes 2017]). Knorr, after discussing at length various application of *neusis* by Archimedes, concludes that his effort with *neuses* gave rise to the search for constructions which might eliminate them [Knorr 1986, 178–187]. This explains both Archimedes' use of *neuses* without hesitation and Apollonius' effort to replace them by other techniques [see also Knorr 1986, 346]. We limit ourselves to underline that in a work on spirals as a special curve, limitations to the construction techniques would have had little sense, because a spiral itself cannot be generated by straight lines and circles, or even by conic sections.

The proof is similar to the "forward" case we have just seen, but there is an important difference which makes the argument far more complicated. In this "backward" part, both the point X on the spiral and the point N on the straight line ΘZ, fall inside the first circle. Thus, the condition for the point N to fall inside the spiral is

$$NP > XP. \tag{14}$$

The direction of inequality is opposite from (3) which was treated in the "forward" case. Therefore, the ratio NP : PΘ will not serve the purpose.

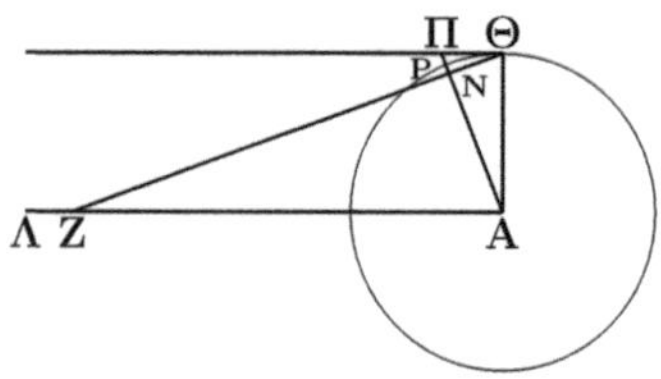

Figure 12: Second half of proposition 18

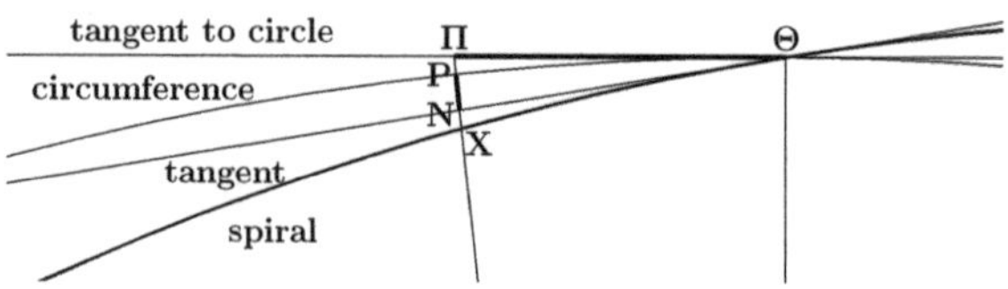

Figure 13: Second half of proposition 18 (enlarged)

The only relation available for XP is always the same

$$XP : \overset{\frown}{\Theta P} = r : c, \tag{4}$$

and as we cannot directly treat the ratio NP : $\overset{\frown}{\Theta P}$, we have to show, for some line x greater than $\overset{\frown}{\Theta P}$, the following

$$NP : x > r : c. \tag{15}$$

Then, since $x > \overset{\frown}{\Theta P}$, we will have

$$NP : \overset{\frown}{\Theta P} > NP : x > r : c = XP : \overset{\frown}{\Theta P}, \tag{16}$$

whence follows (14). Archimedes indeed considers

$$NP : \Theta\Pi, \tag{17}$$

introducing point Π, the intersection of AN and the tangent of the first circle at the point Θ. From these considerations, the inequality

$$\Theta\Pi > \overset{\frown}{\mathrm{P}\Theta} \tag{18}$$

holds, so that if one finds a point N such that

$$\mathrm{NP} : \Theta\Pi > r : c, \tag{19}$$

one can prove (14) as we argued in (15) and (16). This is the outline of the proof of the second part ("backward" case) of the proposition 18.

Archimedes, assuming (13), takes a point Λ on the prolongation of the line AZ (Fig. 12) such that

$$\mathrm{AZ} < \mathrm{A}\Lambda < c \tag{20}$$

and draws the line AN such that

$$\mathrm{NP} : \Theta\Pi = r : \mathrm{A}\Lambda > r : c. \tag{21}$$

The construction of the line AN satisfying (21) which implies (19), is guaranteed by proposition 8, the most difficult one we find in *On Spirals.*

Now we examine this proposition and show that its proof can also be found through geometric analysis.

5.2.3 Reconstruction of the analysis of proposition 8

In the diagram of proposition 8 (Fig. 14), KΛ is parallel to ΥΓ, so that KΥ is equal to ΓΛ.[20]

Moreover, the labels in proposition 8 do not coincide with those in proposition 18. We show here their correspondence here:

Figs. 12, 13	Θ	N	P	Π	Z	Λ
Fig. 14	Γ	E	B	I	(Υ)	(Ψ)

The relation to be realized for NP was (Fig. 13)

$$\mathrm{NP} : \Theta\Pi = r : \mathrm{A}\Lambda. \tag{21}$$

In the context of proposition 8, this becomes (Fig. 14)

$$\mathrm{EB} : \Gamma\mathrm{I} = \mathrm{K}\Gamma : \mathrm{K}\Psi, \tag{22}$$

20. In the diagram of proposition 8 (Fig. 14), we have changed the direction of the whole diagram so that the line ΞΓΛ is horizontal, to make the comparison with the diagram of proposition 18 easier. We have also added the labels Υ, Ψ and the segment AΥ, to explain the relation of this lemma to proposition 18.

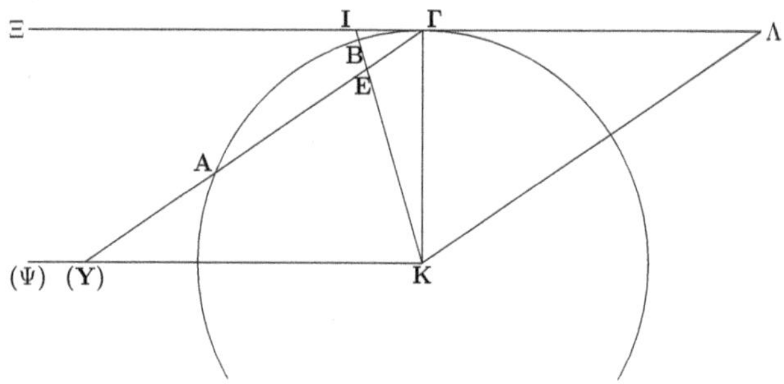

Figure 14: *On Spirals*, Proposition 8

where the ratio on the right side is smaller than KΓ : ΓΛ, for the consequent KΨ is greater than ΓΛ.

Archimedes does not introduce the points Y and Ψ in proposition 8. Instead, he proves that for any ratio Z : H which satisfies the ratio inequality

$$\mathrm{Z : H < K\Gamma : \Gamma\Lambda}, \tag{23}$$

it is possible to draw a line KI such that

$$\mathrm{EB : \Gamma I = Z : H}. \tag{24}$$

Indeed, if (23) and (24) hold, one can take a point Ψ such that

$$\mathrm{K\Gamma : \Gamma\Lambda > K\Gamma : K\Psi = Z : H = EB : \Gamma I}, \tag{25}$$

and hence also (22) holds. This corresponds to the construction of the line KI which satisfies (24). If this is done, the point N in proposition 18 falls inside the point X, so that ΘN is not tangent (Fig. 13).

Our reconstruction of the analysis leading to these claims starts from the assumption that the line KI which satisfies (24) is drawn. Let us remember that the following property will be used somewhere in the course of the argument.

$$\mathrm{K\Lambda \parallel E\Gamma} \tag{26}$$

The expression of the given ratio by Z and H, which has no position in the figure, is useless. Let us "visualize" this ratio following Archimedes. He takes KΓ as antecedent, and sets the consequent as ΓΞ, which is the prolongation of ΓΛ in the opposite direction. Since this ratio has a certain relation to the ratio KΓ : ΓΛ through (23), it is natural to visualize it in this way. Therefore, we have

$$\mathrm{K\Gamma : \Gamma\Xi = Z : H}. \tag{27}$$

Then, from (23),

$$\Gamma\Xi > \Gamma\Lambda. \tag{28}$$

This relation will be used later.

Then, from (24) and (27), the condition to be fulfilled is

$$\mathrm{K}\Gamma : \Gamma\Xi = \mathrm{EB} : \Gamma\mathrm{I}, \tag{29}$$

or

$$\mathrm{I}\Gamma : \mathrm{BE} = \Xi\Gamma : \Gamma\mathrm{K}, \tag{30}$$

which is difficult to handle, because BE is not related to any other line segment in this proportion. So, making use of the radius of the circle (KΓ or KB), let us transform the ratios and change BE into KE. Since

$$\mathrm{K}\Gamma = \mathrm{KB}, \tag{31}$$

we have, from (30),

$$\mathrm{I}\Gamma : \mathrm{BE} = \Xi\Gamma : \mathrm{KB}. \tag{32}$$

Taking the remainder (*Elements* V.19) and replacing KB by KΓ, we have

$$\Xi\mathrm{I} : \mathrm{KE} = \Xi\Gamma : \mathrm{K}\Gamma. \tag{33}$$

Now, to follow the direction of Archimedes' argument further (in reverse order), one has to draw the circle passing through Ξ, Λ and K—an unexpected idea, a *deus ex machina.* Netz points out that the "ankle" ΞΓ, ΓK in the ratio ΞΓ : KΓ, is "highly suggestive of the property of proportion with the meeting of chords in a circle" [Archimedes 2017, 62]. So one may well introduce a circle passing through Ξ and K. True, an excellent mathematician like Archimedes might have immediately seen the circle KΛΞ in the proportion (33), but a ratio of an "ankle" like ΞΓ : KΓ appears quite often, and it is not always handled by drawing a circle.

Instead of assuming that a genius like Archimedes must have seen a circle in this situation, we try to show that even a mediocre mathematician would have ended up drawing the circle, if the given conditions had been carefully examined. Let us suppose that with (33) we have come to a deadlock, not being able to "invent" the circle KΛΞ. In such a case, it is useful to enumerate the given conditions, especially those which are not yet used. There are two such conditions:

$$\mathrm{K}\Lambda \parallel \mathrm{E}\Gamma, \tag{26}$$

$$\Gamma\Xi > \Gamma\Lambda. \tag{28}$$

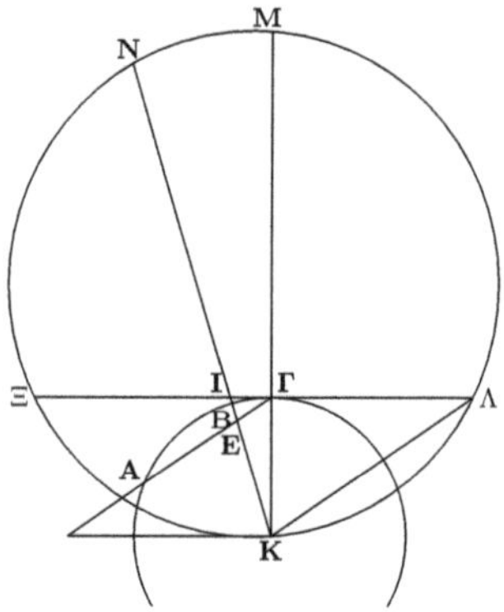

Figure 15: Proposition 8: circle KΛΞ drawn

The former turns out to be helpful. Although there is more than one way to express parallelism by a proportional relation, it seems reasonable to adopt an expression containing the term KE which appears in the relation (33). So from the parallelism of lines (26),

$$\mathrm{KE} : \mathrm{KI} = \Gamma\Lambda : \mathrm{I}\Lambda. \tag{34}$$

Then, the term KE—the consequent of the left side of (33) and the antecedent of the left side of (34)—jumps to eye. Compounding the ratios in (33) and (34), one gets

$$\Xi\mathrm{I} : \mathrm{IK} = r(\Xi\Gamma, \Gamma\Lambda) : r(\mathrm{K}\Gamma : \mathrm{I}\Lambda). \tag{35}$$

A similar relation can be obtained in another way, without compounding of ratio. Transform (34) into the equality of rectangles:

$$r(\mathrm{KE}, \mathrm{I}\Lambda) = r(\mathrm{KI}, \Gamma\Lambda). \tag{36}$$

Since the left side of (33) has KE as consequent, it is convenient to change it to $r(\mathrm{KE}, \mathrm{I}\Lambda)$ by introducing IΛ as a side common to two rectangles. Then from (33) we have

$$r(\Xi\mathrm{I}, \mathrm{I}\Lambda) : r(\mathrm{KE}, \mathrm{I}\Lambda) = \Xi\Gamma : \mathrm{K}\Gamma. \tag{37}$$

The consequent on the left side can be replaced by $r(\mathrm{KI}, \Gamma\Lambda)$ because of (36), leading to

$$r(\Xi\mathrm{I}, \mathrm{I}\Lambda) : r(\mathrm{KI}, \Gamma\Lambda) = \Xi\Gamma : \mathrm{K}\Gamma. \tag{38}$$

So we have either (35) or (38). They are equivalent to each other, but it is easier to "find' the circle KΛΞ in (38). Hence, we start from (38). In this proportion, the antecedent of the ratio on the left side is a rectangle contained by $\Xi\mathrm{I}, \mathrm{I}\Lambda$, i.e., two continuous segments on the line $\Xi\Lambda$, and moreover, the consequent of the ratio $r(\mathrm{KI}, \Gamma\Lambda)$ includes KI, a segment which ends at the point I, the dividing point of the segments of the antecedent. At this point, even a mediocre mathematician would be induced to draw the circle $\mathrm{K}\Lambda\Xi$ (Fig. 15), because the left side ratio of (38) can be transformed as follows (we introduce point N, the intersection of the prolongation of KI and the circle $\mathrm{K}\Lambda\Xi$):[21]

$$r(\Xi\mathrm{I}, \mathrm{I}\Lambda) : r(\mathrm{KI}, \Gamma\Lambda) = r(\mathrm{NI}, \mathrm{IK}) : r(\mathrm{KI}, \Gamma\Lambda) = \mathrm{NI} : \Gamma\Lambda. \tag{39}$$

And the right side ratio of (38) can be transformed to

$$\Xi\Gamma : \mathrm{K}\Gamma = \mathrm{M}\Gamma : \Gamma\Lambda. \tag{40}$$

Now substituting the left sides of (39) and (40) into (38), we get

$$\mathrm{NI} : \Gamma\Lambda = \mathrm{M}\Gamma : \Gamma\Lambda. \tag{41}$$

Therefore,

$$\mathrm{NI} = \mathrm{M}\Gamma. \tag{42}$$

Since the circle $\mathrm{K}\Lambda\Xi$ and the line $\Xi\Gamma\Lambda$ are given in position, $\mathrm{M}\Gamma$ is given in position and in magnitude. Therefore, if we can construct the straight

---

21. We know, of course, the chord theorem (*Elements* III.35, 36), but not all of us are familiar enough with it to be able to use it in analysis when it is needed. There are at least two useful tips for its application.

1. For any triangle ABC and a point D on the side BC, if one draws a circle ABC and AD is prolonged to meet the circle at E,

   $$q(\mathrm{AD}) : r(\mathrm{BD}, \mathrm{CD}) = \mathrm{AD} : \mathrm{DE}.$$

   See Apollonius, *Conics* II.52, for an example of this claim in use.

2. In the same figure,

   $$\mathrm{AD} : \mathrm{BD} = \mathrm{CD} : \mathrm{DE}$$

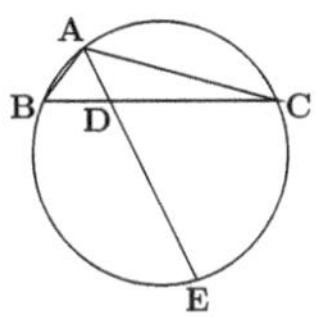

Both are simple consequences of the chord theorem, but usually we are not conscious of them as possible tools for solution of geometric problems.

Greek mathematicians had these and other tips in their "tool-box" which enhanced the power of analysis. If the role of analysis in Greek mathematics tends to be underestimated by us moderns, it is perhaps because we do not know their tool-box, which is equipped with many useful tools, well enough.

line NI satisfying (42) between the circle and the line ΞΓ, verging toward K (this is again a *neusis* construction), we can show, by following the analysis in reverse order, that this line satisfies (24). We can then easily give the proof by reversing the order of our analysis. The construction of the line NI by *neusis* satisfying (42) is indeed the starting point of Archimedes' demonstration of the proposition 8.[22]

We have thus shown that the proof of proposition 8 can be found by way of analysis. Our analysis takes a different route from the reverse of Archimedes' proof between (33) and (42), because the reconstructed analysis from Archimedes' proof would require an ingenious leap (invention of the circle ΚΛΞ from few clues), and we wanted to show that an analysis accessible even to mediocre minds is also possible. Anyway, the equality (42), which resolves the problem can be found by analysis, and we have also shown that an analysis of a problem is not unique, but is flexible to some extent.

Bibliography

APOLLONIUS [1706], *Apollonii Pergaei de sectione rationis libri duo*, Oxford: Theatro Sheldoniano, ed. by E. Halley.

—— [1891-1893], *Apollonii Pergaei quae graece exstant, cum commentariis antiquis*, Leipzig: B. G. Teubner, ed. by J. H. Heiberg.

—— [1987], *On Cutting Off a Ratio*, Fairfield: Golden Hind Press, ed. by E. M. Macierowski & R. H. Schmidt.

—— [2008*a*], *Apollonius de Perge, Coniques. Commentaire historique et mathématique, édition et traduction du texte arabe*, vol. I.1, Berlin; New York: de Gruyter, ed. by R. Rashed.

—— [2008*b*], *Apollonius de Perge, Coniques. Édition et traduction du texte grec*, Berlin; New York: de Gruyter, ed. by M. Decorps-Foulquier and M. Federspiel.

22. Archimedes first takes the point Ξ on the prolongation of ΓΛ by the proportion (27), then draws the circle ΚΛΞ, and constructs the chord KIN satisfying (42) by means of the *neusis* construction, affirming its possibility in a terse phrase:

> since ΞΓ is greater than ΓΛ, and ΚΓ, ΞΛ are at right angles with each other. (Translation by Netz in [Archimedes 2017, 59]. I have deleted the bracket of the word "angle".)

Although Archimedes is laconic, we can see that he is right. For example, draw the diameter of the circle ΚΛΞ parallel to KM (Fig. 15), and let its extremity on the side of the point M be O. Draw KO and let it meet ΞΛ at Π. Then ΟΠ > ΜΓ. Therefore there exists a chord NIK nearer to Ξ than KO, of which the segment NI is equal to ΜΓ.

—— [2010], *Apollonius de Perge. La section des droites selon des rapports*, Berlin; New York: de Gruyter, ed. R. Rashed and H. Bellosta.

ARCHIMEDES [1910-1915], *Archimedis Opera Omnia, cum Commentariis Eutocii*, Leipzig: B. G. Teubner, ed. by J. H. Heiberg.

—— [2017], *The Works of Archimedes: Translation and Commentary*, vol. 2, Cambridge: Cambridge University Press, translation and commentary by R. Netz.

BEHBOUD, Ali [1994], Greek geometrical analysis, *Centaurus*, 37(1), 52–86, doi: 10.1111/j.1600-0498.1994.tb00002.x.

CHEMLA, Karine [2012], Prologue: historiography and history of mathematical proof: a research program, in: *The History of Mathematical Proof In Ancient Traditions*, edited by K. Chemla, Cambridge: Cambridge University Press, 1–68.

DIJKSTERHUIS, Eduard Jan [1987], *Archimedes*, Princeton: Princeton University Press, with a new bibliographic essay by W. R. Knorr. (Original Dutch edition in 1938).

EUCLIDE [2007], *Euclide: Tutte le opere*, Milano: Bompiani, ed. by F. Acerbi.

HEATH, Thomas L. [1921], *A History of Greek Mathematics*, vol. I: From Thales to Euclid, Oxford: Clarendon Press, 2nd edn.

HINTIKKA, Jaakko & REMES, Unto (eds.) [1974], *The Method of Analysis: Its Geometrical Origins and Its General Significance*, *Boston Studies in the Philosophy of Science*, vol. XXV, Dordrecht; Boston: Reidel.

JONES, Alexander [1986], *Pappus of Alexandria: Book 7 of the Collection*, New York: Springer.

KNORR, Wilbur R. [1978], Archimedes' Neusis-constructions in spiral lines, *Centaurus*, 22(2), 77–98, doi: 10.1111/j.1600-0498.1978.tb00453.x.

—— [1986], *The Ancient Tradition of Geometric Problems*, Boston: Birkhäuser.

MAHONEY, Michael S. [1968], Another look at Greek geometrical analysis, *Archive for History of Exact Sciences*, 5(3), 318–348, doi: 10.1007/BF00411631.

NETZ, Reviel [1999*a*], Archimedes transformed: The case of a result stating a maximum for a cubic equation, *Archive for History of Exact Sciences*, 54(1), 1–47, doi: 10.1007/s004070050032.

—— [1999*b*], *The Shaping of Deduction in Greek Mathematics: A Study in Cognitive History*, Cambridge: Cambridge University Press.

—— [2004], *The Transformation of Mathematics in the Early Mediterranean World*, Cambridge: Cambridge University Press.

PAPPUS [1876-1878], *Pappi Alexandrini Collectionis quae supersunt*, Berlin: Weidmann, ed. by F. Hultsch.

SAITO, Ken & SIDOLI, Nathan [2012], Diagrams and arguments in ancient Greek mathematics: lessons drawn from comparisons of the manuscript diagrams with those in modern critical editions, in: *The History of Mathematical Proof In Ancient Traditions*, edited by K. Chemla, Cambridge: Cambridge University Press, 135–162.

Rigorous Purposes of Analysis in Greek Geometry

Viktor Blåsjö
Mathematical Institute, Utrecht University (Netherlands)

Résumé : Dans la géométrie grecque, l'analyse est traditionnellement vue comme une technique heuristique. Cependant, de nombreuses analyses dans les traités mathématiques anciens sont difficiles à expliquer en ces termes. Cet article vise à montrer que l'analyse géométrique grecque peut aussi servir des enjeux mathématiques déterminés, qui, sans son apport, rendraient la synthèse incomplète. D'abord, lorsque la solution d'un problème est précédée par une analyse, celle-ci démontre rigoureusement qu'il n'y a pas d'autres solutions au problème que celles offertes dans la synthèse. Ensuite, chaque fois qu'on est en présence d'une hypothèse de construction qui dépasse l'utilisation de la règle et du compas, l'analyse démontre que le problème n'est pas seulement résolvable à partir de cette assomption, mais qu'il est en fait rigoureusement équivalent à elle.

Abstract: Analyses in Greek geometry are traditionally seen as heuristic devices. However, many occurrences of analysis in formal treatises are difficult to justify in such terms. I show that Greek analysies of geometrics can also serve formal mathematical purposes, which are arguably incomplete without which their associated syntheses are arguably incomplete. Firstly, when the solution of a problem is preceded by an analysis, the analysis latter proves rigorously that there are no other solutions to the problem than those offered in the synthesis. Secondly, whenever some construction assumption beyond ruler and compass is made, the problem is not only solvable by that assumption but is in fact equivalent to that assumption in a rigorous sense.

1 Why analyse?

Arguments called "analysis" occur a number of times in ancient geometry, but the precise meaning, nature, and purpose of analysis remains elusive.

Philosophia Scientiæ, 25(3), 2021, 55–80.

Analysis is traditionally viewed as a kind of method of discovery.[1] Faced with a geometrical problem, the method of analysis consists in assuming that it has been solved and then "reasoning backwards" from there in some sense. This is then followed by the "synthesis" in which the problem is solved in the "forward" direction, mirroring the steps of the analysis. Since the synthesis on its own solves the problem, it seems natural to interpret the analysis as a mere preliminary aid that is not logically necessary but heuristically helpful: in other words, a free-wheeling exploration that has no formal value until it is "confirmed by subsequent synthesis" [Heath 1925, I.140]. Thus, according to this view, analysis is "a heuristic method, essentially"; an "investigative tool that does not have proof character" [Sefrin-Weis 2010, 305].

Yet there are many indications that there must be more to Greek analysis, for if discovery and heuristic is all there is to it, then many aspects of the classical corpus of analysis are inexplicable and perplexing. It is not rare to find cases where the alleged heuristic advantages of analysis are not apparent, yet the analyses are carefully spelled out. For example, there are not a few cases in the Greek corpus where an analysis is spelled out even though the synthesis is obvious and clearly just as easy to come up with as the analysis.[2] Indeed, one can legitimately question or problematise the common assumption that analysis is more heuristic or easier to come up with than synthesis [Behboud 1994, 75], [Netz 2000, 143], and whether the analysis, once accomplished, is necessarily much help in finding the synthesis [Netz 2004, 191, 207, 217–218]. There are many examples where analysis does serve these purposes, but there are also not a few instances where it does not, yet is still included by Greek geometers. This suggests that the heuristic role of analysis is not the whole story. The Greeks seem to have felt that it served some other purpose as well.

By far the most substantial ancient account of what analysis is that has come down to us is that given by Pappus in his introduction to *Collection* VII [Jones 1986, 82–85]. But there are reasons to think that this classic description of analysis is misleading in some respects. In particular, it is perhaps deceptively susceptible to being interpreted in terms of modern conceptions of mathematics, which tend to take an axiomatic-deductive paradigm as primary and hence downplay the prominence of construction problems in the Greek tradition. Pappus seems to be speaking of relating propositional statements to one another as consequences and antecedents very much in the mould of deductive logic. Some older scholarship on analysis took this conception as its starting point and hence looked at the difference between analysis and synthesis as being fundamentally about direction of logical

---

1. This view is expressed in late ancient sources by Pappus (beginning of *Collection* VII, [Jones 1986, 82]), Proclus [Proclus 1970, 165], and Marinus [Taisbak 2003, 248]. It is still generally endorsed, for instance by [Robinson 1936, 464], [Knorr 1975, 9], [Jones 1986, 66], [Menn 2002, 195, 198, 204, 215, 223], [Fournarakis & Christianidis 2006, 47–48], [Sefrin-Weis 2010, xxii, 184].

2. E.g., Archimedes *Sphere and Cylinder* II.1 ("in this case, there is nothing 'heuristic' about analysis", [Netz 2004, 191]) II.3, Pappus *Collection* IV.39.

deduction [Heath 1925, I.139]. This has led to extensive debates as to whether analysis should be seen as consisting in deductions from the assumed result, or in looking for things that would imply the assumed result, or in a chain of reversible two-way implications from the assumed result down to something known. These debates have been inconclusive. More recently, many have felt that a focus on logical direction is not the best way to understand analysis [Behboud 1994, 52–57], [Hintikka & Remes 1974, 11, 31–32], [Berggren & Van Brummelen 2000, 2–8], [Sefrin-Weis 2010, 185–188], [Saito & Sidoli 2010, 583]. In fact, one very striking aspect of the Greek use of analysis is that it is almost always used for problems (that is, requests to construct a geometrical object with given properties) and rarely for theorems. This is contrary to what one would expect both from a modern point of view (where starting from Q when proving $P \implies Q$ is a standard trick often covered in "Intro to Proofs" books) and from the account given by Pappus (who mentions analysis as applied to theorems and to problems on seemingly equal footing). But "a consensus in the current literature", based on the actual Greek analytical corpus, is that "whatever analyses do, they do it better for problems than for theorems" [Netz 2000, 147].[3] Some have gone so far as to argue that "the instances of theoretic analysis [that is, analysis applied to theorems rather than to problems], rare on any account, all seem to be due to later commentators" and are often "artificial and unnecessary" [Knorr 1975, 360, 358].[4] This strongly suggests that the Greek conception of analysis cannot naturally be fitted into a modern axiomatic-deductive picture of mathematics. Instead it appears to have served a purpose that was somehow closely tied to problems and constructions.

The assumption that the synthesis formally speaking makes the analysis superfluous is commonly accepted.[5] According to such a view, the purpose of analysis would be external to technical mathematics itself. Instead it must serve something like heuristic, pedagogical, or rhetorical purposes.[6] But any such interpretation gives rise to the problem: "Why did the Greeks

3. For example, Pappus *Collection* VII, which consists of hundreds of propositions as a commentary following very closely key works in the analytical canon, uses the analysis-synthesis form for virtually all problems and only a tiny fraction of the theorems [cf. Behboud 1994, 57]. In Archimedes there are six analyses for problems (*Sphere and Cylinder* II: 1, 3–7) and none for theorems.

4. This interpretation may well be a bit on the extreme side. For example, Sidoli & Saito note that there are theoretic analyses in Apollonius *On Cutting Off a Ratio* [Apollonius 1987] (although these are lemmas to construction problems) [Sidoli & Saito 2012, 27]. In any case, the general picture that analyses are especially associated with problems remains undeniable.

5. "The analysis [...] contains the creative mathematical work [but] the synthesis nevertheless is the part that carries the proof" [Sefrin-Weis 2010, xxiii]. "The synthesis will often be easy after a successful analysis, but it is the part that carries the formal proof" [Sefrin-Weis 2010, 188].

6. Knorr argues that analyses make the steps of the synthesis appear more naturally motivated [Knorr 1975, 9]. Similarly, Netz construes analysis as a "rhetorical tool" that mathematicians use to make their solutions appear more

publish their analyses?" This would seem to be "something strange, a puzzle: because, after all, the synthesis is sufficient. There seems to be no obvious function for the analysis, once it is directly followed by a synthesis. It is a duplication, doubly strange inside the Greek, highly economical, mathematical presentation" [Netz 2000, 146]. All the more so when the synthesis is simple, as happens regularly. Consider for example Archimedes's *Sphere and Cylinder*. This is a very advanced and authoritative masterpiece, in which, arguably, "intricacy and surprise govern the arrangement of the text" [Netz 2004, 21] in its theoretical development. Yet when treating problems Archimedes suddenly provides even the most elementary solutions with a meticulous analysis—such as in II.3, for example, where the synthesis is so straightforward and obvious that it make little sense to speak of any psychological need for the analysis as a tool of discovery or exposition or teaching. It seems more plausible that Archimedes considered the analysis somehow essential from a logical or mathematical point of view.

Furthermore, attempts to justify the purpose of analyses in extra-mathematical terms do not explain why analyses should be confined to problems only: why would the Greeks not seek such pedagogical and rhetorical advantages for theorems as well?[7] This again suggests that analyses were included for internal mathematical purposes.

Taken together, these considerations strongly suggest that the conception of analysis as a heuristic technique cannot be the whole picture. There must be something else to it, and this seems to be something that serves a formal (not psychological) role for problems (but not theorems). I shall highlight two purposes of analysis that fit precisely this explanatory gap.

2 Analysis as exhaustiveness

The first formal function of analysis I wish to highlight may be called *analysis as exhaustiveness*. I claim that the analysis not only uncovers how a problem can be solved; it also proves that this solution strategy covers all possible solutions.[8] By "solution" I shall mean, throughout this section, a solution configuration—that is, a geometrical object having the property demanded in the enunciation of the problem. For instance, the "solution" of the problem illustrated in Figure 2 consists of the lines DC, EA, AC, which are mentioned in the problem enunciation. It does not include the point F and associated lines

inevitable and definitive [Netz 2000, 153]; "a sort of apology for the synthesis" to make it "appear a bit more 'natural' " [Netz 2004, 207].

7. There is no consensus answer to this question. For some attempts, see [Jones 1986, 67], [Netz 2000, 153].

8. My thesis is exactly that expressed very clearly, but very briefly and in a footnote, by [Zeuthen 1886, 17] (also somewhat less directly in [Zeuthen 1896, 95]). Some modern scholarship has touched on similar connections between analysis and uniqueness [Saito & Sidoli 2010, 591, 600], [Acerbi 2011, 146–148].

which are merely stepping stones needed to construct and verify the solution, rather than being part of the solution object itself. By exhaustiveness I mean finding all solution objects in this sense. This is not to be confused with all possible solution strategies or methods. Of course one could always come up with other ways of producing the same final configuration through other intermediary steps, but this is not relevant to my interpretation of analysis.

The synthesis alone is *not* logically self-sufficient for a complete and exhaustive solution of the problem, contrary to what is commonly assumed. For the synthesis alone only proves that the particular construction offered in the synthesis in fact solves the problem. It typically says nothing about whether other solutions are possible. It is easy to imagine situations where a construction recipe could produce *a* solution to a given problem, yet fail to solve it generally. This can easily happen in underdetermined problem situations such as constructing a triangle with two given side lengths and a given angle other than the one enclosed by these sides, which often has two solutions. A synthesis might give one solution, and indeed prove that it is a true solution. But it would be a grave error to think that this exhausted the problem.

I say that, in many cases, the purpose of the analysis is precisely to ensure that the synthesis has not missed possible alternative solutions. Indeed, the analysis rigorously proves that no such omission is committed. The analysis starts by supposing the problem to have been solved in order to show that *any* solution to the problem leads to the setup of the synthesis. In this way, the analysis proves rigorously that there are no *other* solutions to the problem than those constructed in the synthesis.

A simple example is Apollonius *Conics* II.44: "Given [a parabola], to find a diameter" [Apollonius 2013, 154].[9] The definition of a diameter (Figure 1) makes the synthesis obvious: simply draw any two parallel lines crossing the parabola, bisect them, and join the two midpoints.[10] Clearly we can produce "an indefinite number of diameters" this way, as Apollonius observes. But can we produce *any* diameter this way? The synthesis does not answer this question, but the analysis does. The analysis starts with an arbitrary diameter, cuts across it with two parallels, and infers that by definition the diameter bisects them. This shows that any diameter is one of those generated in the synthesis, because it is producible from the bisection of a pair of parallels, which is exactly what the synthesis covers.

More formally, my general thesis can be stated as follows. Let S be the set of all solutions of a given problem, and let C be the set of all solutions constructed in the synthesis. The synthesis (including its demonstration) alone

9. Sidoli & Isahaya discuss this proposition in detail and argue that it is likely typical of geometrical analyses in the time of Euclid and Apollonius [Sidoli & Isahaya 2018, 17–20].

10. An earlier proposition (II.28) showed that bisecting a pair of parallel lines contained in a parabola implies bisecting all other lines parallel to them as well.

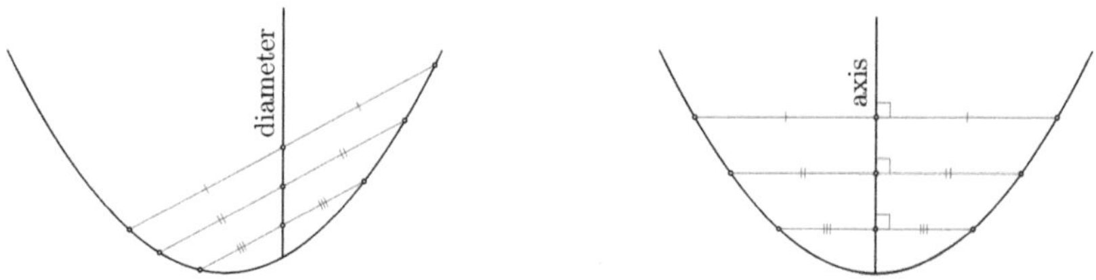

Figure 1: Left: A diameter of a parabola is a straight line that bisects each line in a family of parallel lines contained in the parabola. Right: An axis of a parabola is a diameter that cuts the parallel lines at right angles.

proves that $c \in C \implies c \in S$. The analysis, on the other hand, proves that $S \subseteq C$. It does this in the logically obvious way, namely by considering an arbitrary element $s \in S$ (that is, by starting with any solution of the problem) and proving that it is also an element of C (that is, that it is obtainable by the construction of the synthesis). From $c \in C \implies c \in S$ and $S \subseteq C$ it follows that $C = S$. That is, the analysis and synthesis together prove rigorously not only that the construction is correct but also that it covers all possible solutions.

Exhaustiveness is not the same thing as uniqueness. Many construction problems in the Greek corpus have one unique solution ($|S| = 1$). In such a case the subtleties of the above logical schema collapses. But there are good reasons to approach geometrical problem solving in terms of sets of solutions rather than individual solutions. One indication that Greek geometers were aware of this is that they sometimes explicitly prove that the solution they have given is unique, directly after a full analysis and synthesis have been successfully completed, even in cases where it is intuitively quite obvious that there is only one solution.[11] This suggests that in the preceding analysis and synthesis they allowed the possibility of sets of solutions and intended their arguments to apply to these sets, just as outlined above.

An example of this is Apollonius's *Conics* II.46. This is the same proposition as II.44, which we discussed above, but for an axis instead of a diameter (cf. Figure 1). The analysis and synthesis proceed in a manner analogous to II.44: the synthesis produces an axis and verifies that it is an axis, while the analysis shows that any axis could be obtained in that manner. This shows $C \subseteq S$ and $S \subseteq C$ respectively, which already proves that the synthesis has not missed any solutions. But this still does not say how many solutions there are, that is, the cardinality of S. Hence Apollonius adds a proof (by contradiction) that there could not be more than one axis of a parabola.

11. Apollonius *On Cutting Off a Ratio* I.1.1 [Apollonius 1987] and many times after that; Pappus *Collection* VII: 72, 85, 164, 218.

However, such cases do not validate the above schema completely, because in such cases there is no necessity for the logical function of the analysis that I have provided above. The synthesis (which proves $C \neq \emptyset$ and $c \in C \implies c \in S$) and the uniqueness proof ($|S| = 1$) alone prove that we have exhausted the problem ($C = S$). At least insofar as the uniqueness proof is independent of the analysis, which it sometimes is not (e.g., Pappus *Collection* VII.85). So this may appear to undermine the logical function I have assigned to analysis: in cases where a simple and brief uniqueness proof can be given, and this establishes exhaustiveness, why not do this instead of going through the sometimes rather laborious process of analysis just to accomplish the same goal? To this I have several replies. First of all, uniqueness is often not so straightforward. Already *Elements* I.1 arguably produces two equilateral triangles rather than one, and similar situations where solutions are unique only up to a mirror image or other trivial variations are commonplace in Greek geometry. I furthermore note that almost all of the uniqueness proofs just mentioned are little more than statements that uniqueness is obvious. They say something like: if I cut the thing on that side it would be too small and if on the other side it would be too big; therefore only the point I chose works. But this conclusion is not established by an application of a postulate or proposition, but rather seems to be considered intuitively evident. The analysis allows for a more formal argument. Finally, the analysis way of establishing exhaustiveness is a much more general method since it works regardless of how many solutions there are, whether none or one or many.

We can see the latter point in action in Apollonius's *On Cutting Off a Ratio* [Apollonius 1987].[12] Take for instance I.6.4, which is thoroughly discussed in [Saito & Sidoli 2010, 601–608]. Here the analysis proves that the problem reduces to what is in effect a quadratic equation. It has different numbers of solutions accordingly: 0, 1, or 2, depending on the parameters of the problem. The analysis is eminently useful: it proves that any solution must satisfy the quadratic equation in question. From this it follows rigorously that there are no solutions in certain cases (when the equation has no real roots). The synthesis only states and verifies solutions. The analysis, on the other hand, can prove the impossibility of solutions, by showing that any solutions would have to satisfy an impossible relation. Similarly in the cases where there are solutions. Again the synthesis states and verifies the various solutions. How do you know there are not further ones? You know this because any solution must correspond to the root of a quadratic equation, and this problem can be exhaustively treated. The uniqueness-proof strategy for proving exhaustiveness is not available when there are 0 or 2 solutions, but the analysis way of dealing with exhaustiveness handles it elegantly.

As this example illustrates, analysis is very useful for answering the questions: Under what conditions is the problem unsolvable? Or (more rarely and generally): How many solutions are there? The Greeks had a formal

12. Modern editions of this work are [Rashed & Bellosta 2010], [Apollonius 1987].

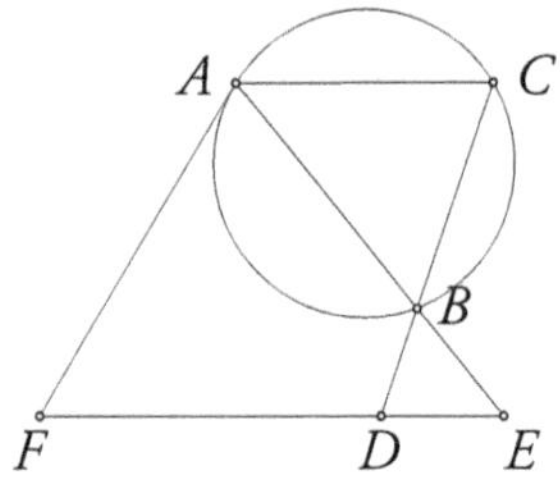

Figure 2: Pappus *Collection* VII.105.

name for arguments answering these questions: diorism. Unlike analysis itself, diorisms are generally recognised as formal arguments serving a rigorous role in showing that the problem has been completely solved. It is a mistake, in my view, to draw such a distinction between the two. Indeed, the diorism often immediately follows the analysis and relies on it.[13] On my reading, the analysis and diorism are both equally rigorous and indispensable arguments for establishing that the construction offered is the definitive one. When the problem is solvable, the analysis proves that the construction given in the synthesis covers *all* possible solutions ($S \subseteq C$), by an argument of the form $s \in S \implies s \in C$. When the problem is unsolvable, however, no set C is defined, so this argument cannot work. To ensure that we are not missing any solutions we must prove that the problem is unsolvable ($S = \emptyset$). The natural way to do this is to assume that there is a solution and prove that this leads to an impossibility ($s \in S \implies \perp$). The initial assumption of the analysis (let $s \in S$) is thus the natural starting point in both cases. In this respect, diorism and analysis are naturally related.

Let us spell out in more detail how exactly the analysis proves that $S \subseteq C$. To this end it is useful to employ the modern conventional division of an analysis-synthesis proof into four stages.[14] I shall illustrate these stages by a prototype example: Pappus *Collection* VII.105 (Figure 2). I shall give the full text of this problem and proof in the translation by [Jones 1986, 236] with minor adaptations and labelling of stages added in brackets. I also add footnotes explicating the steps of the proof. Importantly, the problem in fact has a second solution (Figure 3) which is not that of Pappus's figure. A second purpose of my notes on the proof is to verify that it applies equally well to this alternate configuration.

13. A canonical example is Archimedes *Sphere and Cylinder* II.7.
14. Introduced by [Hankel 1874, 144].

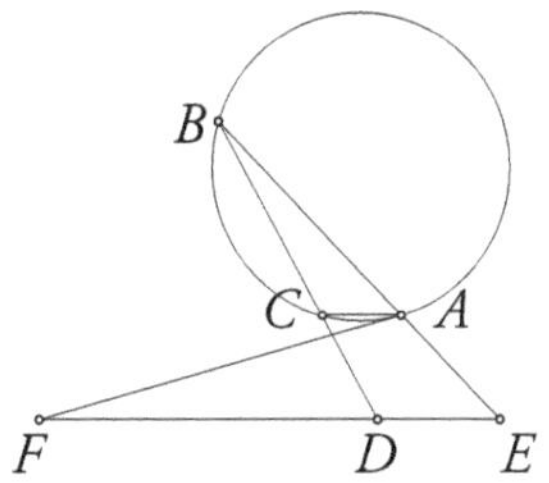

Figure 3: Alternate configuration for Pappus *Collection* VII.105.

Problem Given circle ABC in position, and two points D, E given,[15] to inflect a straight line DBE and, with it produced, to make AC parallel to DE.[16]

Analysis. Transformation. Let it be accomplished, and let FA be drawn tangent. Then since AC is parallel to DE, angle C equals angle CDE [*Elements* I.29]. But angle C equals angle FAE, because FA is tangent to, and AC cuts, the circle.[17] And hence angle FAE equals angle CDE. Thus points A, B, D, F are on a circle.[18] Hence the rectangle contained by AE, EB equals the rectangle contained by FE, ED.[19]

Resolution. But the rectangle contained by AE, EB is given, because it equals the square of the tangent from E to circle ABC.[20] Therefore also the rectangle contained by DE,

15. It is implicitly assumed that DE is outside the circle. This is evident for example in the synthesis where it is assumed that one can draw "the tangent [to the circle] from E".

16. In other words the problem is: Given a line segment DE and a circle, find a point B on the circle, such that the points C and A of intersection of DB and EB with the circle define a line AC parallel to DE.

17. *Elements* III.32, with our C = Euclid's D, our B = Euclid's C, given supplementary angle of FAC = angle CBA. Considering angle sum of triangle ABC, this means angle ACB = angle FAB = angle FAE. In the alternate case: *Elements* III.32, with our B = Euclid's D, our C = Euclid's C, gives supplementary angle of FAB = angle ACB. Hence angle ACB = angle FAE since angle FAE is the vertical angle of the supplementary angle of FAB.

18. By the converse of *Elements* III.22. angle FAE = supplementary angle of its opposite angle FDB. In the alternate case: Use instead the theorem that a quadrilateral is cyclic if the angle between a side and a diagonal (in our case angle BAF) is equal to the angle between the opposite side and the other diagonal (angle FDB).

19. By a common variant of *Elements* III.35–36, noted for instance in Heath's commentary thereon.

20. By the *Data* or "given" equivalent of *Elements* III.35.

EF is given.[21] And DE is given. Hence EF too is given. But it is also given in position; and E is given. Hence F too is given. But from a given point F a straight line FA has been drawn tangent to a circle ABC given in position. Hence FA is given in position and magnitude.[22] And F is given. Therefore A too is given. But E too is given. Therefore AE is given in position. But the circle too is given in position. Therefore point B is given. But each of D, E is given. Hence each of DB, BE is given in position.

Synthesis. The synthesis of the problem will be made as follows. **Construction.** Let the circle be ABC, and the given two points D, E, and let the rectangle contained by DE and some other line[23] EF be made equal to the square of the tangent from E, and from F let a straight line FA be drawn tangent to circle ABC,[24] and let AE be joined, and let DB be joined and produced to C,[25] and let AC be joined. I say that AC is parallel to DE.

Demonstration. For since the rectangle contained by FE, ED equals the square of the tangent from E,[26] while the rectangle contained by AE, EB too equals the square of the tangent,[27] therefore the rectangle contained by AE, EB equals the rectangle contained by FE, ED. Hence points A, B, D, F are on a circle.[28] Therefore angle FAE equals angle BDE.[29] But angle FAE also equals angle ACB in the alternate segment.[30] Hence angle ACB equals angle BDE. And they are alternate angles. Thus AC is parallel to DE.

---

21. As in note 19.

22. It is obvious that FA is not uniquely determined and that there are in fact two possible tangents.

23. It is implied that F is taken on the extension of ED.

24. Again, it is obvious that FA is not uniquely determined and that there are in fact two possible tangents.

25. Of course, in the alternate case, it is AE that needs to be produced (that is, extended) rather than DB, but this is a cosmetic matter. In these kinds of situations, the logic of the proof only concerns points defined as intersections of lines (that may be thought of as infinite). Whether the lines need to be produced or not is not relevant to the proof, only to the practical drawing. As is well known, there are many instances already in the *Elements* where the proof should be taken to apply also to variants of the figure that "would require a slight modification in the wording", not least with regard to whether certain segments need to be produced or not [Heath 1925, I.245]. The same goes for the phrasing in terms of "produced" in Pappus's statement of the problem itself.

26. By definition of the point F.

27. *Elements* III.36.

28. By the converse of the theorem used in note 19.

29. By the converse of the reasoning in note 18.

30. As in note 17.

We can formulate the principles of this and other analysis-synthesis arguments in general terms as follows. In the transformation stage, we assume a solution to be available to us, and draw constructions and inferences from this starting point. In this way we prove that solving the problem amounts to producing some auxiliary configuration (in our example, to finding an auxiliary point F that stands in a certain relation to given entities).

Typically, the transformation uses only reversible inferences and constructions [Behboud 1994, 65], so that solving the problem is strictly equivalent to finding the auxiliary configuration. This is certainly very natural and useful since the steps will be reversed later in the proof. Nevertheless, on my reading, it is not necessary to stipulate this as a logical requirement of the transformation per se. The important thing, rather, established in the transformation is that *any* solution maps to the auxiliary configuration in question.

The resolution confirms that the scaffolding built up in the transformation is indeed sufficient to bridge the gap between the givens and the sought. Unlike the transformation, the resolution is not reasoning "backwards" from the solution but rather forwards *from* the givens of the problem *to* the solution via the auxiliary configuration. This confirms that the solution is recoverable from the auxiliary configuration.

The transformation and resolution together prove that any solution to the problem can be obtained via the auxiliary configuration.

The construction gives a recipe for producing the solution configuration from scratch, going through the path laid out in the analysis. The important thing for our logical purposes is that the synthesis clearly covers all possible auxiliary configurations of the type established in the analysis. In fact, in our example as in many others, the first step of the construction is virtually *defined* as the act of accomplishing the auxiliary configuration in question. While it is not evident that there could not be other solutions of some completely different kind, it is evident that no auxiliary configuration of this type is missed by the construction. But since the analysis proved that all solutions are recoverable from such an auxiliary configuration, it follows that the construction produces all possible solutions. The subsequent demonstration of course verifies that the construction indeed fulfils the requirements of the problem. In other words, the construction defines C, and the demonstration proves that $c \in C \implies c \in S$.

It is not necessary for this argument that the point F should be unique. Indeed, one could argue that the analysis and synthesis also cover the cases in Figure 4, insofar as the point labelling A, C and D, E can be considered pairwise interchangeable.[31] It is not important to my purposes whether Pappus or other Greek mathematicians intended the scope of their proofs to be

31. It is evident that the same proof applies to these configurations. They produce the same segment AC as in the previous figures, but as far as my account of analysis is concerned this is not important. The analysis shows that the synthesis covers all solutions without saying anything about how many solutions there are.

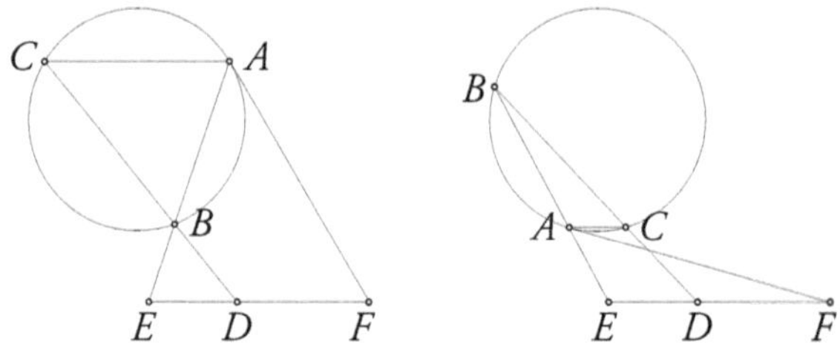

Figure 4: Other alternate configurations for Pappus *Collection* VII.105.

interpreted in this kind of way. My reading works whether this interpretation is granted or not. But let us suppose for the sake of argument that Pappus's proof should be read in this more flexible sense that includes the configurations of Figure 4, because this will allow us to highlight some general points about how far uniqueness requirements can be relaxed with the analysis still being able to perform the task I ascribe to it.

In general terms, we can state the logical schema of the analysis in my sense as follows. We are interested in linking the set of solution configurations S to the given initial configuration (which we may think of as a set G consisting of a single configuration). We do this by means of a set of auxiliary or intermediate configurations I. In our example we can define these sets as follows (cf. Table 1). The elements of the set of solutions S are geometrical configurations, so essentially the figures shown above. Except the solutions only concern what is mentioned in the problem, so we must delete the point F and its associated lines. The set G contains the given configuration, meaning the circle and the segment DE only. The set I can be defined as the set of configurations that contain the givens and an additional point F on the extension of the given line DE on the side of D such that $DE \cdot EF = ET^2$, where ET is a tangent to the circle. Allowing for Figure 4, we should consider all of these elements as concerning only the geometric entities, not their lettering. Thus, in our example, S and I have two elements (corresponding to the two possible ACs and the two possible Fs, respectively), while G has one.

The constructions involved in the analysis and synthesis are effectively mappings between these sets. A construction can be thought of as a function that takes one geometrical configuration as input and produces one or more geometrical configurations as output. In simple cases where there is a single unique solution, we typically have simple bijections $S \longleftrightarrow I \longleftrightarrow G$. But more generally we can think of the relations between these sets in terms of multivalued functions. Thus, for example, the transformation stage of the analysis shows that any solution $s \in S$ is associated with some auxiliary configuration $i \in I$, but the analysis does not care whether the construction that produces this i is uniquely determined or not. It could just as well involve ambiguous or case-splitting steps, such as taking the tangent to a circle from a point. So really the transformation is about a multivalued function $S \longrightarrow I$. The transformation shows that any solution $s \in S$ maps to some auxiliary configuration(s), that is, some subset of I.

The resolution then looks at a multivalued function in the other direction, $I \longrightarrow S$. Again, multivaluedness does not matter. The goal of the resolution is to prove that any $s \in S$ can be obtained from some $i \in I$. It does this by confirming that the s we started with—which was an arbitrary element of S—can indeed be recovered from I, that is, that this s is among the outputs of the multivalued function $I \longrightarrow S$ defined by the construction (the construction in the resolution is implied by the chain of givens; later in the synthesis the same construction is spelled out more explicitly). The analysis transformation already outlined a path connecting any $s \in S$ to some $i \in I$. It remains for the resolution to verify that this path is constructively traversable in the reverse direction, and that the construction covers all such paths. See Section 3 for more detail on how the machinery of "givens" contributes to this.

In the same way the resolution also confirms that the multivalued function $G \longrightarrow I$ defined by the construction in the synthesis does indeed cover all of I. Note indeed in our example that the first step of the construction is in effect the definition of I, as is very typical.[32]

These things taken together prove that the composite multivalued function $G \longrightarrow I \longrightarrow S$ is onto. Since the image of this composite multivalued function is C, by definition, this proves that all of S is contained in C, that is, that the synthesis produces all possible solutions. (Of course, these explications in terms of sets and functions must not be taken too literally. They are not meant as a rigorous formalisation of analysis-synthesis proofs altogether, but only as a schematic representation of how analysis-synthesis proofs can deal with sets of solutions and branching constructions and still serve the purpose I have attributed to them.)

This account shows the viability of conceiving analyses and syntheses as describing sets of solutions rather than individual solutions. As I have shown, in our example, there are two solutions that are both covered by the same analysis and synthesis, so the figure can be considered a particular case whereas the proof applies generally to the full set of solutions. By thinking in terms of sets of solutions in the manner I have outlined, this is handled just as easily as if there had been only one solution. Indeed, the existence of situations like this, where there are multiple solutions, is all the more reason to make sure that the set of solutions provided in the synthesis is exhaustive, which is exactly what the analysis does.

In conclusion, I have outlined a general account of how analysis can serve a particular formal function. I believe analyses in the Greek corpus are typically

32. An analogous example is Pappus *Collection* VII.72, where H is the point defining I. Also analogous are cases where I consists in a point defined as the intersection of conic sections, as in for example Pappus *Collection* IV.31.

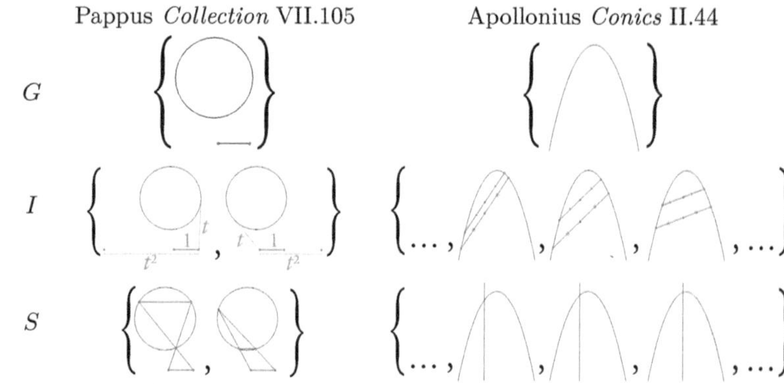

Table 1: The sets G, I, S in the case of two illustrative problems. Light-grey elements are explanatory notes, not themselves part of the set elements.

susceptible to such a reading. At the very least, I have shown that my reading works for Pappus *Collection* VII.105, which is a prototype example of an analysis-synthesis argument often expressly used as a generic illustration of the entire genre,[33] and a complex one in that there are non-trivially distinct solutions.

3 Role of the *Data* and meaning of "given"

The resolutions of analyses are characterised by inferences of the form "X is given, so Y is given". The precise meaning of "given" in Greek geometry has been the subject of much scholarly attention but has eluded simple characterisation. To understand the meaning of "given", the key source is Euclid's *Data*, which proves theorems of the form "if X is given then Y is given", and is hence the canonical source for establishing the validity of the inferences made in analysis resolutions. Just as the resolution of a problem analysis matches up step by step with the construction in the synthesis, so also the *Data* provides direct companions for many constructions in the *Elements*. For example, *Data* 39 ("if each of the sides of a triangle be given in magnitude, the triangle is given in form") corresponds to *Elements* I.22 ("to construct a triangle from three straight lines which are equal to three given [straight lines]"), and *Data* 90 ("if from a given point a straight line be drawn tangent to a circle given in position, the straight line drawn will be given in position

33. [Hankel 1874, 143], [Heath 1925, I.141], [Ito 1980, 10], [Fournarakis & Christianidis 2006, 48] all use VII.105 to illustrate analysis generally. [Behboud 1994, 57] uses the very similar variant proposition VII.107 in place of VII.105 as his prototype example.

and in magnitude") corresponds to *Elements* III.17 ("from a given point to draw a straight line touching a given circle").

It is evident that being "given" is very closely related to being "determined" in some sense. However, for the purposes of my account of analysis, it is essential that this not be confused with "uniquely determined". Being "given" does not entail uniqueness. Indeed, the proof of *Data* 39 follows *Elements* I.22 (which shows the possibility of constructing a triangle with three given sides), not I.7–8 (which proves that there is only one such triangle). *Data* 90 too is evidently not bothered by the fact that the object shown to be "given" is not uniquely determined by the conditions imposed on it (this is the ambiguity which corresponds precisely to the step at note 22 above).[34] This is necessary for my account, because, as I argued above, the logic of the analysis is best phrased in terms of sets of solutions. If "given" meant "uniquely determined", then this point of view would collapse.

Nevertheless, I propose that "given" does indeed mean "determined", but in the following sense. The key purpose of the concept of "given" for the purposes of my account of analysis is this: the *Data* version of a construction from the *Elements* confirms that the construction is done *without loss of generality*. On its own, a solution to a problem in the *Elements* produces an object that satisfies the problem posed, and verifies that it does so. As such, it leaves the question open whether this is the most general solution possible, or whether there could be other solutions missed by this construction. A key concern of the *Data*, I believe, is to alleviate this worry. The *Data* does this by verifying, anytime a construction involves some apparent specificity (such as placing a given length along a particular line, or constructing a tangent of a particular length), that this level of specificity is not gratuitous but rather forced upon us by the specifications given in the problem statement. The proofs of the *Data* check that the specificity assumed in each step of a construction is truly "given"—that is to say, implied by the conditions imposed by the statement of the problem itself—rather than a substantive restriction of the generality of the problem.

It is because the *Data* has done this work that a problem analysis such as that of the Pappus problem above can verify that the synthesis construction does not miss any solutions. Inferences of the form "X is given, so Y is given" means not only that Y is constructible from X, but also that this construction operates without loss of generality, so that it will not miss any such Y. Recall that, on my account, the goal of the resolution is to prove that $I \longrightarrow S$ is onto. It is for this purpose that it is important to know that each step of the

34. Another example of a similar nature is *Data* 31: "If from a given point a straight line given in magnitude be drawn to meet a straight line given in position, the line drawn is also given in position". Thus "either the proposition is false or 'given in position' does not mean 'unique'—unless we extend the property 'given in position' to cover *symmetrical* positions" [Taisbak 2003, 105]. I note that even if this very liberal notion of "uniqueness" is granted the argument against uniqueness based on *Data* 39 still stands.

construction does not introduce overspecificity, but rather solves its subtask with full generality. This ensures that the mapping $s \mapsto i$ is reversible since it rules out the possibility that the construction ran back up again starting from i "branches off" into a restricted subset of S.

4 Analysis as justification of means

I shall now argue that in some cases analysis serves a second rigorous function, in addition to proving exhaustiveness as above. This point of view comes into play when the solution assumes a construction method other than ruler and compass, or the Euclidean postulates.

Consider for example Archimedes's *Sphere and Cylinder* II.1. I will summarise the basic structure of it in modern terms.[35] This is the problem: given a cylinder (say with diameter d and height h), to find a sphere (say with diameter x) with the same volume. Archimedes has already proved the basic volume relation, $\frac{3}{2}d^2h = x^3$, as a theorem earlier in the treatise (I.34). The problem therefore amounts to extracting a cube root (or, in more classical language, taking two mean proportionals). The structure of the analysis is in effect: suppose such a sphere has been found; then $x = \sqrt[3]{\frac{3}{2}d^2h}$. The structure of the synthesis is in effect: form $\frac{3}{2}d^2h$ and extract its cube root and make a sphere with this diameter; then this is the sought sphere.

In the synthesis, Archimedes simply stipulates that the cube root can be extracted ("let two mean proportionals be taken"). The proof of the synthesis shows that, if this is granted, then the problem can be solved. In the analysis, the implication goes the other way, so that together the analysis and synthesis show that not only can the problem be solved by taking mean proportionals, but the problem is in fact *equivalent* to doing so. This two-way implication aspect is known in the literature.[36]

But I shall go further and argue that this can be read as a justification of the tools assumed in the solution in that it serves to answer the possible objection that the synthesis has assumed too advanced a method. In a sense the analysis shows that we have not assumed too advanced means for the problem, and hence justifies the use of this additional construction rule. This may be called *analysis as justification of means.*

---

35. Thus I am using algebraic formulations whereas Archimedes of course writes purely geometrically. These differences are immaterial to my argument. A detailed exposition using both geometric and algebraic explications of Archimedes's proofs is [Dijksterhuis 1987, chap. V].

36. [Berggren & Van Brummelen 2000, 8, 16]. Closely related to this is the idea that and analysis shows of what kind or degree a problem is, in the sense of something like Pappus's classification of problems into plane, solids, and linear. It is evident that analyses of non-plane problems is linked to such questions, as has often been noted [e.g., Knorr 1975, 344], [Sefrin-Weis 2010, xxx, 188, 274, 293, 301, 305].

In Archimedes's case, nobody knew how to take two mean proportionals with ruler and compass,[37] so if the problem could in fact be solved by ruler and compass, then Archimedes could be criticised for assuming unnecessarily advanced methods where simple ones would do. But the analysis proves that Archimedes is completely safe from such a critique. For while the synthesis proves that the ability to extract cube roots implies the ability to solve the problem, the analysis shows that the ability to solve the problem implies the ability to extract cube roots. So if in fact someone would come along and solve the problem by ruler and compass, then the analysis shows that the extraction of cube roots too can be done by ruler and compass.[38] Hence Archimedes has proved rigorously that it is impossible to find a simpler construction than the one he has given, for any possible "simpler" solution must in fact entail the ability to extract cube roots and hence be logically on par with Archimedes's solution rather than simpler than it.

My point can be stated more explicitly as follows. Geometrical problems have the form: "given X, construct Y". To construct something means to reach it by applying a small set of approved construction rules. These rules can be thought of as problems of the same form as above—such as "given two points, construct a straight line joining them"—but whose solution is assumed rather than proved. Let E be the set of construction rules allowed in the *Elements*,[39] and let $P(E)$ be the set of all problems that can be solved by these means. Higher Greek geometry deals with problems that are not in $P(E)$. Their solution therefore involves some additional construction step, that introduces a point determined by means of neusis, conic sections, or higher curves such as the conchoid or quadratrix. Let p denote such a problem and let f denote the additional construction rule assumed for its solution.[40]

37. This is of course impossible, as we now know and as the Greeks in all likelihood strongly suspected.

38. In effect, by tacking the steps of the analysis on at the end of the ruler-and-compass solution of the problem. To turn this composite construction into a recipe for finding the cube root of any given x one only needs to restrict it to a suitable choice of cylinder, such as $d = 1$, $h = \frac{2}{3}x$.

39. This means essentially Postulates 1–3 and 5 of Book I, with some minor accommodations for informal assumptions that Euclid does not articulate explicitly. See, e.g., [Sidoli 2018], where, in particular, Euclid's postulates (419–424) and problems (426–431) are both interpreted as functions introducing certain geometrical entities.

40. We must understand f here as being restricted to the precise point-introduction rule used in the particular construction in question. For example, the Greeks knew how to duplicate a cube by conic sections. In modern terms, the intersection of the hyperbola $xy = 2$ and the parabola $y = x^2$ has x-coordinate $\sqrt[3]{2}$, which is the side of a cube with twice the volume of a unit cube. But we must not think of the assumption of this solution as being the ability to draw conic sections and taking their intersections. That would be much too general. All the solution really needs is the ability to produce a point that stands in a specific relation to the existing geometrical configuration already in place at that stage of the proof. Characterising this point as the intersection of two conics is a natural way of formulating and conceptualising this

Then solving p really means showing that $p \in P(E, f)$, that is, that p is in the set of all problems that can be solved by Euclidean means together with the additional rule f. Now, as we observed, problems and construction rules formally have the same structure and the only thing that separates one from the other is whether we have decided to accept it as a "primitive" given or not. Hence it makes just as much sense to think of f as a problem and p as a construction rule. I claim that this is in effect what the analysis does. In fact, the analysis shows that $f \in P(E, p)$.

One important purpose of doing this, I claim, is to justify the use of the additional construction rule f. Ideally, to justify the use of f, you would want to show that the problem cannot be solved by Euclidean means alone ($p \notin P(E)$). As is well known, results of this type for the main classical construction problems were proved only in the 19th century. Nevertheless, analysis can provide the next best thing. By proving $f \in P(E, p)$, the analysis shows that *any* solution of the problem implies the ability to do f. Thus, in a rigorous sense, we did not assume "too much" when we allowed ourselves to take f as given.

Another way of putting it is that the analysis shows that it is impossible to solve the problem by "simpler" means than f in a certain rigorous sense. For suppose the problem could be solved by ruler and compass, $p \in P(E)$. Then the analysis shows that f itself can be done by ruler and compass, $f \in P(E, p) = P(E)$. Hence when we assumed f we did in fact *not* assume anything beyond the reach of ruler and compass, and hence the supposedly "simpler" solution by ruler and compass is as a matter of fact not simpler at all (in the sense of being based on a more restrictive set of assumptions). In other words, although the analysis itself does not answer the question of whether or not $P(E) = P(E, f)$, the analysis *does* show that there is no set of assumptions $A \supseteq E$ such that $p \in P(A) \subsetneq P(E, f)$: there is no "simpler"—meaning more restrictive—set of assumptions that accomplishes the solution. This fits with a documented concern in the Greek tradition of hierarchy of methods issues. The methodological dictum that it is "not a small error for geometers" to solve a problem "from a non-kindred kind", that is, using more advanced assumptions or methods than necessary, is found in Pappus and seems to have been a prominent concern for Apollonius as well [Knorr 1975, 346], [Sefrin-Weis 2010, 145, 271–275], [Jones 1986, 530], [Knorr 1982, 272], [Acerbi 2018, 273, 276].

Consider for example Pappus *Collection* IV.31 (Figure 5). Everything in the analysis and synthesis of this problem proceeds by ruler and compass, except the introduction of the hyperbola. One might therefore object: yes, this solves the problem, but by advanced means—perhaps a simpler solution is possible, that does not require the ability to draw hyperbolas but only ruler

in the Greek framework, but this does not mean that the proof relies in an essential way on the ability to draw these conics, let alone any two conics. We shall see an example of this below.

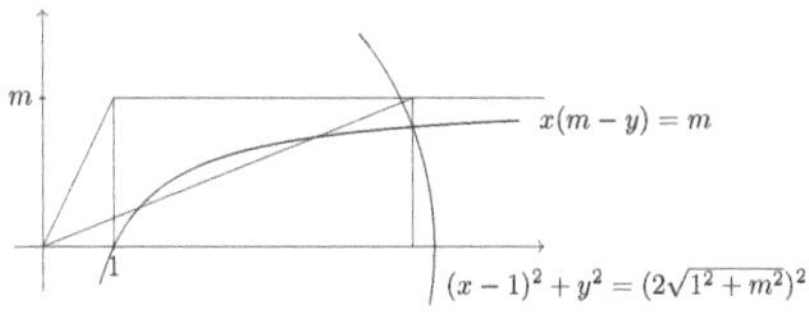

Figure 5: Angle trisection by conics.

and compass? Ideally, we would like to be able to show that such a thing is not impossible. Unfortunately the Greeks did not have the tools to do this. Nevertheless, with the help of the analysis we could still give at least some reply to the sceptical question. The first step in defending ourselves against such an objection could be to say: yes, the synthesis is best formulated in terms of drawing a conic section, but really all it actually requires is the ability to find one single point of intersection (the intersection of the hyperbola and the circle), not the ability to draw the entire curve. The analysis proves that *any* solution to the problem implies the ability to find that intersection point (in other words: if you can trisect the angle you can also recreate the intersection point by ruler and compass from there). Thus we have rigorously proved that it is impossible to solve the problem by more restrictive means than the ones we employ in the synthesis, for if any purportedly simpler solution was provided, it would entail our assumption and hence not be based on more restrictive assumptions after all.

In the notation introduced above, the additional construction rule f assumed in this case would be: given line segments 1 and m, to construct the point of intersection of $x(m-y)=m$ and $(x-1)^2+y^2=(2\sqrt{1^2+m^2})^2$. This formulation is agnostic as to how this point of intersection is found. The logical function of analysis that I have outlined is based on this f only, and hence does not capture the idea that the problem is solvable *by conics*, but rather focusses only on one very specific, technical construction principle. In this way my account of analysis misses what is arguably a fundamental point of the proof and others like it. This is indeed a drawback. The function of analysis that I have outlined in this section is not the greatest thing a geometer might wish for. It would be more interesting indeed to have systematic results characterising the scope of ruler and compass constructions, the scope of constructions by conics, and so on, in general terms. For example, Viète later showed that

$$\text{any cubic or quartic equation} \in P(E, p_1, p_2) \subseteq P(E, F)$$

where

$$p_1 = \text{cube duplication}$$
$$p_2 = \text{angle trisection}$$
$$F = \text{neusis}$$

But such results were not forthcoming in Greek times. The function of analysis I have outlined doesn't say anything about such "general scope" (of conics, neusis, etc.) questions. This is indeed another respect in which this function of analysis doesn't give the most complete answer to means-justification-questions. Nevertheless, the form of analysis I have highlighted is at any rate better than merely assuming the method f without justification (as would have been the case if the problem was solved by the synthesis alone).

There are a few rare cases in the Greek geometric corpus where neusis or conics are used to solve a certain problem even though it would have been possible to solve it purely with ruler and compass.[41] These problems do not come with analyses, but, if we tried to supply analyses for such cases, how would my account of analysis as justification of means play out? There are two possibilities: either f can be effected by ruler and compass, or it cannot. My analysis applies in either case.

Consider the case where f can be constructed by ruler and compass. Then an analysis is perfectly possible. The interpretation of analysis as a justification of means is applicable, but what it justifies is the use of f, not the use of neusis or conics. Those advanced methods may give a more compact way of expressing the step f, but that step in and of itself does not actually depend on those means. So in this case $P(E, f) = P(E) = P(E, p)$. As always, the analysis proves that $f \in P(E, p)$ and that there is no more restrictive set of assumptions that solves the problem, which is correct. One may feel that this analysis "misses the point", because it doesn't take into account that f was described in terms of conics or neusis. The analysis is indeed blind to this fact and would have said the exact same thing if f had been done by ruler and compass. This could be perceived as a drawback or limitation, since analysis in this sense is somewhat divorced from certain elements of the mathematical practice. On the other hand, one could argue that the analysis is doing the right thing in that it focusses on what the proof actually needed formally speaking, namely f, and not the manner in which f was described, which is arguably a cosmetic or psychological question.

Next consider the case where f cannot be constructed by ruler and compass. Then the solution to the problem via f depends in an essential way on the extra means (conics, neusis, etc.), although there would be another path, not via f, that led to the solution without such means. So the means truly are not justified, and indeed the analysis cannot be used to prove that they are. For in this case $f \notin P(E, p) = P(E)$, so the analysis transformation can never arrive at f, and hence the analysis for this case can never be completed. (It is understood, of course, that in any analysis-synthesis pair,

41. [Dijksterhuis 1987, 138–139], [Heath 2002, c–ciii], [Heath 1921, 183, 196], [Heath 1896, cxxix]. All of these examples are from works where the overall purpose of the treatise means that a reduction to ruler and compass in those isolated cases would arguably have been pointless, since those works as a whole are concerned precisely with things that cannot be reduced to ruler and compass.

f must be the only non-ruler-and-compass step. Any analysis transformation uses only ruler-and-compass steps until it reaches the point corresponding to f, or, what is the same thing, to the intermediate configuration(s) I.) Hence it is impossible for the analysis to give a "false positive" justification of the means f in any such case.

5 Summary of the two purposes of analysis

Any problem has a set S of solutions. For example, there is one triangle with three given sides (Euclid *Elements* I.22),[42]

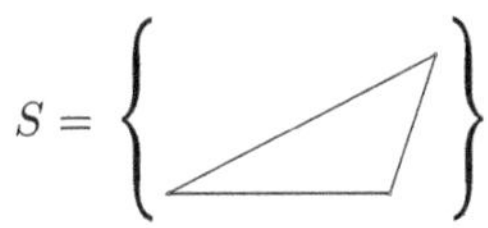

$|S| = 1$

two tangents to a given circle from a given point (Euclid *Elements* III.17),

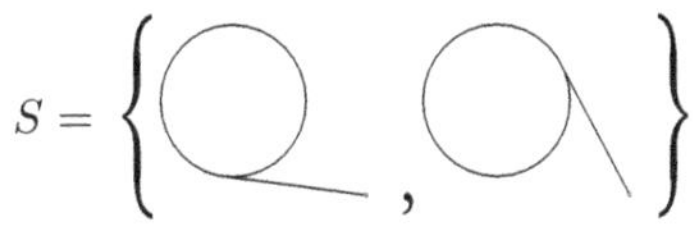

$|S| = 2$

and infinitely many diameters for a given parabola (Apollonius *Conics* II.44),

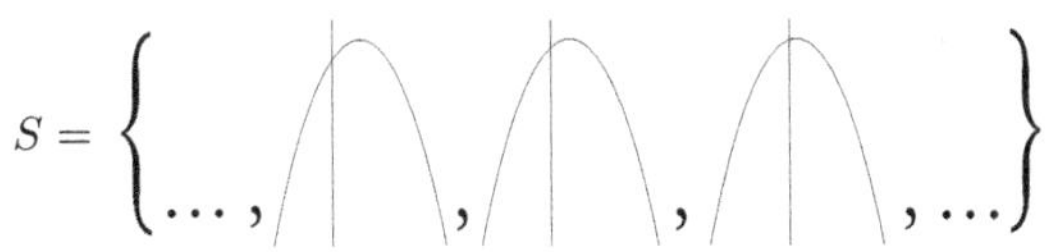

$|S| = \infty$

A solution to a problem is a construction recipe that produces some set of purported solution objects C. Constructions typically produce not just one object but a set of objects, due to case-splitting steps. For example, Euclid's construction of an equilateral triangle (*Elements* I.1) produces two of them:

42. Strictly speaking, whenever we speak of enumerations of elements such as these, we are assuming implicitly some notion of equivalence under which two figures are regarded as "the same". The *Data* has the necessary technical language for this: we speak of geometrical entities being "given in form" if we only care about the shape and not where it is located, but "given in position" if we distinguish between identical shapes differently located. I shall leave this technical issue implicit. But I note that my account of analysis, by being based on cardinalities of sets, naturally raises such issues. So this squares well with the technical attention to exactly such issues in the *Data*.

$C = \{$ 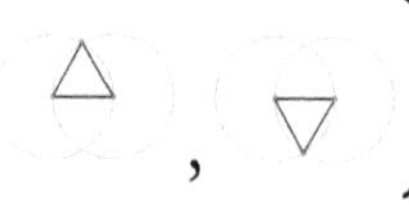 $\}$

The synthesis proves that constructed objects are solutions: $C \subseteq S$. But it leaves open the question: are they *all* the solutions? $C = S$? The analysis proves that all possible solutions are among those constructed: $C \supseteq S$. Hence the analysis-synthesis pair altogether proves that the construction is exhaustive: $C = S$.

The synthesis defines a construction $G \longrightarrow I \longrightarrow S$ from the set of the given configuration G, via some set of intermediate configurations I, to the set of solutions S. The analysis transformation $I \longleftarrow S$ shows that any solution is obtainable by "the kind of construction" that the synthesis uses. It remains (for the analysis resolution, i.e. chain of givens) to verify that the synthesis includes *all constructions of that kind*, i.e., that *no step limits the generality of the construction.* This is purpose of the machinery of "givens". "If X is given, then Y is given" means: We can construct Y from X in such a way that any specificity that Y has is unavoidable (i.e., a consequence of the the specificity of X). In other words, the construction does not introduce specificity or limit the generality of the problem.

The purpose of analysis is to show that the synthesis construction $G \longrightarrow S$ is *onto* (i.e., hits all of S). The analysis transformation verifies the onto-ness of the synthesis construction *globally* by showing that any solution is obtainable by the type of construction given in the synthesis, while the analysis resolution verifies the onto-ness of the individual steps of this construction *locally* by showing that no step introduces overspecificity.

A second purpose of analysis applies for non-ruler-and-compass problems. If a problem p is not solvable by ruler and compass, it is solved by some additional construction rule f (such as an application of conics, neusis, etc.). Problems and construction rules have the same form: "given X, construct Y". So it makes just as much sense to think of f as the problem and p as the construction rule. This is precisely what the analysis does.

Let $P(X)$ be the set of all problems solvable by means X, and let E be the set of Euclidean means (ruler and compass). The synthesis proves $p \in P(E, f)$. The analysis proves $f \in P(E, p)$.

Do we "assume too much" when we take f as given? The analysis enables us to answer: No. The analysis result $f \in P(E, p)$ means that *any* solution of the problem implies the ability to do f. Hence there is no set of assumptions $A \supseteq E$ such that $p \in P(A) \subsetneq P(E, f)$: there is no "simpler" (= more restrictive) set of assumptions that accomplishes the solution. In other words, since *any* set of assumptions sufficient for p are also sufficient for f, it is impossible to solve the problem by simpler methods (= methods whose scope includes p but not f).

The analysis does not show that the problem cannot be solved by Euclidean means alone ($p \notin P(E)$). But it still justifies the use of the means f in that:

either	the problem *is not* solvable by ruler and compass	$p \notin P(E)$
$\Longrightarrow$	additional means necessary	
$\Longrightarrow$	f is justified	
or	the problem *is* solvable by ruler and compass	$p \in P(E)$
$\Longrightarrow$	f can be done by ruler and compass	$f \in P(E, p) = P(E)$
$\Longrightarrow$	f doesn't assume anything beyond ruler and compass	$P(E, f) = P(E)$
$\Longrightarrow$	f is justified	

6 Conclusion

The two functions of analysis I have outlined have much in common. In terms of logic, they both start from the supposition that the problem has been solved because this is the proper logical starting point for a rigorous derivation of *properties that any solution must have.* In terms of purpose, they are both essential parts of a completely satisfying solution, since they rigorously dismiss certain critical objections, to which the solution would have been susceptible if the synthesis alone had been given.

Prominent aspects of the classical corpus that are not easily explained by other means make perfect sense on my reading. The functions of analysis I have highlighted have nothing to do with the notion of analysis as a method of discovery, so they explain why analyses occur in sparsely worded formal treatises and even where heuristic or pedagogic motives seem inapplicable. They also explain why analyses are particularly relevant to problems, and hardly at all to theorems. Indeed, my interpretation fits well with the documented concern for constructions and the scope of particular construction methods in Greek geometry.

If my account is correct, the famous description of analysis by Pappus—the only surviving methodological description of analysis in ancient sources of any detail—is inadequate and incomplete. Pappus states, correctly, that analysis starts by assuming that a solution has been affected and proceeds to reason from this assumption onwards. But he fails to highlight what is in my view the reason for doing so, and instead overemphasises, in my view, the exploratory, heuristic purpose of analysis.

But there are good grounds for not according Pappus's passage too much weight. "Pappus is often careless and sometimes demonstrably in error [...] about earlier Greek geometry" [Toomer 1976, 14], and his mathematical credentials are far from impeccable [Knorr 1975, 339], [Knorr 1989, 31, 226–228], [Knorr 1982, 253], [Jones 1986, 1], [Neugebauer 1975, 968]. His description of analysis is vague and seemingly incoherent, to the extent that a number of scholars have felt that interpretations assuming textual corruption is the only way to make coherent sense of it [Berggren & Van Brummelen 2000, 8]. And, in what may be a product of Platonic bias [Knorr 1975, 360], he seemingly construes analysis as applicable to problems and theorems in equal measure, which is at odds not only with my view but with the Greek geometrical record generally. Furthermore, Pappus was far removed from the leading geometers who had actually done the real work, writing many hundreds of years after the composition of all the works that by his own reckoning constitute the "treasury of analysis". Finally, Pappus most likely did not intend his brief characterisation of analysis to be complete, but rather as "remarks to introduce a broad field expounded in a number of treatises that he expected his reader to be able to read" [Saito & Sidoli 2010, 583]. For these reasons I do not see it as a problem that my account of analysis does not align perfectly with Pappus's description.

Bibliography

ACERBI, Fabio [2011], The language of the Givens: Its forms and its use as a deductive tool in Greek mathematics, *Archive for History of Exact Sciences*, 65(2), 119–153, doi: 10.1007/s00407-010-0072-z.

—— [2018], Hellenistic mathematics, in: *The Oxford Handbook of Science and Medicine in the Classical World*, edited by P. T. Keyser & J. Scarborough, New York: Oxford University Press, chap. 3, 269–298, doi: 10.1093/oxfordhb/9780199734146.013.69.

APOLLONIUS [1987], *On Cutting Off a Ratio*, Fairfield: Golden Hind Press, ed. by E. M. Macierowski & R. H. Schmidt.

—— [2013], *Conics Books I–IV*, Santa Fe: Green Lion Press, ed. by C. R. Taliaferro & M. N. Fried.

BEHBOUD, Ali [1994], Greek geometrical analysis, *Centaurus*, 37(1), 52–86, doi: 10.1111/j.1600-0498.1994.tb00002.x.

BERGGREN, Lennart J. & VAN BRUMMELEN, Glen [2000], The role and development of geometric analysis and synthesis in Ancient Greece and Medieval Islam, in: *Ancient & Medieval Traditions in the Exact Sciences: Essays in Memory of Wilbur Knorr*, edited by P. Suppes, J. M. Moravcsik, & H. Mendell, Stanford, CA: CSLI Publications, 1–31.

DIJKSTERHUIS, Eduard Jan [1987], *Archimedes*, Princeton: Princeton University Press, with a new bibliographic essay by W. R. Knorr. (Original Dutch edition in 1938).

FOURNARAKIS, Philippos & CHRISTIANIDIS, Jean [2006], Greek geometrical analysis: A new interpretation through the "givens"-terminology, *Bollettino di Storia delle Scienze Matematiche*, 26(1), 33–56.

HANKEL, Hermann [1874], *Zur Geschichte der Mathematik in Alterthum und Mittelalter*, Leipzig: Teubner.

HEATH, Thomas L. [1896], *Apollonius of Perga: Treatise on Conic Sections*, Cambridge: Cambridge University Press.

—— [1921], *A History of Greek Mathematics*, vol. I: From Thales to Euclid, Oxford: Clarendon Press, 2nd edn.

—— [1925], *Euclid: The Thirteen Books of the Elements*, Cambridge: Cambridge University Press.

—— [2002], *The Works of Archimedes*, Mineola: Dover Publications.

HINTIKKA, Jaakko & REMES, Unto (eds.) [1974], *The Method of Analysis: Its Geometrical Origins and Its General Significance*, *Boston Studies in the Philosophy of Science*, vol. XXV, Dordrecht; Boston: Reidel.

ITO, Shuntaro [1980], *The Medieval Latin Translation of the Data of Euclid*, Tokyo: University of Tokyo Press.

JONES, Alexander [1986], *Pappus of Alexandria: Book 7 of the Collection*, New York: Springer.

KNORR, Wilbur R. [1975], *The Ancient Tradition of Geometric Problems*, Boston: Birkhäuser.

—— [1982], The hyperbola-construction in the *Conics*, Book II: ancient variations on a theorem of Apollonius, *Centaurus*, 25(4), 253–291, doi: 10.1111/j.1600-0498.1981.tb00647.x.

—— [1989], *Textual Studies in Ancient and Medieval Geometry*, Boston: Birkhäuser.

MENN, Stephen [2002], Plato and the method of analysis, *Phronesis*, 47(3), 193–223, doi: 10.2307/4182698.

NETZ, Reviel [2000], Why did Greek mathematicians publish their analyses?, in: *Ancient & Medieval Traditions in the Exact Sciences: Essays in Memory of Wilbur Knorr*, edited by P. Suppes, J. M. Moravcsik, & H. Mendell, Stanford, CA: CSLI Publications, 139–157.

—— [2004], *The Works of Archimedes*, vol. 1, Cambridge: Cambridge University Press.

NEUGEBAUER, Otto [1975], *A History of Ancient Mathematical Astronomy*, New York: Springer.

PROCLUS [1970], *A Commentary of the First Book of Euclid's Elements*, Princeton: Princeton University Press.

RASHED, Roshdi & BELLOSTA, Hélène [2010], *Apollonius de Perge, La section des droites selon des rapports*, Berlin: Walter de Gruyter.

ROBINSON, Richard [1936], Analysis in Greek Geometry, *Mind*, 45(180), 464–473, doi: 10.1093/mind/XLV.180.464.

SAITO, Ken & SIDOLI, Nathan [2010], The function of diorism in ancient Greek analysis, *Historia Mathematica*, 37(4), 579–614, doi: 10.1016/j.hm.2009.12.003.

SEFRIN-WEIS, Heike [2010], *Pappus of Alexandria: Book 4 of the Collection*, London: Springer.

SIDOLI, Nathan [2018], Uses of construction in problems and theorems in Euclid's *Elements* I–VI, *Archive for History of Exact Sciences*, 72(4), 403–452, doi: 10.1007/s00407-018-0212-4.

SIDOLI, Nathan & ISAHAYA, Yoichi [2018], *Thābit ibn Qurra's Restoration of Euclid's Data*, Cham: Springer.

SIDOLI, Nathan & SAITO, Ken [2012], Comparative analysis in Greek geometry, *Historia Mathematica*, 39(1), 1–33, doi: 10.1016/j.hm.2011.09.002.

TAISBAK, Christian Marinus [2003], *Euclid's Data*, Copenhagen: Museum Tusculanum Press.

TOOMER, Gerald J. [1976], *Diocles on Burning Mirrors*, Berlin: Springer.

ZEUTHEN, Hieronymus Georg [1886], *Die Lehre von den Kegelschnitten im Altertum*, Copenhagen: A. F. Höst & Sohn.

—— [1896], *Geschichte der Mathematik im Altertum und Mittelalter*, Copenhagen: A. F. Höst & Sohn.

Diagrams in Intra-Configurational Analysis

Marco Panza
IHPST, CNRS, Université Paris I (France)
Chapman University, CA (USA)

Gianluca Longa
PHIER, Université Clermont-Auvergne (France)

Résumé : Dans cet article, nous tentons de clarifier la manière dont les diagrammes interviennent dans la pratique de l'analyse géométrique grecque ancienne. Pour cela, nous distinguons d'abord entre deux principales formes de cette pratique, les formes trans-configurationnelles et intra-configurationnelles. Nous soutenons ensuite que dans la première forme les diagrammes sont introduits dans la preuve essentiellement de la même manière (*mutatis mutandis*) qu'ils le sont dans les démonstrations synthétiques canoniques, alors que dans la seconde forme ils participent à l'argument analytique d'une manière spécifique, sans rapport direct avec d'autres aspects de la géométrie classique. En effet, dans l'analyse intra-configurationnelle, les diagrammes constituent le résultat d'un geste purement matériel, non codifié par un quelconque canon de construction, mais permis uniquement par la pratique (théorique) de la méthode de l'analyse et de la synthèse.

Abstract: In this paper we would like to attempt to shed some light on the way in which diagrams enter into the practice of ancient Greek geometrical analysis. To this end, we will first distinguish two main forms of this practice, i.e., trans-configurational and intra-configurational. We will then argue that, while in the former diagrams enter in the proof essentially in the same way (*mutatis mutandis*) they enter in canonical synthetic demonstrations, in the latter, they take part in the analytic argument in a specific way, which has no correlation in other aspects of classical geometry. In intra-configurational analysis, diagrams represent in fact the result of a purely material gesture, which is not codified by any construction canon, but permitted only by the (theoretical) practice of the method of analysis and synthesis.

Philosophia Scientiæ, 25(3), 2021, 81–102.

1 Introduction

A common question that many works on mathematical diagrams have tried and still try to answer is whether pieces of mathematical activity that indispensably require diagrams to achieve or justify some relevant result exist [Giaquinto 2007], [Carter 2010], [De Toffoli 2017]. In this context, one of the most studied domains is Euclidean (synthetic) geometry—the first four books of Euclid's *Elements* in particular. By contrast, diagrams in ancient Greek geometrical analysis represent an almost unexplored territory. As pointed out by Kenneth Manders:

> The role of diagram use in ancient geometric analysis is highly non-trivial, and 20th-century discussions have shed little light on this. [...] one as yet undescribed factor in geometrical analysis is the sense of what-determines-what that only one obtains by actually constructing diagrams. [Manders 2008, 77]

In this paper, we would like to attempt to shed some light, at least tentatively, on how diagrams enter the practice of the method of analysis and synthesis in ancient Greek geometry. To this end, following [Panza 2007], we will distinguish two main forms of analysis, i.e., trans-configurational and intra-configurational. We will then argue that, while the former diagrams enter in the proof essentially in the same way (*mutatis mutandis*) they enter in canonical synthetic demonstrations, in the latter, they take part in the analytic argument in a specific way, which does not correlate with other aspects of classical geometry. The thesis we want to put forward is that, while diagrams in trans-configurational and synthetic arguments can be identified as the material counterpart of the κατασκευή (i.e., a canon of construction), in the intra-configurational analysis, they represent the result of a purely material gesture, which is not codified by any constructive canon but permitted only by the (theoretical) practice of the method of analysis and synthesis.

The paper is structured in three sections. We will first examine some examples of the interaction between texts and diagrams in trans-configurational analysis, both in modern and ancient times. In the second section, we will deal with diagrams in intra-configurational analysis. In this part, we will try to explain how diagrams take part in these types of arguments and how this is somewhat different from synthetic and trans-configurational proofs. Finally, in the third section, by examining the manuscript tradition of some Greek mathematical texts, we will provide some historical and philological evidence in support of our thesis. In particular, we will highlight that, at least in the classic geometric corpus, the writing of the intra-configurational analyses has a peculiarity which is absent in the synthetic demonstrations: in a significant number of cases, we find two somewhat visually identical diagrams, one for the analysis and the other for the synthesis. As we will see, this specificity, absent in synthetic proofs, finds an explanation in the theses set out in the second section.

2 Trans-configurational analysis

Trans-configurational analysis is typical of the use of algebra in geometry.[1] Viète's *Zeteticorum Libri* [Viète 1591*a*], a collection of problems both stated and solved employing the language of algebra, provides several examples of this kind of reasoning. Let us consider, for instance, proposition 17 of the second book [Viète 1591*a*, 54]:

> Data differentia laterum, & differentia cuborum: invenire latera.[2]

Viète takes B to be the difference of sides [*differentia laterum*], D the difference of cubes [*differentia cuborum*] and E the sum of sides. In his notations, capital consonants denote known quantities, and capital vowels unknown ones. Solving a problem within his collection requires making the latter known in terms of the former. In the case in question, the problem requires making the sides known in terms of B and D. Though making E known is not enough, it makes the task quite easier, and it is, however, an important stage in the solution.

By adapting Viète's language and notation to our modern ones (for the sake of simplicity), his argument goes as follows: Let x and y be the two (unknown) sides, then:

$$x - y = B \quad x^3 - y^3 = D \quad x + y = E$$

$$E + B = 2x \quad E - B = 2y$$

$$(E+B)^3 - (E-B)^3 = 6E^2B + 2B^3 = 8(x^3 - y^3) = 8D$$

$$E^2 = \frac{4D - B^3}{3B}$$

This reduces the given problem to another, already solved [Viète 1591*a*, 2]:

> *Zeteticum* I.1: Data differentia laterum & aggregato eorundem invenire latera.[3]

1. Within classical mathematics, algebra was in no way opposed to geometry as a different branch of mathematics. It was rather a common "art" for solving problems both in arithmetic and geometry, going together with a common language, admitting different interpretations in the two cases. A crucial aspect of the deep innovation promoted by Descartes's *Géométrie* pertains to the introduction of a new way to interpret this language in geometry (also going together with a new and particularly performant notation).

2. "Given the difference of the sides and the difference between their cubes, to find the sides." For a slightly different translation, see [Viète 1983, 108].

3. "Given the difference of the sides and their sum, to find the sides."

If the difference of sides is B and their sum ["*aggregato eorundem*"] is $\sqrt{\frac{4D-B^3}{3B}}$, the two sides are of course

$$x = \frac{B + \sqrt{\frac{4D-B^3}{3B}}}{2} \qquad \text{and} \qquad y = \frac{\sqrt{\frac{4D-B^3}{3B}} - B}{2},$$

which makes them known in terms of B and D.

By its nature, analysis supposes the problem is solved and works on the supposed solution to indicate a way for actually solving it. Here, supposing the problem solved consists in expressing an unknown quantity (the sum of sides), whose knowledge makes the actual solution easier, through a given letter, namely 'E'. Though this is a vowel rather than a consonant, the difference is purely typographic and does not forbid working on it just as on the consonants expressing the known quantities. In other words, what analysis does, here, is supposing the problem is solved and working on the supposed solution in order to modify the configuration of data to transform the given problem into another and simpler one (one that, by the way, has been already solved). This is just what makes it trans-configurational: it does not operate within a given configuration of data but, instead, transforms it into a new configuration, corresponding to a more straightforward problem.

There is no diagram here. But there is quite a codified formalism at work. When presented in the notation we used above, this formalism is not so dissimilar from the elementary algebraic one still used today. It is true that Viète uses another notation, quite unlike our present one, and justifies the formalism in a different way than we would do (and Descartes himself will do, only a few decades later). Though quite convenient for the purpose of trans-configurational analysis, this formalism is however not indispensably required by it.

To see why, we first need to understand what makes it so convenient. This is not only about its deductive agility. It is also, and even overall, about its neutrality regarding the possible interpretations of the problem at issue and the analysis itself. Are Viète's "*latera*", and "*cubi*", just geometrical segments and solids? They can certainly be taken as such. But not necessarily, and Viète is quite explicit about it in his *In artem anayticem Isagoge* [Viète 1591*b*], a sort of foundational essay from which *Zeteticorum Libri* openly depends on. They are just scalar quantities [Bos 2001, 143] admitting different possible instantiations: as numbers, or as the mentioned geometrical objects, or even as other magnitudes sharing with those some crucial metric properties. Viète's formalism and notation are just conceived to render this generality explicit.

At this level, diagrams (or, at least, the usual geometrical diagrams, which are the only ones we are considering here) can at most help offering palpable illustrations of the general arguments. But they are certainly not indispensable as such and are potentially misleading. What is relevant here is the capacity to fix the formalism appropriately to make the required inferences licensed.

But when one comes back from this level to the particular case of geometrical segments and solids, the formalism that makes them both dispensable and equivocal can be replaced by classical geometry's ordinary language without making trans-configurational analysis impossible at all.

To show this,[4] let us consider four segments, B, E, x and y (with B and E representing, respectively, the difference and the sum of x and y) so that

$$E + B = (x + y) + (x - y) = 2x \quad \text{and} \quad E - B = (x + y) - (x - y) = 2y$$

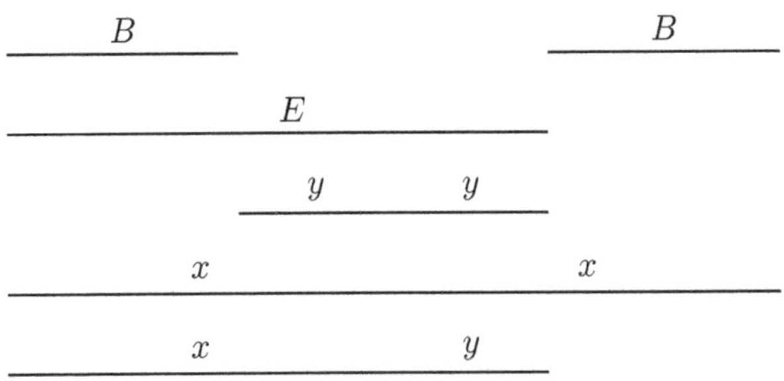

Notice that the diagram includes two distinct representations for B and three for x and y. This is possible because of the purely quantitative nature of the problem at issue. This means that what the problem is asking for is not (the construction of) a pair of particular segments, but rather the identification of the metric relations they must have with the given segment B and the given difference of cubs D. The metric nature of these relations makes the only relevant property of the given and searched for segments be their length, which, in classical geometry, was not conceived as a real number (as we do today) but as the property that a segment shares with all other segments equal to it. In modern terms, this means that what is relevant here are not single segments but equivalent classes of equal segments. Hence, what 'B', 'x' and 'y' properly denote are not single segments but circumstantial representatives of these equivalence classes.

Now, for whatever segments a, b, and c, let $\mathcal{C}(a)$ be the cube of the side a, and $\mathcal{P}(a, b, c)$ the parallelepiped with sides a, b, and c. Hence, from the elementary properties of cubes and parallelepipeds, immediately made manifest by the following diagrams,

4. We adopt here a convent notation, but we do it only for reasons of brevity. The argument we present here does in no way require this notation and can perfectly be restated in the (codified but) discursive language of the Euclidean geometry, merely appealing to the composition and decomposition of cubes and parallelepipeds, indispensably supplemented by appropriate diagrams (possibly only imagined, but not for this less indispensable in this intellectual activity).

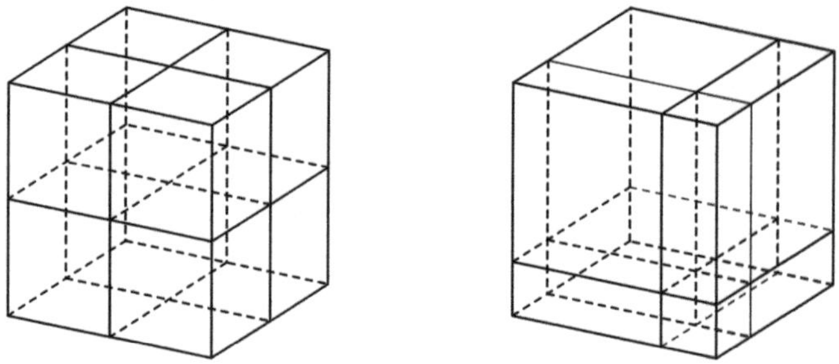

and taking D to be the difference between $\mathcal{C}(x)$ and $\mathcal{C}(y)$, we will have that

$$\mathcal{C}(E+B) = \mathcal{C}(2x) = 8\,\mathcal{C}(x)$$

$$\mathcal{C}(E-B) = \mathcal{C}(2y) = 8\,\mathcal{C}(y)$$

$$\mathcal{C}(E+B) - \mathcal{C}(E-B) = 8\,[\mathcal{C}(x) - \mathcal{C}(y)] = 8\,D$$

and

$$\mathcal{C}(E{+}B) = \mathcal{C}(E) + \mathcal{C}(B) + 3\,\mathcal{P}(E,B,B) + 3\,\mathcal{P}(E,E,B)$$

$$\mathcal{C}(E{-}B) = \mathcal{C}(E) - \mathcal{C}(B) - 3\,\mathcal{P}(B,B,E{-}B) - 3\,\mathcal{P}(B,E{-}B,E{-}B)$$

$$\mathcal{P}(B,E{-}B,E{-}B) = \mathcal{P}(E,E,B) - \mathcal{C}(B) - 2\mathcal{P}(B,B,E{-}B)$$

$$\mathcal{P}(B,B,E{-}B) = \mathcal{P}(E,B,B) - \mathcal{C}(B)$$

so that

$$\mathcal{C}(E{-}B) = \mathcal{C}(E) - 3\mathcal{P}(E,E,B) + 3\mathcal{P}(E,B,B) - \mathcal{C}(B)$$

and

$$\mathcal{C}(E{+}B) - \mathcal{C}(E{-}B) = 6\mathcal{P}(E,E,B) + 2\mathcal{C}(B) = 8D$$

which is just the geometrical interpretation of the equality

$$(E+B)^3 - (E-B)^3 = 6E^2B + 2B^3 = 8D$$

already obtained through Viète's formalism. There is, however, no need to appeal to this last equality and this formalism to go ahead and conclude that

$$\mathcal{P}(E,E,B) = \frac{1}{3}\,[4D - \mathcal{C}(B)]\,.$$

This conclusion does not directly correspond to what is obtained through Viète's formalism, namely:

$$E^2 = \frac{4D - B^3}{3B}$$

since nothing allows to decompose $\mathcal{P}(E, E, B)$ in the square $\mathcal{S}(E)$ with the side E and the segment B. But it still makes the original problem reduced to a new simpler one, easily solvable by ruler and compass.

For the sake of simplicity, let us take the difference of cubes D to be a parallelepiped $\mathcal{P}(B, B, a)$ constructed on the the square $\mathcal{S}(B)$, where, according to *El.* XI.32 and VI.1, a is such that $\mathcal{C}(B) : D : B : a$. Insofar as B is given, admitting that this is also for D is the same as admitting that the segment a is given. This makes $4D$ equal to $\mathcal{P}(B, B, 4a)$, $4D - \mathcal{C}(B)$ equal to $\mathcal{P}(B, B, 4a - B)$, and $\frac{1}{3}[4D - \mathcal{C}(B)]$ equal to $\mathcal{P}\left(B, B, \frac{4a-B}{3}\right)$, all of which will also be given by quite easy constructions. Let this last parallelepiped be C. The new problem is, then, the following:

> On a given side (B), construct a square-based parallelepiped equal to a given parallelepiped (C).

This is nothing but a relatively simple particular case of *El.* XI.27, and can then be solved through the construction spelt out there.

The reduction of the given problem—i.e., *Zeteticum*, II.17—to *El.* XI.27 is a clear case of trans-configurational analysis performed with no help of Viète's formalism or of any other similar algebraic formalism. It shows, then, that this form of analysis does in no way require such a formalism.

Insofar as it is a form of analysis, it involves, of course, also in this version, some work on unknown quantities. In this case, this work consists of reasoning on the unknown segments E, x and y, together with the known segment B and solid D, without making any difference among them, that is dealing with the former just as with the latter. This includes representing both the former and the latter by appropriate diagrams, where no difference is at work among them. These diagrams undoubtedly play an indispensable role in the argument, perfectly in line with the essential role they play in the whole *EPG*, as accounted for in [Panza 2012]. However, this role is relatively marginal in this case—or better—not so explicitly manifest. The most explicit role diagrams have, in this context, is keeping fixed the reference of the names of the relevant geometrical objects or equivalence classes, and to allow proving the primary results about the appropriate segments, cubes and parallelepipeds appealed to, by the consideration of how they mutually compose and decompose.

More important for our purpose is what diagrams do not do here. Considering the last two diagrams—representing a cube decomposed into eight cubes and into two cubes and six (non–cubic) parallelepipeds—makes this immediately manifest. Even though these diagrams are visually and intuitively different, they are in fact perfectly equivalent in relation to the role they have within the previous argument: either can be replaced by the other. This is because all they do is representing how a cube can be decomposed when all of its sides are cut into two parts. All that the argument requires to the diagram(s) is showing how the cut of sides propagates on the whole solid, which is just the same regardless if these sides are cut in equal parts or not, and even if they are not all cut in the same proportion. The relevant information to decide whether the parts that are so obtained in the whole solids are cubes or (non-cubic) parallelepipeds is neither provided nor reflected by the diagrams but rather by the problems' assumption.

This is an obvious consequence of the fact the equality is not a diagrammatic relation. In a cursory way, we could say that it is in no way accounted for in diagrammatic terms. Still, this consequence has, here, a crucial effect on the logical nature of the argument: it allows avoiding requiring that the relevant unknown segments are properly supposed to be constructed; it makes inessential, to let the diagrams play their role, whether these segments are known or not, and actually, satisfy the conditions of the problem; what is relevant is that they are taken as sides of a cube or a parallelepiped, or as parts of such sides. In other terms, what is relevant here is that we reason on cubes or parallelepipeds, and their respective parts and sides, whatever they might be given, one with respect to another, both in magnitude, position and ratio (to use the three modalities in which geometrical objects can be given according to Euclid's *Data*).

This is what makes diagrams play their role in the argument. But the argument does not only go ahead because of diagrams. It also depends on additive relations and rules of replacements proper to any magnitudes, for example to the fact that

$$(\alpha+\beta)-(\alpha-\beta)=2\beta \quad \text{and} \left(\begin{array}{l} \alpha=\beta-\gamma-3\delta-3\varepsilon \\ \varepsilon=\zeta-\gamma-2\delta \\ \delta=\eta-\gamma \end{array} \right) \Rightarrow \alpha=\beta-3\zeta+3\eta-\gamma$$

whatever quantities α, β, γ, δ, ε, ζ, η might be. These relations and rules are essential for making analysis proceeds, but they do not depend on any constructive clause, and diagrams have no role in fixing them (or, at least, not a direct role).

The analytical argument justifying the reduction to the given problem to another is, then, perfectly independent of the way the relevant segments, cubes, and parallelepipeds are given or supposed to be given, provided they enduringly belong to the same equivalence classes, and they bear the relevant additive relations and obey the relevant substitution rules. There is no need to suppose that they have been constructed since they are not identified in the force of their actual or supposed constructions, but rather of their staying to each another in the relevant additive relations and of the fact that the segments are taken to be as sides or parts of sides of the relevant cubes and parallelepipeds.[5]

Mutatis mutandis, this happens in any instance of geometrical trans-configurational analysis, even in theorematic cases.[6] Some clear examples are provided in the alternative proofs of *El.* XIII.1–5 [Euclid 1883-1899, IV, 364.18–376.22], usually attributed to Heron of Alexandria [Euclid 2001, 390–400], who probably lived in the first century AD [Masià 2015]. All of them are preceded by an explicit analysis, which is openly trans-configurational indeed. Let us consider the case of *El.* XIII.1 [Euclid 1883-1899, IV, 366.5–24]:[7]

> Let some straight line, AB, be cut in extreme and mean ratio at Γ, and let there be a greater segment, $A\Gamma$, and let an equal to half of AB be set out, $A\Delta$. I say that <the square> on $\Gamma\Delta$ is quintuple of <the square> on $A\Delta$. For since <the square> on $\Gamma\Delta$ is quintuple of <the square> on $A\Delta$, and <the square> on $\Gamma\Delta$ is <the square> on $A\Gamma$, $A\Delta$ plus twice <the rectangle contained> by $A\Gamma$, $A\Delta$, therefore <the square> on $A\Gamma$, $A\Delta$ plus twice <the rectangle contained> by $A\Gamma$, $A\Delta$ are quintuples of <the square> on $A\Delta$. Therefore, *separando* [διελόντι],[8] <the square> on $A\Gamma$ plus twice <the rectangle contained> by $A\Gamma$, $A\Delta$ is quadruple of <the square> on $A\Delta$. But <the rectangle contained> by BA, $A\Gamma$ is equal to twice <the rectangle contained> by $A\Gamma$, $A\Delta$—for BA <is> double of $A\Delta$—and <the rectangle contained> by AB, $B\Gamma$ is equal to <the square> on $A\Gamma$—for AB has been cut in extreme and mean ratio. Therefore <the rectangle contained> by BA, $A\Gamma$ plus <the rectangle contained> by AB, $B\Gamma$ is quadruple of <the square> on $A\Delta$. But <the rectangle contained> by BA, $A\Gamma$ plus <the rectangle contained> by AB, $B\Gamma$ is <the square> on AB. Therefore <the square> on AB is quadruple of <the square> on $A\Delta$. And it is [ἔστι δέ]: for AB is double of $A\Delta$.

5. For further clarifications of trans-configurational (problematic) analysis in connection with the classical and Arabic mathematical tradition, see [Panza 2007].

6. Problematic analysis is usually opposed to theorematic analysis: while the former aims to construct a geometrical object satisfying certain given conditions, the latter is aimed to prove the truth of theorems. This distinction, and that between problems and theorems come back to ancient sources, like Proclus's *Commentary on the First Book of Euclid's Elements* [Proclus 1873, 77–80], and the Seventh Book of Pappus's *Collectio* [Pappus 1876-1878, VII.1, 634.24–636.14].

7. Unless otherwise specified, the translations from ancient Greek are done by G. Longa. A special thank to A. Jones and N. Sidoli and for their kind help in this regard.

8. We read this "separation" [διελόντι] as a way of applying the ratio operation of *El.* V.17, different from a simple division.

Using the previous notations the theorem can be expressed in this way:[9]

$$(b+c=a \ \& \ a:b=b:c) \Rightarrow \mathcal{S}\left(b+\frac{a}{2}\right)=5\,\mathcal{S}\left(\frac{a}{2}\right)$$

The analysis goes, then, as follows:

Let's suppose that	$\mathcal{S}\left(\frac{a}{2}+b\right)=5\,\mathcal{S}\left(\frac{a}{2}\right).$	1
For *El.* II.4	$\mathcal{S}(b)+\mathcal{R}(a,b)=\mathcal{S}\left(\frac{a}{2}+b\right)-\mathcal{S}\left(\frac{a}{2}\right).$	2
Hence	$\mathcal{S}(b)+\mathcal{R}(a,b)=4\,\mathcal{S}\left(\frac{a}{2}\right).$	3
For *El.* VI.17	$\mathcal{S}(b)=\mathcal{R}(a,c).$	4
Hence	$\mathcal{R}(a,c)+\mathcal{R}(a,b)=4\,\mathcal{S}\left(\frac{a}{2}\right).$	5
For *El.* II.2	$\mathcal{R}(a,c)+\mathcal{R}(a,b)=\mathcal{S}(a).$	6
Hence	$\mathcal{S}(a)=4\,\mathcal{S}\left(\frac{a}{2}\right).$	7

As this last equality is an obvious particular case of *El.* II.4, the proof can start from it and go ahead by merely reversing the analysis.

Here all the segments, squares, and rectangles are given. So, the analysis does not work on any unknown object as if it were known. It rather starts from a statement that is not (yet) proved and deduces an already established theorem from it suggesting that the required proof starts from it. Diagrams can at most enter it, then, insofar as they are required to perform the deduction or, indirectly, to prove the theorems that the deduction has recourse to. As it happens for trans-configurational problematic analysis, also trans-configurational theorematic analysis does neither require that the unknown geometrical objects are supposed to have been constructed nor does any specific use of diagrams, apart from that which classical geometry requires to conduct non-analytical arguments.

3 Intra-configurational analysis and the purely material role of diagrams

A crucial difference arises in intra-configurational analysis. Unlike the trans-configurational one, this form of analysis cannot avoid assuming the relevant unknown objects as constructed and, thus, have a specific constructive relation to the given ones. At issue here are not equivalence classes of (equal)

9. With respect to the text, a stands for AB, b for $A\Gamma$ and c for $B\Gamma$ (therefore, $A\Delta$ is 1/2 of a).

segments and the additive relation of the figures that have them as sides, but rather particular points or segments in an identified position, to be obtained by a specific construction. This construction has to be disclosed since it makes the searched points or segments known and characterizes them as points and segments.

Consider a simple example: proposition II.3 of Archimedes's *On the Sphere and Cylinder* asks:

> To cut the given sphere by a plane, so that the surfaces of the segments have to each other a ratio the same as the given one. [Archimedes 1910-1915, I 184.2–4]

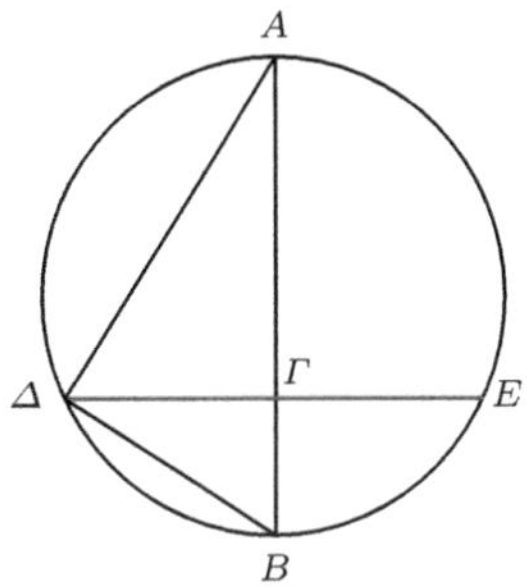

The analysis goes as follows:

Consider a great circle, $A\Delta BE$, of the sphere with diame- 1
ter AB.

Let the problem supposed to be solved by cutting the sphere 2
with a plane perpendicular to AB, which cuts $A\Delta BE$ in Δ and E and the diameter in Γ.

Then, the surface of the spherical segment ΔBE will be to the 3
surface of the spherical segment ΔAE in the given ratio.

According to *On the Sphere and Cylinder*, I.42-43, these sur- 4
faces are equal to the circles of radii ΔB and ΔA, respectively.

By *El.* XII.2, then, these circles are to one other as the 5
squares $\mathcal{S}(\Delta B)$ and $\mathcal{S}(\Delta A)$ on the radii.

According to the Pythagorean theorem, these squares are to 6
one other as the segments ΓB and $A\Gamma$.

Hence, these segments are to one another as the surfaces of 7
spherical segments ΔBE and ΔAE.

The synthesis becomes, then, obvious :

> And it will be put together [συντεθήσεται] thus: let there be a sphere with great circle $AB\Delta E$ and diameter AB, and <let> the given ratio <be> that of Z to H, and let AB be cut at Γ so as to be: as $A\Gamma$ to $B\Gamma$, so Z to H, and let the sphere be cut by a plane through Γ at right <angles> to the line AB, and let there be a common section, ΔE, and let $A\Delta$, ΔB be joined, and let there be set out two circles, Θ, K: Θ having the radius equal to $A\Delta$, K having the radius equal to ΔB. [Archimedes 1910-1915, 184.21–186.3]

To construct the object solving the problem (and its diagrammatic representation), the diameter AB has to be cut at a certain point Γ, so that $A\Gamma$ and ΓB are equal to one another in the given ratio (that of Z to H). Since this ratio is given insofar the two segments Z and H are given [*Data* 1], then the construction can easily be carried out by applying the procedure for finding the fourth proportional between $Z + H$, AB and Z (or H). This is quite obvious [following *El.* I.2, I.11, I.31 and VI.9], and Archimedes does not detail it. Here is as it might go.

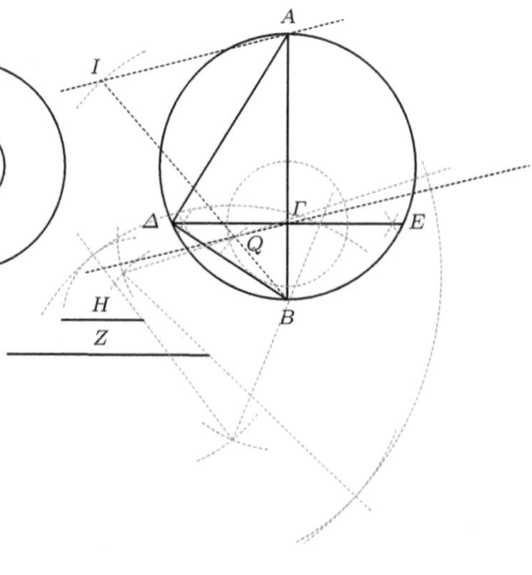

In agreement to *El.* I.2 or I.3, construct a segment BQ, starting from B and equal to Z. Then, by Post. 2 and *El.* I.2 or I.3 draw a segment QI, starting from Q, collinear to BQ, and equal to H. Join I and A [Post. 1]. Construct the parallel $Q\Gamma$ to IA passing through Q [*El.* I.31]. The intersection point of this parallel and the diameter AB—i.e., the point Γ—cuts AB in such a way that as $A\Gamma$ is to ΓB so H is to Z. Finally, draw the perpendicular ΔE to AB through Γ [*El.* I.11]. Therefore, the plane perpendicular to AB passing through ΔE cuts the sphere so that the surface of relation between the two spherical segments ΔBE and ΔAE is equal to the given ratio of Z to H.

Here the diagram takes part in the argument just as it participates in the synthesis of our previous examples of trans-configurational analysis, but with an essential difference. In the latter, the given segments are whatever elements of the relevant equivalence class of equal segments, working as incidental representatives of these classes. By contrast, here, the given segments are particular individual objects, working as incidental representatives or whatever segments, and they provide a basis for the construction of other particular segments and points forming a geometrical system. This system works, as a whole, as an incidental representation of any other (topologically) equivalent geometrical system. In other terms, in these last two cases, the focus is no more on equivalence classes of equal segments but on a(n equivalence class of) particular system(s) of geometrical objects.

What makes this (equivalence class of) system(s) represented by a diagram is that the diagram is drawn, step by step, in agreement to some constructive clauses belonging to a constructive canon which is, as such, an essential component of the theory within which the argument is conducted. Even the given segments, squares, and circles are given only since they are supposed to have been constructed in advance through a licensed constructive procedure, which is simply not detailed here (since the focus is not on it but on a further construction): their drawing is nothing but a (material) counterpart of a constructive argument, which details, step by step, the whole process of this drawing; each diagrammatic gesture that is here at issue obeys a constructive clause licensed by the relevant canon; and it is just this, rather than the actual features of the material drawing, that makes the diagrams represent the relevant objects and play, then, their role in the geometrical argument.

However, this is what happens in Archimedes's synthesis, not in his analysis. What makes the latter an analysis is just that its starting point—the act of taking Γ as a given particular point on AB—is not the outcome of a licensed construction. This makes the dot representing this point in the diagram not drawn in agreement to any constructive clause, but rather freehand, so to say. The diagrammatic gesture making this point represented is a purely material act, which enters the argument as such, rather than as the counterpart of a licensed constructive step. It is just this material act—this free diagrammatic gesture, as it were—that makes the analysis possible, by allowing taking the searched for point as given; it is this act that triggers an effective (but conditional) construction, making, all along with the analytical argument itself, other diagrams constructed in agreement with appropriate constructive clauses. In short, we could say that diagrams indispensably play, in intra-configurational analysis, a purely material role.

Whereas in a geometrical trans-configurational analysis, what makes it possible to work on unknown objects is, as said above, the fact that analytical arguments do not require these objects to be supposed to have been constructed, since these objects are not identified in the force of their actual or supposed construction, this is what happens here, as well as in any other instance of intra-configurational geometrical analysis: the point Γ is here properly supposed to have been constructed, and solving the problem just consists in detailing its construction, which is, then, what identifies it as such. Then one of the crucial roles of diagrams is here supporting the very possibility of working on a non-constructed point as if it were provided, by displaying it in a discretionary position: a role that can only be played by diagrams drawn freehand, or, as it were, thanks to a purely material act.

It has often been argued that geometrical analysis, although certainly present, is not very frequent in the mathematical works of the Hellenistic period.[10] For instance, it has been maintained that analysis is missing from Euclid's *Elements*—interpolations apart, of course. This depends on a restricted way of understanding geometrical analysis, which we think is not appropriate, conceptually speaking. If geometrical analysis is concerned with some sort of item that is not at hand, but is nevertheless supposed to be at our disposal, or with a statement not justified, but anyway taken for granted, then an instance of intra-configurational geometrical analysis is at work any time a certain geometrical object that is supposed to be constructed, though not being so. This happens, in particular, when a geometrical object is proved to be not constructible by means of a demonstration showing that, if it were so, a contradiction would arise, that is, any time a *reductio ad absurdum* is performed in geometry. If this is the case, then intra-configurational geometric analysis is largely present, if not pervasive, in the mathematical works of the Hellenistic Period and, of course, also in Euclid's *Elements*.

Here is a simple example. It concerns a case of intra-configurational analysis drawn from Euclid's proof of *El.* I.7. This is properly a proof, since this proposition is properly a theorem, not a problem. Still, strictly speaking, the analysis is problematic, even if it concludes that proof. Since what is to be proved is that a certain construction cannot be performed: a certain triangle is supposed to have been constructed, and it is shown that this supposition leads to a contradiction. What makes the analysis provide a proof is just a last meta-geometric step, in which it is implicitly admitted that no licensed constructions can lead to a contradiction. It is, then, concluded that no such construction could make the relevant triangle constructed.

Euclid's theorem is the following:

> On the same straight-line, there will not be constructed [οὐ συσταθήσονται] two other straight-lines towards different points on the same side, equal, respectively, to the same two straight-lines and having the same limits as the initial straight-lines. [Euclid 1883-1899, I, 24.12–16]

Euclid takes three given segments—AB, $A\Gamma$, and $B\Gamma$—so as to form a triangle $AB\Gamma$, and proves, by a *reductio ad absurdum*, that no other point Δ, which is not symmetric to Γ with respect to AB, can be constructed, such that $A\Delta = A\Gamma$ and $B\Delta = B\Gamma$. More generally, his argument actually proves

10. See, for example, [Netz 2000, 140–1].

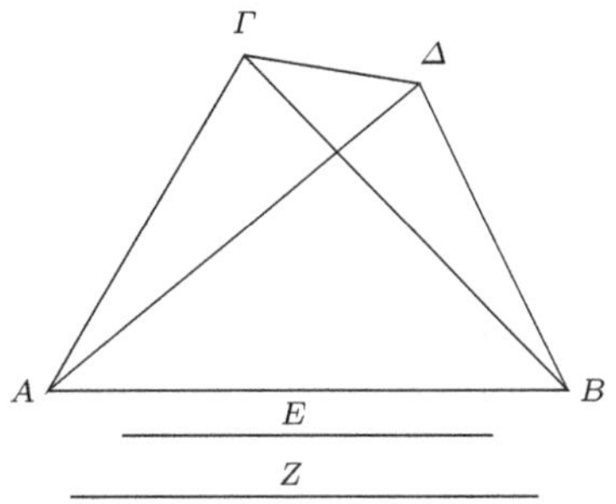

that if whatever three distinct segments AB, E, Z, and a triangle $AB\Gamma$ are given, such that $A\Gamma = E$ and $B\Gamma = Z$, then, up to symmetry, no other triangle can be constructed on AB, whose other sides are respectively equal to E and Z. Hence, three segments being given, only one triangle can be constructed, up to symmetry, such that its sides are equal to these segments. Here is Euclid's argument.

> Let a point Δ other than Γ supposed given "on the same side" of AB than Γ, such that $A\Delta = A\Gamma$ and $B\Delta = B\Gamma$. 1
>
> In agreement to *El.* Post. 1, let the segment $\Gamma\Delta$ be traced. 2
>
> The isosceles triangles $A\Delta\Gamma$ and $B\Delta\Gamma$ are, then, given. 3
>
> According to *El.* I.5, the angles $A\Gamma\Delta$ and $A\Delta\Gamma$ are equal. 4
>
> As the angle $B\Gamma\Delta$ is part of the angle $A\Gamma\Delta$, in agreement to *El.* Com. Not. 5, the latter is greater than the former, which also makes the angle $A\Delta\Gamma$ greater than the angle $B\Gamma\Delta$. 5
>
> As the angle $A\Delta\Gamma$ is part of the angle $B\Delta\Gamma$, in agreement to *El.* Com. Not. 5, the latter is greater than the former, which makes the angle $B\Gamma\Delta$ greater than the angle $B\Delta\Gamma$. 6
>
> But according to *El.* I.5, these last two angles are equal. 7
>
> Contradiction. 8
>
> Hence, no point Δ other than Γ can be given "on the same side" of AB than Γ, such that $A\Gamma = A\Gamma$ and $B\Delta = B\Gamma$. 9

This argument can be extended to prove that, up to symmetry, no triangle other than $AB\Gamma$ can be constructed on AB, whose other sides are equal to E and Z, which is obvious, and there is no need to detail it.

The steps *1–7* of this argument clearly form a problematic intra-configurational analysis. If, on the one side, this is made possible by the drawing of the diagram representing the two segments $A\Delta$ and $B\Delta$, sharing the extremity Δ, which allows supposing that the triangles $A\Delta\Gamma$ and $B\Delta\Gamma$ are given, this same argument proves that these segments are not only supposed to be constructed without being actually so, but even can actually not be constructed. This diagram is, then, not only traced freehand, but it cannot but be so traced. Tracing is necessarily a free diagrammatic gesture, that is, as we have said below, a purely material act.

Such a gesture or act is an indispensable component of intra-configurational geometric analysis, which entails, in turn, that diagrams indispensably enter Greek geometry not only as counterparts of licensed constructions, but, in the case of intra-configurational analysis, also as material devices, independent of any construction, but still belonging to a perfectly codified theoretical procedure.

4 Some historical confirmations

In this section, we intend to provide a historical and philological argument in favour of the thesis we have presented in the previous section. If we examine, even superficially, the manuscript tradition of the Greek mathematical texts, we'd notice that the arguments we have called "intra-configurational" exhibit often a peculiarity that is almost absent in synthetic proofs and, to a minor extent, in trans-configurational analyses, i.e., the presence of two diagrams, one for the analysis and one for the synthesis.

Let us take the example of the Archimedean corpus:[11] there, we find only six problems solved through the method of analysis and synthesis, all included in the second book of *On the Sphere and Cylinder* [II.1 and II.3–7].[12] With regards to diagrams, among the six propositions mentioned, four have two diagrams [II.4–7], [Archimedes 1910-1915, I, 190.11–194.10, 206.1–234.30] one placed at the end of the analysis and one at the end of the synthesis—or, to be more precise, one at the beginning of the synthesis (that of the analysis) and one at the beginning of the subsequent proposition (that of the synthesis).[13] Consider, for instance, proposition II.7: it requires to cut a given sphere $AB\Gamma\Delta$ in such a way that the spherical segment $AB\Gamma$ has a given ratio (that of ΘK to $K\Lambda$) to the cone $AB\Gamma$, i.e., the cone having the base and the height equal to the cones of the spherical segment.

11. Archimedean diagrams are reproduced according to their critical edition included in [Archimedes 2004]. Likewise, the reproduction of Apollonius' diagrams will follow the critical edition included in [Apollonius 2010]. Different choices, due to a different reading of the manuscripts, will be indicated whenever it is necessary.

12. We have already encountered proposition II.3 of the Archimedean treatise in the previous section.

13. In almost every Greek mathematical text, diagrams are placed after the proposition [Acerbi 2020].

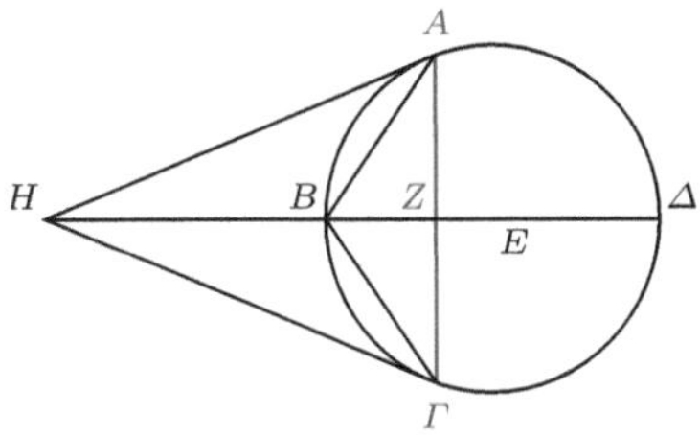

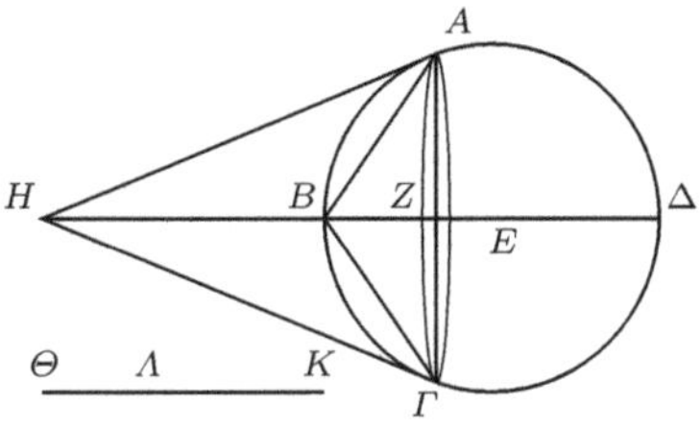

The diagram of the analysis and the diagram of the synthesis are partially different: in the latter, there is a graphical representation, besides of the base of the cone or the spherical segment $AB\Gamma$, also of the ratio of ΘK to $K\Lambda$ (through a segment $\Theta\Lambda K$). According to the thesis we have stated in the previous paragraph, this difference has a crucial importance: in the analysis, in fact, the assumption that the spherical segment $AB\Gamma$ has a certain given ratio to the cone $AB\Gamma$ is only hypothetical. The given ratio of ΘK to $K\Lambda$ is not present there because it is not necessary to the analytic argument, which consists only in showing that the plane solving the problem is given, that is, constructible.[14] In the synthesis, instead, this ratio is required to carry out the constructive procedure leading to the determination of the point Z on AB such that, tracing a plane through it and perpendicular to the diameter AB, the spherical segment $AB\Gamma$ has, with the cone $AB\Gamma$, the same ratio as the given one (that of ΘK to $K\Lambda$). By mirroring the analysis [Berggren & Van Brummelen 2000, 13] the problem has then turned into finding the fourth proportional ΔZ between segments $\Theta\Lambda$, ΛK, and ΔE (a straightforward application of *El.* VI.10). However, to apply the constructive procedure exposed in *El.* VI.10 one needs three segments in input (so to say). For this reason, $\Theta\Lambda K$ has to be represented in the diagram of the synthesis, where the constructive procedure has to be actually exhibited and not simply assumed hypothetically as realized. In this sense, in the diagram of the analysis, Z cannot but be drawn freehand and is not intended to result from the application of a constructive procedure. In the synthesis, instead, Z is determined by a construction procedure (that of *El.* VI.10)[15] and the diagram is drawn accordingly.

In the Apollonian corpus preserved in direct tradition, we find the same kind of phenomenon, albeit a bit more complex from a philological point of view. Only an isolated group of six propositions exists here as well

14. For the meaning of the term "given" as constructible in Greek mathematics, see [Sidoli 2018, 381–382].

15. This examination is identical to that we have proposed for *SC* II.3, even though we only find one diagram in the manuscript tradition in this proposition. As a matter of fact, also in that case the given ratio, as in *SC* II.7, is never used in the analysis but is employed only in the synthesis. In a certain sense, therefore, we can see the diagram of II.3 is like two different diagrams.

proved by analysis and synthesis, in a sort of appendix to the second book [propositions II.44, 46, 47, 49–51].[16] Concerning the presence of double diagrams, it only occurs in the proposition II.50b [Apollonius 2010, 122.12–126.24], in which a tangent to a given hyperbola has to be constructed, making with the axis an angle equal to the given acute angle:

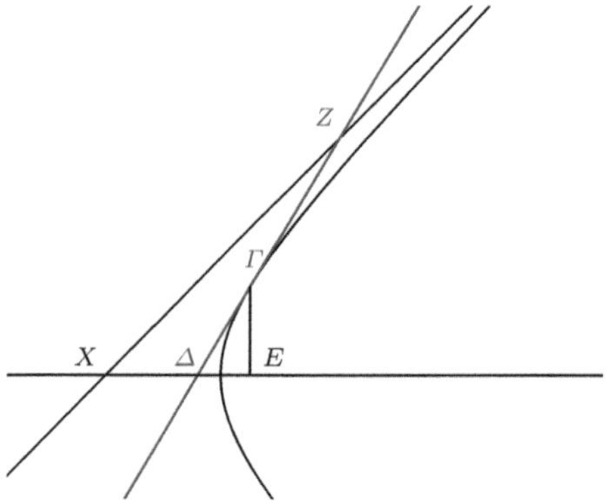

In the analysis, it is assumed that a tangent $\Lambda\Delta$ to the given hyperbola has already been drawn [γεγονέτω καὶ ἔστω ἡ $\Lambda\Delta$], making an angle with the axis equal to a given acute angle (not represented in the diagram). The ordinate ΓE of point Γ and an asymptote XZ are then drawn, with Z as the point of intersection between the asymptote and the tangent $\Gamma\Delta$. Finally, the center X and Γ are joined. This is sufficient to see the possibility of applying the fundamental result of *Conics* I.37 [Apollonius 2010, 87]: Since $\Gamma\Delta$ is assumed to be a tangent (analytical assumption), ΓE is the ordinate (Γ) and EX is a diameter, then:

$$\mathcal{R}(E\Delta, EX) : \mathcal{S}(E\Gamma) :: \textit{latus transversum } (=2XA) : \textit{latus rectum}$$

On the other hand, the ratio of the *latus transversum* to the *latus rectum* is obviously given (since the hyperbola is given). Therefore the ratio of the rectangle contained by $E\Delta$ and EX to the square on the ordinate $E\Gamma$ is also given [*Data* def. 2]. From here, by means of a chain of givens that are not difficult to decode,[17] Apollonius demonstrates that the object solving the problem, the tangent $\Gamma\Delta$, is indeed given in position [θέσει ἄρα ἡ $\Gamma\Delta$].

Leaving aside the diorism,[18] we see in the synthesis that the given angle (presented in the enunciation and never used in the analysis) comes to be actively involved and, therefore, is represented in the diagram, in this case by

16. On the problem of the authenticity of these propositions, see [Federspiel 2008].
17. By using *Data* def. 2 and props. 8, 25, 29, 40, and 50.
18. Which establishes that the problem is soluble if and only if the given angle is greater than half the angle between the asymptotes.

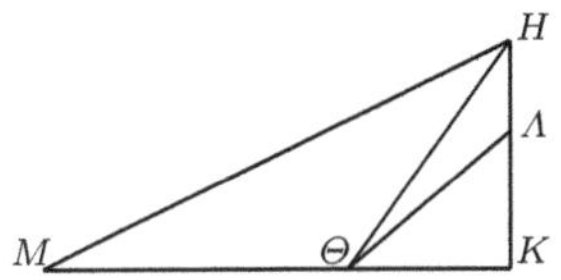

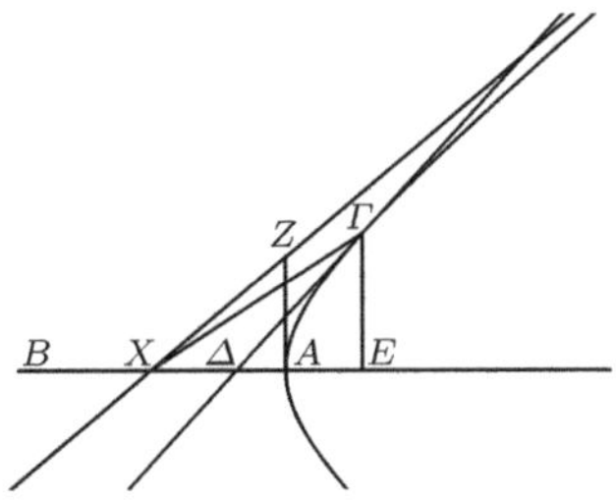

$K\Theta H$.[19] This allows, through means of a manipulation of proportions and the application of some procedures of construction taken from the sixth book of Euclid's *Elements*, to reach the actual construction of the tangent $\Gamma\Delta$ making an angle equal to the given acute angle $K\Theta H$ with the axis of the hyperbola. Beyond the demonstrative details, here we only aim to point out that, also in this case, the presence of the two diagrams is explicable in the same way we have proposed for the previous examples taken from Archimedes. Here too, we have an action free from constructive constraints (the drawing of the tangent $\Gamma\Delta$ in the analysis) in the first diagram and an effective construction only in the synthesis.

Although *Conics* II.51b is the only explicit case, in the Apollonian corpus, of the introduction of two diagrams, it is possible to suppose that other propositions, at least a certain stage of their transmission, had the same feature. This could have been the case for *Conics* II.44 and II.46, for example. We find an argument in favor of this in (an interesting) mistake of the copyist of the manuscript *Vat. gr.* 206 (siglum *V*), the archetype from which all the later manuscript tradition and the modern editions of the Apollonian treatise derive directly or indirectly [Decorps-Foulquier 2000, 180–3]. Here is how M. Decorps-Foulquier accounts for this error in his remarks on the manuscript tradition of the *Conics*:

> On a ainsi un espace réservé pour les propositions 45*V* et 48*V*, qui sont les synthèses de nos propositions 44 et 46, ce qui n'offre pas d'intérêt en soi, puisque les figures sont les mêmes que celles des analyses correspondantes. En tout cas, l'existence de ces espaces a favorisé l'erreur d'un copiste antérieur à celui de V, puisque l'emplacement réservé pour la figure de la proposition 45*V*, au début de la proposition 46*V*, n'a pas été rempli par la figure attendue (la même figure que la prop. 44), mais par les figures de la prop. 46*V*. De ce fait, l'espace réservé pour les figures de la proposition 46*V* (au début de la prop. 47*V*) est resté vide, et le copiste de *V* écrit au milieu de l'emplacement (cela devait

19. Greater than the half-angle between the asymptotes, in compliance with the diorism just mentioned, i.e., greater than $K\Theta\Lambda = AXZ$.

être dans son modèle) : ἐγράφη τὸ σχῆμα ἄνω ("La figure a été représentée plus haut"). [Apollonius 2010, II.3, 159]

Without entering into the details of the discrepancies between *V* and the modern editions of the *Conics*,[20] for our purposes, it is enough to say that the copyist's error shows indirectly that, in the manuscript at his disposal, for the two propositions in question, there were two diagrams,[21] not subsequently copied because one of them was considered as a mere (useless) repetition of the other. This is also confirmed by the fact that in the Arabic version of the *Conics*, an independent witness of the Apollonian text from our Eutocian edition, we find a double diagram for both propositions [Apollonius 2010, II.1, 199–203].[22]

From this brief overview of the available sources, we can therefore reasonably conclude that, with regard to the classic corpus, the practice of inserting two diagrams was present in a significant number of cases in the analysis of problems (7/12, 58%). This particularity can be explained by the different logical statutes that the object solving the problem (of which the diagram is a representation) assumes in analysis, and in synthesis. As we have explained in the previous paragraph, and reiterated in the examples cited here, such an object is not presented as the result of an actual construction procedure, but simply as hypothetically existing (by recourse to the classical expression γεγονέτω). On the other hand, in the synthesis, the same object takes on a different connotation: it is no longer an assumption, but rather the result of a construction procedure that reproduces the resolution, or chain of givens [Acerbi 2011], as a series of constructive actions/steps. In this sense, the diagrams of the analysis and synthesis, although almost identical, have a completely different status. Hence, the need to reproduce them twice.

Bibliography

Acerbi, Fabio [2011], The language of the Givens: Its forms and its use as a deductive tool in Greek mathematics, *Archive for History of Exact Sciences*, 65(2), 119–153, doi: 10.1007/s00407-010-0072-z.

—— [2020], Interazioni fra testo, tavole e diagrammi nei manoscritti matematici e astronomici greci, in: *La conoscenza scientifica nell'Alto Medioevo*,

20. Decorps-Foulquier [2000] provides a detailed examination of this intricate issue.

21. Or, at least, a diagram and an empty indentation intended to contain the diagram of the syntheses of propositions 44 and 46.

22. In the Arabic tradition, we find another possible confirmation of the presence of two diagrams in the writing of intra-configurational analyses. In Apollonius's *De Sectione Rationis*, a work entirely written using analysis and synthesis, all propositions (or cases) present a double diagram (in many cases even a triple diagram, the extra diagram being reserved for diorism), one for analysis and the other for synthesis. See [Saito & Sidoli 2010] for a careful examination of these cases.

Centro Italiano di Studi sull'Alto Medioevo, *Settimane di Studio del CISAM*, vol. 67, 585–621.

APOLLONIUS [2010], *Apollonius de Perge, Coniques*, Berlin; New York: de Gruyter, ed. by M. Decorps-Foulquier and M. Federspiel.

ARCHIMEDES [1910-1915], *Archimedis Opera Omnia, cum Commentariis Eutocii*, Leipzig: B. G. Teubner, ed. by J. H. Heiberg.

—— [2004], *The Works of Archimedes: Translation and Commentary*, vol. 1, Cambridge: Cambridge University Press, ed. by R. Netz.

BERGGREN, Lennart J. & VAN BRUMMELEN, Glen [2000], The role and development of geometric analysis and synthesis in Ancient Greece and Medieval Islam, in: *Ancient & Medieval Traditions in the Exact Sciences: Essays in Memory of Wilbur Knorr*, edited by P. Suppes, J. M. Moravcsik, & H. Mendell, Stanford, CA: CSLI Publications, 1–31.

BOS, Henk J. M [2001], *Redefining Geometrical Exactness: Descartes' transformation of the early modern concept of construction*, Berlin; New York: Springer Science & Business Media.

CARTER, Jessica [2010], Diagrams and proofs in analysis, *International Studies in the Philosophy of Science*, 24, 1–14, doi: 10.1080/02698590903467085.

DE TOFFOLI, Silvia [2017], Chasing the diagram. The use of visualizations in algebraic reasoning, *The Review of Symbolic Logic*, 10, 158–186, doi: 10.1017/S1755020316000277.

DECORPS-FOULQUIER, Micheline [2000], *Recherches sur les Coniques d'Apollonios de Pergé*, Paris: Klincksieck.

EUCLID [1883-1899], *Euclidis Opera Omnia*, Leipzig: B. G. Teubner, ed. by J. H. Heiberg and H. Menge.

—— [2001], *Les Éléments*, vol. 4, Paris: Presses Universitaires de France, traduction et commentaires par B. Vitrac.

FEDERSPIEL, Michel [2008], Les problèmes des livres grecs des *Coniques* d'Apollonius de Pergé. Des propositions mathématiques en quête d'auteur, *Études Classiques*, 76, 321–360.

GIAQUINTO, Marcus [2007], *Visual Thinking in Mathematics*, Oxford: Oxford University Press.

MANDERS, Kenneth [2008], Diagram-based geometric practice, in: *The Philosophy of Mathematical Practice*, edited by P. Mancosu, Oxford: Oxford University Press, 65–79, doi: 10.1093/acprof:oso/9780199296453.003.0004.

Masià, Ramon [2015], On dating Hero of Alexandria, *Archive for History of Exact Sciences*, 69, 231–255, doi: 10.1007/s00407-014-0148-2.

Netz, Reviel [2000], Why did Greek mathematicians publish their analyses?, in: *Ancient & Medieval Traditions in the Exact Sciences: Essays in Memory of Wilbur Knorr*, edited by P. Suppes, J. M. Moravcsik, & H. Mendell, Stanford, CA: CSLI Publications, 139–157.

Panza, Marco [2007], Qu'est-ce qui est neuf et qu'est-ce qui est ancien dans l'*analysis restituta* et l'*algebra nova* de Viète et quelle en est leur provenance? Quelques réflexions sur les relations entre l'algèbre et l'analyse avant Viète, *Revue d'histoire des mathématiques*, 13(1), 85–113, doi: 10.24033/rhm.48.

—— [2012], The twofold role of diagrams in Euclid's plane geometry, *Synthese*, 186, 55–102, doi: 10.1007/s11229-012-0074-2.

Pappus [1876-1878], *Pappi Alexandrini Collectionis quae supersunt*, Berlin: Weidmann, ed. by F. Hultsch.

Proclus [1873], *Procli Diadochi in primum Euclidis Elementorum librum commentarii*, Leipzig: Teubner, ed. by G. Friedlein.

Saito, Ken & Sidoli, Nathan [2010], The function of diorism in ancient Greek analysis, *Historia Mathematica*, 37(4), 579–614, doi: 10.1016/j.hm.2009.12.003.

Sidoli, Nathan [2018], The concept of given in Greek mathematics, *Archive for History of Exact Sciences*, 72(4), 353–402, doi: 10.1007/s00407-018-0211-5.

Viète, François [1591*a*], *Francisci Vietae Zeteticorum libri quinque ex Opere Restitutæmathematicæanalysaeos, seu algebra nova*, Turonis: Apud I. Mettayer.

—— [1591*b*], *In Artem analyticem Isagoge. Seorsim excussa ab Opere restitutae Mathematicae Analyseos, seu Algebra nova*, Turonis: Apud I. Mettayer.

—— [1983], *The Analytic Art. Nine Studies in Algebra, Geometry and Trigonometry from the "Opus Restitutæ Mathematicæ Analyseos, seu Algebra Nova"*, Kent, Ohio: State University Press, ed. by T. R. Witmer.

Analytical Reasoning and Problem-Solving in Diophantus's *Arithmetica*: Two Different Styles of Reasoning in Greek Mathematics

Jean Christianidis
National and Kapodistrian University of Athens (Greece)
Centre Alexandre Koyré, Paris (France)

Résumé : Depuis quelques décennies, la question d'une compréhension historiquement correcte de la méthode de Diophante a attiré l'attention des chercheurs. « L'algèbre moderne (c'est-à-dire, post-viètienne) », « la géométrie algébrique », « l'arithmétique », « l'analyse et la synthèse » sont parmi les contextes proposés par certains historiens pour interpréter les procédures résolutoires de Diophante, tandis que la catégorie de « l'algèbre prémoderne » a été proposée récemment par d'autres dans la même finalité. Le but de cet article est d'argumenter contre l'idée de contextualiser le *modus operandi* de Diophante dans le cadre conceptuel de l'analyse ancienne et d'examiner les quelques exemples, dans les livres conservés des *Arithmétiques*, qui pourraient être considérés comme liés aux pratiques qui appartiennent au domaine analytique.

Abstract: Over the past few decades, the question regarding the proper understanding of Diophantus's method has attracted much scholarly attention. "Modern (i.e., post-Vietan) algebra", "algebraic geometry", "arithmetic", "analysis and synthesis", have been suggested by historians as suitable contexts for describing Diophantus's resolutory procedures, while the category of "premodern algebra" has recently been proposed by other historians to this end. The aim of this paper is to provide arguments against the idea of contextualizing Diophantus's *modus operandi* within the conceptual framework of the ancient analysis and to examine the few instances, in the preserved books of the *Arithmetica*, which might be regarded as linked to practices belonging to the field of analysis.

Philosophia Scientiæ, 25(3), 2021, 103–130.

1 Introduction[1]

According to a well-known passage in Proclus's *Commentary on the First Book of Euclid's Elements* [Proclus 1873, 203.1–207.25], the formal division of a mathematical proposition comprises six parts: πρότασις (proposition), ἔκθεσις (setting-out, exposition), διορισμός (definition of goal, problem/proof-specification), κατασκευή (construction), ἀπόδειξις (proof, demonstration), and συμπέρασμα (conclusion).[2] No matter whether this scheme is suitable for describing the canonical exposition of any geometrical (theorem/problem) or arithmetical (like those of Books VII–IX of the *Elements*) proposition,[3] it is certainly not appropriate to describe a problem worked-out by algebra, like those in Diophantus's *Arithmetica.*[4] For example, Diophantus's solutions do not feature any stage corresponding to κατασκευή, with its accompanying diagram.[5] Moreover, the crucial stage of ἀπόδειξις, in the sense of a textual unit containing chains of deductive steps, like the proofs we read in the *Elements*, is downgraded in Diophantus to a mere test-proof, that is, a verification, which is very often skipped in the Greek books of the *Arithmetica*. Likewise, the part that is designated by διορισμός almost never appears in the Greek books, and only in the books which are preserved in Arabic translation it appears with remarkable consistency. The word itself does not appear in the Greek books, in which we find to be employed four times the cognate noun προσδιορισμός [Diophantus 1893-1895, I, 36.3; 340.9],[6] and the verb διορίζεσθαι [424.14;

1. This paper was presented to the conference on "Greek Geometrical Analysis: Problems and Prospects" (Clermont-Ferrand, France, March 4–6, 2020). The author would like to thank the organizers for the invitation to participate in the conference, and the anonymous reviewers for their constructive comments.

2. The beginning of this passage is also found in the pseudo-Heronean *Definitions* [Heron 1912, 120.21–122.19]. Translations of the Greek terms have been proposed, among others, by [Netz 1999], [Vitrac 2005], [Acerbi 2011], and [Sidoli 2018b].

3. Sidoli points out that the Proclean scheme is suitable for the simpler problems of the *Elements*, but it fails to capture all of the possible components of the more complicated problems [Sidoli 2018b, 410]. For example, in Euclid's treatment of Proposition III.1 Sidoli distinguishes the following parts: "enunciation", "exposition", "problem-specification", "problem-construction", "proof-specification", "proof-construction", "demonstration", etc.

4. Cf. [Netz 1999, 293]. However, some scholars still think that the Euclidean format applies to Diophantus's propositions. See for example [Meskens 2010, 57–58], and, more recently, Rashed & Houzel, who claim that "du point de vue architectonique, l'exposé de Diophante épouse délibérément la forme et l'ordre de l'exposé euclidien" [Rashed & Houzel 2013, 23].

5. Cf. Acerbi's statement "In the Diophantine problems construction is almost absent" [Diofanto 2011, 67].

6. References to the Greek books of Diophantus are given according to Tannery's edition [Diophantus 1893-1895]: Vol. I: *Diophanti quae exstant omnia continens* (1893). Vol. II: *Continens pseudepigrapha, testimonia veterum, Pachymerae paraphrasis, Planudis commentarium, scholia vetera, omnia fere adhuc inedita, cum prolegomenis et indicibus* (1895). References to the first volume of this work are

428.21], but with the totally different meaning of the condition of solubility (determination).[7] By virtue of the above, the scheme described by Proclus is evidently not suitable to describe the structure of the Diophantine proposition.

Recognizing the unsuitability of the Proclean scheme, Sesiano proposed another one, according to which the presentation of a Diophantine worked-out problem comprises the following parts: πρότασις (described as "statement of the problem, in terms of required magnitudes and given ones, if any"); διορισμός (described as "limiting condition"); ἔκθεσις (described as "numerical setting of the given magnitudes"); ἀνάλυσις (not described at all); σύνθεσις (not described at all); and συμπέρασμα (described as "final statement") [Sesiano 1982, 49]. Sesiano, therefore, regards analysis and synthesis as components of the Diophantine resolutory procedure.

It is true that a characteristic of the Diophantine procedure is to operate with the *quaesitum*—provided that the latter has been named—and this makes the Diophantine solutions apparently analytical [cf. Acerbi in Diofanto 2011, 49].[8] Interpretations of the Diophantine solutions through the machinery of the ancient analysis are witnessed in the scholarship. Besides Sesiano, one might mention for example the study of [Netz 2012], while the influential [Klein 1968] still remains the *locus classicus* for the idea of contextualising Diophantus's approach within the framework of the ancient analysis.[9] Concerns about this viewpoint have been raised by Acerbi in the introduction of his [Diofanto 2011]. Acerbi rightly remarks that there are modalities in the Diophantine approach which do not square with the analytical paradigm [Diofanto 2011, 49], and wonders if Diophantus himself

---

given by simply writing the page number and the line numbers, separated by a dot (.). There are two editions of the Arabic books: [Sesiano 1982] and [Diophante 1984]. References to these books are given according to the edition of Sesiano. All translations from Diophantus are taken from the forthcoming [Christianidis & Oaks 2021].

7. See "Index graecitatis apud Diophantum" [Diophantus 1893-1895, II, 281], s.v. προσδιορισμός, and Tannery's explanation "conditio, limitatio datorum ita ut problema possibile sit". According to Acerbi, the word προσδιορισμός with the meaning of a condition of solubility may originate in Diophantus himself [Diofanto 2011, 16].

8. Of course this feature is common to any algebraic solution as well. More specifically a solution in premodern algebra comprises naming the unknown(s) in terms of preassigned names of the powers, and working through the operations called for in the enunciation with the named terms, to set up (ideally) a polynomial equation, which is then simplified and solved; finally, the *quaesitum* is calculated by means of the solution of the equation and the assigned name(s). The above are discussed in a number of recent studies, including [Christianidis 2018a,b], [Christianidis & Oaks 2013], [Oaks 2009, 2010a,b], [Oaks & Alkhateeb 2005, 2007] and in the forthcoming [Christianidis & Oaks 2021]. For the algebraic character of Diophantus's *Arithmetica* see, in addition to the above, [Christianidis 2015], [Christianidis & Megremi 2019], [Christianidis & Oaks 2021], [Christianidis & Skoura 2013], [Sialaros & Christianidis 2016].

9. Cf. however n. 23 below.

would have considered his own solutions as analyses. He points out that "he never speaks of 'synthesis', but only of 'demonstration', which however is always 'manifest'" [Diofanto 2011]. Besides, even if one were to "qualify the approach in *Arithmetica* not as 'analytic' but as operating by 'reduction'", as Acerbi suggests, even then the reductions cannot be regarded as relating to an analytical undertaking, since the reasoning is devoid of any connotation of search for preconditions [Diofanto 2011, 50].

The concerns expressed by Acerbi are legitimate.[10] Be that as it may, the issue deserves further investigation, especially since the previous discussions fail to take into account the premodern algebra as interpretative context for Diophantus's problem solving. The present paper has therefore a twofold aim: first, to provide additional arguments against the idea that Diophantus proceeds in his solutions by analysis-and-synthesis; second, to discuss the very few propositions of the *Arithmetica* which are referred to as "analysis" or "synthesis".

2 Some discrepancies between Diophantus's solutions and analytical reasoning

Starting with the first, it is important to note that linguistic analysis does not support subsuming the Diophantine solutions into the field of ancient analysis. An essential feature of any ancient Greek analytical text, either geometric or metrical,[11] is the use of the technical language of "givens" [δοθέν and/or δεδομένον] and the unfolding of mathematical arguments shaped as chains of givens, through which the predicate "given" is transferred from one object to another.[12] In Acerbi's words, the language of the "givens" is "one of the major features of the proof format of analysis and synthesis" [Diofanto 2011, 119]. Yet, this is not the case in Diophantus's *Arithmetica*. Although the term "given" appears quite often in it, it is not employed in the core part of the propositions, where the working out of the task set forth in the enunciation takes place, nor are the solutions carried out through any chain of givens.

10. However, Acerbi's reservations are expressed within an interpretative framework which considers Diophantus's solutions as solutions which proceed by "reductions", and not as solutions by premodern algebra. In his words "*Arithmetica* are a gigantic heap of reductive procedures" [Diofanto 2011, 50].

11. The term "metrical analysis" was introduced by [Sidoli 2004] to designate analytical practices concerning numerical mensuration of geometrical objects.

12. For recent studies on the meaning and use of the concept of "given" in Greek analytical practices, see [Acerbi 2011], [Sidoli 2018a]. For the historiographical questions concerning the understanding of Greek geometric and metrical analysis see the bibliography provided in Sidoli's study. For Marinus's definition of "given", see [Sialaros, Matera *et al.* 2019].

Let us be more precise. The technical term "given" which is used in analytical texts should be distinguished from the general usage of the term, as, for example, when we say "to write a given number as a sum of two square numbers" or "given a number, to find in how many ways it can be polygonal", and so on. Such usages cannot be classified as related to analytical practices [cf. Sidoli 2018a, 354]. But this is precisely the case of Diophantus's primary use of the word "given" in *Arithmetica.*[13] When this word appears in a proposition it appears in the enunciation (generic and/or instantiated) and in the determination, and not in the core part of the solution, that is, the setting up and the solution of the equation.[14] One might say, by repeating the words of Sidoli [Sidoli 2018a, 358], that, in practicing problem-solving by analysis, given objects are given by the problem-solver, whereas given objects (namely, numbers) in the *Arithmetica* are always given by the problem-setter. Therefore, Diophantus does not use the word "given" with the technical meaning it has in ancient analytical texts, with one exception, Problem 10 of the Greek Book V, to be discussed later.

Moreover, Diophantus's use of the words ἀνάλυσις and σύνθεσις is different from that in the ancient analytical texts. The word ἀνάλυσις is never used in the Greek books of the *Arithmetica* with the technical meaning it has in ancient analysis, while the verb ἀναλύειν is used only with the meaning "to reduce in

---

13. Another use of the word "given", as part of the formulaic expression "triangle given in form", occurs often in the Greek Book VI, which deals with rational right-angled triangles. In this context, if (a, b, c) are the sides of a right-angled triangle (that is, if $c^2 = a^2 + b^2$), the expression "triangle given in form" refers to a triangle whose sides are (ax, bx, cx), which therefore belongs to the class of right-angles triangles which are similar to (a, b, c). This is the technical meaning of triangle "given in form" according to Euclid's *Data*, Def. 3 [Euclid 1896, 2.6–8], that is, a triangle whose angles are given, or for which the ratios of the sides are given. On the other hand, the word "given" with the technical meaning it has in analytical reasoning is used by Diophantus in his *On Polygonal Numbers.* See [Acerbi 2011], [Diofanto 2011].

14. An example of a problem in which the word "given" is employed in the generic enunciation and the determination is Problem I.9: "To subtract the same number from two given numbers and make the remainders have to one another a given ratio. It is certainly necessary for the given ratio to be greater than the ratio which the greater of the givens has to the smaller" [26.13–18]. An example in which the word appears in the generic enunciation and the instantiation is Problem 4 of Greek Book V: "Given one number, to find three numbers such that any one of them, as well as the product of any two, if it lacks the given, makes a square. Let the given number be 6 units" [318.4–7]. Apart from Problem V.10 (see below), in the Greek books of the *Arithmetica* we find only seven instances in which the word "given" is employed in a part of the proposition other than the enunciation and the determination. In two cases (Problems III.19 and V.13) the word is employed in metamathematical comments aiming at reminding the reader something already shown: "we learned how to divide a given square into two squares" [184.3–4; 350.3–4]; in four cases (Problems III.20, IV.1, Lemma to IV.34, and V.4) it is employed to refer to a specific value assigned in the setting-out [188.1; 190.11; 282.2–3; 6; 318.10]; and in one case (Problem V.3) the word is used in the enunciation of a proposition from the lost *Porisms* [316.8].

the same part" [ἀναλύειν εἰς μόριον].[15] As for the word σύνθεσις, it is used in the Greek books with the meaning of "addition, sum",[16] and the corresponding verb συντιθέναι with the meaning "to add".[17] In the Arabic text the words "analysis" and "synthesis" are used a couple of times in Problems 37, 42a, and 43 of Book IV, which will be discussed in the second part of this paper.

Besides linguistic arguments, there is another point on which the problem-solving of Diophantus stands out compared with the analytical problem-solving, as the latter is practiced in the preserved analytical texts. Taking for granted the traditional quadripartite division of a proposition worked-out by analysis-and-synthesis into "transformation", "resolution", "construction", and "demonstration",[18] in Diophantus's solutions we do not observe what is very common in almost every instance of an analyzed proposition, that is, the intermingling of steps belonging to different parts. In propositions treated by analysis, steps belonging to "transformation" are often intermingled with steps belonging to "resolution", as well as steps belonging to "construction" are intermingled with steps belonging to "demonstration" [Sidoli 2018a, 359]. Such intermingling is not possible in Diophantus's solutions, in fact, in any solution by premodern algebra. For example, the treatment of the equation—which includes its simplification (application of the "restoration" and "confrontation" steps)[19] and solution—can only start when the stage of its setting-up has been accomplished. In other words, the production of the equation, and the solution of the equation are two tasks that cannot be intermingled with each other. Likewise, the "demonstration" (test-proof) can only occur at the very end of the solution. So, in a solution by premodern algebra the steps are clearly separated from one another.

More differences between premodern algebra and the sub-category of ancient analysis called "metrical analysis" have been identified by Sidoli:

> There are a number of fundamental differences between the methods of metrical analysis and those of premodern algebra—found, for example, in Diophantus' *Arithmetics.* For one thing, Diophantus' procedures are, at least in principle, purely numerical, and do not rely on any underlying geometric conception.
>
> Next, metrical analysis has no special nomenclature for designating objects to be sought, as is introduced in premodern algebra.

---

15. See "Index graecitatis apud Diophantum" [Diophantus 1893-1895, II, 262], s.v. ἀναλύειν εἰς μόριον, translated by Tannery as "reducere ad denominationem".

16. [Diophantus 1893-1895, II, 283], s.v. σύνθεσις, translated by Tannery as "additio, summa".

17. [Diophantus 1893-1895, II, 283], s.v. συντιθέναι, translated by Tannery as "addere".

18. See [Acerbi 2011, 138–141], [Berggren & Van Brummelen 2000, 5–16], [Fournarakis & Christianidis 2006, 49–50], [Hankel 1874, 137–150], [Hintikka & Remes 1974, 22–26], [Saito & Sidoli 2010, 583–588].

19. For the meaning of these technical terms in the context of the premodern algebraic practice see [Oaks & Alkhateeb 2007].

> In ancient analysis, we deal only with geometric objects and with those same objects when they are *given* in various ways—hence, there is no notational, or conceptual, device that allows us to set up a relation containing both *given* elements and explicitly sought elements. A problem in premodern algebra, however, begins with an instantiation of the stated problem using a certain equation, in which terms to be sought are set into relation with actual numbers that are stated to be *given*.
>
> Finally, although metrical analysis provides an algorithm for computing a definite value, it does so in a different manner than premodern algebra. Diophantus' procedure for setting up the equation with which he will work, allows him to set known and sought values on both sides of his equation, so that he can apply operations mathematically equivalent to the arithmetical operations without regard to the epistemological, or ontological, status of any of the objects in his equation. Of course, in metrical analysis we also find equations, and proportions, with non-*given* objects on both sides of the equation, which are then subjected to arithmetical operations and ratio manipulations, but this is done only as an intermediate step before immediately asserting that some geometrical object is *given* in terms of some computable number. In metrical analysis, it is this series of claims about what is *given* that functions as the primary problem-solving procedure. [Sidoli 2018a, 393–394]

To the above arguments one should add that a feature occurring quite often in problem-solving by analysis, whatever geometric or metrical, is that analysis begins with the initial assumption that the problem is solved in its entirety.[20] Transferred in the setting of problem-solving by premodern algebra, this would mean that all sought-after numbers called for in the enunciation must be assumed to be known, that is, they have to be named right from the outset of the solution. Against this background, one would expect that any algebraic solution begins with assigning names to *all numbers*, the finding of which the enunciation of the problem calls for. This happens, of course, if there is only one unknown, and in some cases if there are just a few. But in more complicated problems, where several numbers are required, the assignments are done gradually, as the resolutory procedure progresses. This is the case, for example, of all "derivative" assignments, that is, assignments which are based on other assignments. For example, the very first problem of the *Arithmetica*, whose instantiated enunciation we write today as

$$\begin{cases} x + y = 100 \\ x - y = 40 \end{cases}$$

20. This rule is not general; for example, it does not apply to locus problems.

is solved by assigning the smaller sought-after number (designated above by y) to be "1 Number" (which we will write "1N"), thus making the greater sought-after number (designated by x) to be "1 Number, 40 units" (which we will write "1N 40u"). The first assignment is "direct", the second is "derivative". The former is made from the outset, the latter presupposes not only the first but also that the addition of "1N" and "40u", stipulated by the second condition of the problem, has been performed, and the sum ("1N 40u") has been found.[21]

The above arguments are enough to dismiss the idea that the analysis-and-synthesis format provides a suitable interpretative framework for Diophantus's method of solution. But there is also another reason for rejecting such an idea: Diophantus describes clearly his method of solution in the introduction of Book I. And he doesn't have a single word to say about "analysis" and/or "synthesis". On the contrary, he speaks about a "way" [ὁδός] for solving arithmetical problems, the stages of which are outlined as follows:

1. Generic enunciation.
2. Determination (if necessary).
3. Instantiation (sometimes accompanied by the instantiated enunciation).
4. Set up of the equation (comprising (a) naming the unknowns and (b) working through the operations stipulated in the problem *on the names*).
5. Treatment of the equation (comprising (a) simplification and (b) solution of the simplified form).
6. Answer to the problem.
7. Test-proof.

That the above list portrays the structure of the Diophantine worked-out problem is shown in a number of recent studies.[22] Now, the core part of this structure, stages 4 and 5, is the main theme discussed by Diophantus in the introduction, and there is nothing in his text suggesting that his undertaking was conceived to be part of the field of analysis-and-synthesis.[23]

21. For the technical terms of premodern algebra, the notions of "assignment", "named" and "unnamed" term, "forthcoming equation", and for the techniques used by Diophantus for assigning names to unnamed terms the reader is referred to the papers mentioned in n. 8 above.

22. See the references given in n. 8 above.

23. The idea of contextualizing Diophantus's *modus operandi* within the conceptual framework of the ancient analysis was advanced by Jacob Klein in his account of Viète's "reinterpretation of the Diophantine procedure" [Klein 1968, 161*ff.*]. Klein's starting point is the idea that the solutions "in the indeterminate form", that Diophantus occasionally employs in his solutions, "represent a properly 'analytic' procedure" [Klein 1968, 164]. Although Diophantus considers such solutions as "merely auxiliary" tools, says Klein, it is possible that a "solution in the indeterminate form" can be applied for every case, with the proviso, of course, that "the numbers 'given' in a problem are also regarded only in their character of being given, and not as just these determinate numbers" [Klein 1968, 134]. This step, says Klein,

As said before there are four instances in the preserved books of the *Arithmetica* which might be regarded as linked to practices belonging to the field of analysis. They are found in Problems $V^g.10$, and $IV^a.37$, 42a, and 43.[24] In what follows, we examine these problems, paying special attention to the relevant aspects.

3 The argument by "givens" in Problem V^g.10 and its function as reduction

Problem $V^g.10$ asks to cut unit into two parts, and add to each part a different given number, and make a square. Its instantiated enunciation corresponds to the problem we write in modern algebra as

$$\begin{cases} x + y = 1 \\ x + 2 = \square \\ y + 6 = \square' \end{cases}$$

The resolution runs as follows: The conditions of the problem entail that $9u = \square + \square'$, with $2u < \square < 3u$.[25] Diophantus assigns the square designated by $\square$ to be 1 Power (we write this assignment as $\square := 1P$), with $2u < 1P < 3u$. Then, he subtracts the $1P$ from $9u$, to obtain $9u$ lacking $1P$ (which we write,

was taken by Viète, who thus arrived at his conception of the "*logistice speciosa*", which is the true parallel to the ancient geometrical analysis [Klein 1968, 165]. Whatever problems there might be with the above account, what is important to be noticed is that: (a) Klein does not consider any Diophantine solution as a solution by analysis, but only the very few solutions that fall into the category of solutions "in the indeterminate"; (b) even then, he does not consider analysis and synthesis as stages of the resolutory procedure. On this, Klein leaves no room for doubt. "For every case", he writes, that is, for every solution cast in the form of a solution "in the indeterminate", "three stages could always be distinguished in the process of solution: (1) the construction of the equation; (2) the transformation to which it is subjected until it has acquired a canonical form which immediately supplies the 'indeterminate' solution; and (3) the numerical exploitation of the last, i.e., the computation of unequivocally determinate numbers which fulfill the conditions set for the problem" [Klein 1968, 164]. The identification of these stages with analysis and synthesis, is due, according to Klein, to Viète; ascribing it to Diophantus we are committing a retrospective reading of history.

24. V^g is the Greek Book V, while IV^a is the Arabic Book IV.

25. The relation $9u = \square + \square'$ (i.e., the sum of the given numbers increased by one unit must be the sum of two squares) constitutes a necessary condition that Diophantus omits to state.

$9u\ \ell^{26}$ 1P). Hence, $9u\ \ell\ 1P = \square'$. This half-constructed equation[27] is easily solved. We simply have to assign the side of the unnamed square to be an expression of the type "$3u$ lacking some Ns",[28] or, in quasi-modern terms, "$3u\ \ell\ mN$", the multitude (i.e., the coefficient m) being any positive rational number. But $1P$ must lie between $2u$ and $3u$. Diophantus takes two squares, one, the smaller, greater than $2u$, the other, smaller than $3u$, and sets out to establish the $1P$ in the interval between the two squares. $\frac{289}{144}u$ (square of $\frac{17}{12}u$), and $\frac{361}{144}u$ (square of $\frac{19}{12}u$), are such squares. So, if we make the multitude (m) to be such that the solution of the equation which emerges from the forthcoming equation satisfies the double inequality $\frac{17}{12}u < 1N < \frac{19}{12}u$, we shall solve the problem.

Now, the equation which arises from the forthcoming equation, after an assignment for the unnamed square of the type mentioned above, is, in quasi-modern terms, $9u\ \ell\ 1P = m^2P\ 9u\ \ell\ 6mN$ (corresponding to $9 - t^2 = m^2t^2 + 9 - 6mt$), thus $1N$ is $\frac{6m}{m^2+1}$. Therefore, we are looking for a value of m which satisfies the double inequality $\frac{17}{12} < \frac{6m}{m^2+1} < \frac{19}{12}$. This is a subsidiary problem, which Diophantus solves by positing $m := 1N$. Working through the operations we obtain the double inequality $\frac{17}{12}u < \frac{6N}{1P1u} < \frac{19}{12}u$, from which two inequalities emerge:

$$(1) \qquad \frac{17}{12}u < \frac{6N}{1P1u}, \text{or, } 72N > 17P\ 17u$$

$$(2) \qquad \frac{6N}{1P\ 1u} < \frac{19}{12}u, \text{or, } 72N < 19P\ 17u.$$

Diophantus solves the two inequalities by applying the rules for solving the corresponding trinomial equations. For the first he finds successively: Square $\frac{1}{2}72u \rightarrow 1296u$; multiply $17u$ by $17u \rightarrow 289u$; subtract this from $1296u \rightarrow 1007u$; take the square root of this, it is $\not> 31u$; take the half of $72u \rightarrow 36u$; add this to $\sqrt{1007}u$, the result is $\not> 67u$; divide this by $17u$, the result is $\not> \frac{67}{17}u$. Thus, the $1N$ is not greater than $\frac{67}{17}u$. Similarly, for the second inequality he finds that the $1N$ is not smaller than $\frac{66}{19}u$. He adopts for $1N$ the numerical value $3\frac{1}{2}u$, so this is the value of the unknown number of the subsidiary problem designated by m.

We are now in place to continue the solution of the original problem, by making a suitable assignment for the side of the $\square'$. The complete solution is shown in the table below:

26. We use ℓ as the sign standing for "lacking", by which we translate the Greek λείψει. The corresponding word which is used in the Arabic books is *illā*.

27. Henceforth the expression "forthcoming equations" will be used to designate such half-constructed equations.

28. Tannery's text has (the abbreviations being resolved) μονάδων γ̄ λείψει ἀριθμοῦ τινος (3 units lacking some Number), but in two of the most important mss., Martitensis 4678 and Marcianus gr. 308, we find for the last two words the writings ἀριθμούς τινας and ἀριθμῶν τινων, both meaning "some Numbers", that is, "some multitude of Numbers".

Assignments	Operations	Equation
$\square := 1P(2u < 1P < 3u)$		
	Subtract $1P$ from $9u \rightarrow 9u \;\ell\; 1P$	
		$9u \;\ell\; 1P = \square'$
$\sqrt{\square'} := 3u \;\ell\; 3\frac{1}{2}N$		
	Square $3u \;\ell\; 3\frac{1}{2}N \rightarrow 12\frac{1}{4}P\; 9u \;\ell\; 21N$	
		$9u \;\ell\; 1P = 12\frac{1}{4}P\; 9u \;\ell\; 21N$

The equation simplifies to $13\frac{1}{4}P = 21N$, hence $1N = \frac{84}{53}u$. The square designated by $\square$ is $\frac{7056}{2809}u$, so, by subtracting $2u$, we find the sought-after number designated by x to be $\frac{1438}{2809}u$, while the number designated by y is found to be $\frac{1371}{2809}u$.

The solution above involves three problems:

$$P1.\begin{cases} x + y = 1 \\ x + 2 = \square \\ y + 6 = \square' \end{cases}$$

$$P2.\quad 9 = \square + \square', 2 < \square < 3$$

$$P3.\quad \frac{17}{12} < \frac{6m}{m^2+1} < \frac{19}{12}$$

At the first stage, the problem $P1$ is reduced to $P2$. At this stage, Diophantus formulates an argument framed in the language of "givens". The argument has the format of analysis, and this happens only once throughout the preserved books of the *Arithmetica*. The text is the following:[29]

> Let a unit, AB, be set out, and let it be cut at Γ, and let a dyad, $A\Delta$, be added to $A\Gamma$, and a hexad, BE, to ΓB. Therefore, each of $\Gamma\Delta$, ΓE is a square. And since AB is 1 unit, while $A\Delta$ and BE together is an octad, therefore ΔE as a whole becomes 9 units, and these need to be divided into two squares, the (squares) $\Gamma\Delta$ and ΓE. But since one of the squares is greater than $A\Delta$, that is, of a dyad, but smaller than ΔB, that is, of a triad, I am reduced to dividing a proposed square, as in the present case the 9, into two

29. For the Greek text see [336.17–338.9]. Tannery followed Bachet by adding the diagram suggested by the text, for which, however, there is no manuscript basis:

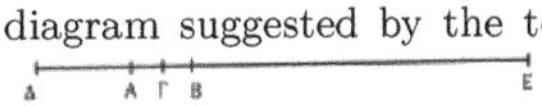

> squares, $\Delta\Gamma$ and ΓE, so that one, $\Gamma\Delta$, is in the interval between the dyad and the triad. Indeed, $\Gamma\Delta$ having been found, and the dyad $A\Delta$ being given, then the remainder $A\Gamma$ is given. But AB is 1 unit; therefore $B\Gamma$, a remainder, is given. Therefore, Γ, at which the unit is cut, is, also, given.

The chain of givens at the end of this argument confirms that once the problem $P2$ is solved, the original problem $P1$ is also solved.[30] So, its aim is not to solve the original problem, but to reduce it. Rather than a complete ἀνάλυσις, therefore, we have here an ἀπαγωγή, in which the analytical procedure stops halfway, reaching another problem to solve [cf. Iwata 2016]. Moreover, the analytical argument does not function as a primary problem-solving procedure. This part of the resolution has nothing to do with algebra. The algebraic part of the solution starts after the reduction, it concerns the reduced problem, and features all key characteristics of a premodern algebraic solution: naming the unknowns, working through the operations stipulated by the enunciation, setting up, simplifying, and solving an equation framed in the language of names, and computing the numerical values of the sought-after numbers.[31]

4 Three instances referred to as "analyses" and "syntheses" from the Arabic Book IV

Problem IV^{a}.37 The problem asks to find a cubic number such that if we multiply the square that comes from its side by two given numbers, and we add what is gathered from each of them to the cubic number, amounts to a square number. Its instantiated version corresponds to the problem we write today as

$$\begin{cases} x^3 + 5x^2 = \square \\ x^3 + 10x^2 = \square' \end{cases}$$

Diophantus's solution runs as follows. He assigns the sought-after cube (x^3) to be 1 Cube (we write this assignment, $x^3 := 1C$), therefore the square that comes from its side (x^2) is 1 *Māl* (we write, $x^2 := 1M$).[32] Working through the operations he obtains the pair of forthcoming equations:

$$\begin{cases} 1C\ 5M = \square \\ 1C\ 10M = \square' \end{cases}$$

30. Proposition 4 of Euclid's *Data* is repeatedly implied in the deductive steps.
31. Displaying all the above characteristics Problem V^{g}.10 is closely aligned with Diophantus's project, so there is no reason for questioning its authenticity.
32. "*Māl*" is a technical term of Arabic algebra, corresponding to the term Power (δύναμις, the square of the algebraic unknown) of Diophantus.

Next, Diophantus must find a square expression (corresponding to $\square$) to equate to the $1C\ 5M$. He wants the side of the square to be "Things",[33] that is, a multitude of Things. Likewise he must find a square expression (corresponding to $\square'$) to equate to the $1C\ 10M$. In order to find conditions on the respective "multitudes" he argues as follows:[34]

> If we make a side of the square that is a Cube and five *Māls* be Things, then its square is *Māls*. Then, if we subtract the five *Māls* in common from both sides, it leaves a Cube Equals[35] *Māls*. Thus it is clear that the number assigned in this problem to be a Thing is equal to the number of the remaining *Māls*. And also, if we make a side of the square that is a Cube and ten *Māls* be Things, then its square is *Māls*. And if we subtract the ten *Māls* in common from both sides, it leaves a Cube Equals *Māls*. Therefore, the number assigned to be a Thing *in this analysis* is equal to the number of remaining *Māls*. So the remaining *Māls* in the first Equation should be equal to the remaining *Māls* in the second Equation. But the remaining *Māls* in the first Equation is a square number less five units, and the remaining *Māls* in the second Equation is a square less ten units, and so we should find two square numbers such that if we subtract ten units from the greater and five units from the smaller, (they) are equal.

Diophantus deploys in this passage a mental reasoning which runs as follows: if we assign the side of the $\square$ to be of the form mT,[36] the square is m^2M, hence the equation that arises from the first forthcoming equation is of the type $1C\ 5M = m^2M$ (corresponding to $t^3 + 5t^2 = m^2t^2$), thus $1T$ is of the form $m^2 - 5$ (*). Likewise, if we assign the side of the $\square'$ to be nT, the square is n^2M, hence the equation that arises from the second forthcoming equation is of the type $1C\ 10M = n^2M$ (corresponding to $t^3 + 10t^2 = n^2t^2$), thus $1T$ is of the form $n^2 - 10$ (**). Now, from (*) and (**) we obtain that $m^2 - 5$ equals $n^2 - 10$, or, by adding 10 in both sides, $m^2 + 5$ equals n^2. Thus, two square numbers must be found whose difference is 5 (the smaller of which must be greater than 5). This is a subsidiary problem coinciding with II.10, so Diophantus gives directly the solution $58\frac{7}{9}u$ and $53\frac{7}{9}u$ for the squares n^2 and m^2 respectively. We assign these numbers to be in terms of a *Māl*, instead of a unit, so the assignments for the two unnamed squares are $\square := 53\frac{7}{9}M$ and $\square' := 58\frac{7}{9}M$. Thus the equations which arise from the two forthcoming

33. "Thing" is a technical term of Arabic algebra, corresponding to the term Number (ἀριθμός, the algebraic unknown) of Diophantus.

34. For the Arabic text see [Sesiano 1982, lines 1115–1127, the emphasis is added].

35. The capitalized "Equals" translates the verb *'adala* which is used in the statement of an algebraic equation. Equating outside the statement of an equation, which is expressed by some other word, is written "equal" in lower case. For details see [Oaks 2010a].

36. mT stands for the word "Things", in plural, that is "a multitude of Things".

equations are:

$$\begin{cases} 1C\ 5M = 53\frac{7}{9}M \\ 1C\ 10M = 58\frac{7}{9}M. \end{cases}$$

After simplification, both equations become $1C = 48\frac{7}{9}M$, therefore $1T = 48\frac{7}{9}u$, so the sought-after cubic number is $\frac{84,606,519}{729}u$.

In the above solution two problems are involved

$$P1. \begin{cases} x^3 + 5x^2 = \square \\ x^3 + 10x^2 = \square' \end{cases}$$

$$P2. \quad m^2 + 5 = n^2, n^2 > 5$$

the latter (P2) being the 10th Problem of Greek Book II. The reduction, which aims at finding suitable assignments for the unnamed squares $\square$ and $\square'$, is expressed as a mental process, and in this context we find the word "analysis" to be used—unlike the above discussed Problem V^{g}.10, where the similar reduction from the second to the third problem involved was not described as "analysis".

Problem IV^{a}.42a Two numbers are required, a cube and a square, such that both the sum and the difference of a cube of the cube and a square of the square are square numbers. In our notation the problem is written:[37]

$$\begin{cases} (x^3)^3 + (y^2)^2 = \square \\ (x^3)^3 - (y^2)^2 = \square' \end{cases}$$

Diophantus proposes three solutions for this problem. The first, for which he gives only the instructions, is by the method of double-equality. Thus, the stage of the final calculation of the sought-after numbers is not actually pursued, Diophantus being satisfied with merely indicating it by the phrase "after knowing the Thing, we can synthesize everything in the problem". The other two solutions are in fact identical, the only difference being that in the latter the pair of forthcoming equations is reduced to another pair with smaller "coefficients" and "powers". Both solutions are described without actually

37. The enunciation calls for the difference to be a square, but it does not say which of the two is the greater. So there are two cases: (1) a cube of the cube subtracting a square of the square, and (2) a square of the square subtracting a cube of the cube. Only the first case is considered here.

working through the calculations. The phrase marking the transition to the stage of the final calculation of the required numbers is, in the second solution, "Then we return to perform the synthesis of the problem", and in the third, "Once we know it [i.e., the numerical value of the "Thing"], we return to synthesize the problem according to the way we set it up in the analysis". Below we present the third solution, by adding all implicit calculations.

We assign the side of the sought-after cube (x^3) to be 2 Things (we write this assignment, $x := 2T$), so the cube is $8C$ and the cube of the cube is 512CCC.[38] Likewise, we assign the side of the sought-after square (y^2) to be 4 *Māls* (we write, $y := 4M$), so the square is $16MM$[39] and the square of the square is $256CCM$.[40] Working through the operations we obtain the pair of forthcoming equations

$$\begin{cases} 512CCC\ 256CCM = \square \\ 512CCC\ \ell\ 256CCM = \square' \end{cases}$$

In order to find suitable assignments for the two unnamed squares Diophantus proceeds in the way we saw in the previous problem. The text runs as follows:

> If we wish, we can say: five hundred twelve Cube Cube Cubes and two hundred fifty-six Cube Cube *Māls* Equal a square, and five hundred twelve Cube Cube Cubes less two hundred fifty-six Cube Cube *Māls* Equal a square. And for any square divided by a square, the result of the division is a square. Thus we divide the five hundred twelve Cube Cube Cubes and the two hundred fifty-six Cube Cube *Māls* by a square, which can be a Cube Cube *Māl* or four Cube Cube *Māls* or nine Cube Cube *Māls* or sixteen Cube Cube *Māls* or by whatever we wish among the square numbers after we make any one of them Cube Cube *Māls*. As for Cube Cube *Māls*, the result of its division by Cube Cube *Māls* is a number, and for Cube Cube Cubes, the result is Things. Let us suppose that we divide them by sixteen Cube Cube *Māls*. Then the result of the division is thirty-two Things and sixteen units. And by the same amount we divide this square, let us divide the other square, which is five hundred twelve Cube Cube Cubes less two hundred fifty-six Cube Cube *Māls*, to get thirty-two Things less sixteen units. Thus thirty-two Things and sixteen units are a square, and thirty-two Things less sixteen units are a square. Let us look for a number that, if we add a given (*mafrūd*) number

38. *CCC*, abbreviation of "Cube Cube Cube", corresponding to the 9th power of the algebraic unknown.

39. *MM*, abbreviation of "*Māl Māl*", corresponding to the 4th power of the algebraic unknown.

40. *CCM*, abbreviation of "Cube Cube *Māl*", corresponding to the 8th power of the algebraic unknown.

> to it, which is sixteen, it gives a square, and if we subtract a given (*mafrūd*) number from it, which is sixteen, it gives a square. Once we have found that number, we divide it by thirty-two, so what results from the division is the Thing. *Once we know it, we return to synthesize the problem according to the way we set it up in the analysis.*[41]

After reduction of "powers" and "coefficients" of the forthcoming equations, by dividing all terms by $16CCM$, a new pair of forthcoming equations is obtained:

$$\begin{cases} 32T\ 16u = \square'' \\ 32T\ \ell\ 16u = \square''' \end{cases}$$

Following the same procedure as in Problem 37, Diophantus assigns the $\square''$ to be a square multitude of units, say m^2u, so the $1T$ is found to be $\frac{m^2-16}{32}u$, and, similarly, he assign the $\square'''$ to be a square multitude of units, say n^2u, thus the $1T$ is $\frac{n^2+16}{32}u$. Thus, we are reduced again to a subsidiary problem of the type of II.10, and, the rest of the resolution is the same as before.

Problem IV^{a}.43 The problem asks to find two numbers, a cube and a square, such that a cube of the cube, if we add a given multiple of a square of the square to it, amounts to a square number, and if we subtract a given multiple of a square of the square from it, leaves a square number. In modern notation its instantiated version is:

$$\begin{cases} (x^3)^3 + 1\frac{1}{4}(y^2)^2 = \square \\ (x^3)^3 - \frac{3}{4}(y^2)^2 = \square' \end{cases}$$

We adopt the assignments $x^3 := 1C$, $y := 2M$, and work through the operations to obtain the pair of forthcoming equations:

$$\begin{cases} 1CCC\ 20CCM = \square \\ 1CCC\ \ell\ 12CCM = \square' \end{cases}$$

In order to find suitable assignments for the unnamed squares Diophantus argues as follows:

41. For the Arabic see [Sesiano 1982, lines 1391–1409, added emphasis].

> So if we assign (*fara.dnā*) a side of the square Equated to the Cube Cube Cube and the twenty Cube Cube *Māls* to be *Māl Māls*, then its square is *Māl Māls* by *Māl Māls*, of which one of them is called a Cube Cube *Māl*. If we Equate it with <the Cube> Cube Cube and the twenty Cube Cube *Māls*, then we subtract the twenty <Cube Cube *Māls*> in common, it leaves a Cube Cube Cube Equals Cube Cube *Māls*, its number being equal to a square less twenty, and that is the assigned (*mafrūd*) number of a Thing in this solution. Likewise, if we assign (*fara.dnā*) a side of the square Equated to the Cube Cube Cube less twelve Cube Cube *Māls* to be *Māl Māls*, then its square is Cube Cube *Māls*. And if we add to it the twelve Cube Cube *Māls* lacking from the Cube Cube Cube and we make them added in common to both sides, it amounts to a Cube Cube Cube Equals Cube Cube *Māls*, its number being equal to a square and twelve, and that is (also) the assigned number of a Thing in the problem. So a [great] square less twenty Equals a small square and twelve. And we add the twenty in common to the two sides together, giving a small square and thirty-two (which) Equal a great square. The small square is four units, and when thirty-two is added to it, it amounts to thirty-six, which is the great square. So we make the square Equated to the Cube Cube Cube and twenty Cube Cube *Māls* be thirty-six Cube Cube *Māls*, and the square Equated to the other square be four Cube Cube *Māls*. Both Equations turn out to be, after the restoration and confrontation and division, a Thing Equals sixteen units. *We will now perform the synthesis of the problem in the way we did the analysis.*[42]

Following the usual procedure Diophantus assigns the side of the $\square$ to be, in quasi-modern terms, mMM, the square is m^2CCM, so the equation $1CCC\ 20CCM = m^2CCM$ (corresponding to $t^9 + 20t^8 = m^2t^8$) arises, which is simplified to $1CCC = (m^2 - 20)CCM$ (i.e., $t^9 = (m^2 - 20)t^8$), and, after division by a CCM the $1T$ is found to be of the form $m^2 - 20$. Likewise, if we assign the side of the $\square'$ to be nMM the square is n^2CCM, and so the equation $1CCC\ \ell\ 12CCM = n^2CCM$ (corresponding to $t^9 - 12t^8 = n^2t^8$) arises, which is simplified to $1CCC = (n^2 + 12)CCM$, and, after division by a CCM the $1T$ is found to be of the form $n^2 + 12$. So, $m^2 - 20 = n^2 + 12$. Thus, we are led to a subsidiary problem, namely to find two square numbers whose difference is 32. This problem was solved in II.10, so Diophantus gives directly the solution $36u$ for m^2 and $4u$ for n^2. We assign these numbers to be in terms of a Cube Cube *Māl*, so the assignments for the two unnamed squares are $\square := 36CCM$ and $\square' := 4CCM$. Thus the equations which arise from the two forthcoming equations are:

42. For the Arabic text see [Sesiano 1982, lines 1474–1494; emphasis added].

$$\begin{cases} 1CCC\ 20CCM = 36CCM \\ 1CCC\ \ell\ 12CCM = 4CCM. \end{cases}$$

After simplification each equation becomes $1CCC = 16CCM$, and, by division, $1T = 16u$. Therefore, the sought-after cube is $4096u$, and the sought-after square is $262{,}144u$.

Discussion of the three problems of the Arabic Book IV As we saw the words "analysis" and "synthesis"/ "synthesize", with a meaning which might be regarded as relating to ancient analysis, appear within *Arithmetica* only in Problems 37, 42a, and 43 of the Arabic Book IV. These problems belong to a larger group consisting of Problems IV^{a}.34–43, whose enunciations are (in our notation):

$$34. \begin{cases} x^3 + y^2 = \square \\ x^3 - y^2 = \square' \end{cases}$$

$$35. \begin{cases} y^2 + x^3 = \square \\ y^2 - x^3 = \square' \end{cases}$$

$$36. \begin{cases} x^3 + 4x^2 = \square \\ x^3 - 5x^2 = \square' \end{cases}$$

$$37. \begin{cases} x^3 + 5x^2 = \square \\ x^3 + 10x^2 = \square' \end{cases}$$

$$38. \begin{cases} x^3 - 5x^2 = \square \\ x^3 - 10x^2 = \square' \end{cases}$$

$$39. \begin{cases} 3x^2 - x^3 = \square \\ 7x^2 - x^3 = \square' \end{cases}$$

$$40. \begin{cases} (x^2)^2 + y^3 = \square \\ (x^2)^2 - y^3 = \square' \end{cases}$$

$$41. \begin{cases} x^3 + (y^2)^2 = \square \\ x^3 - (y^2)^2 = \square' \end{cases}$$

$$42a. \begin{cases} (x^3)^3 + (y^2)^2 = \square \\ (x^3)^3 - (y^2)^2 = \square' \end{cases}$$

$$42b. \begin{cases} (x^3)^3 + (y^2)^2 = \square \\ (y^2)^2 - (x^3)^3 = \square' \end{cases}$$

$$43. \begin{cases} (x^3)^3 + 1\tfrac{1}{4}(y^2)^2 = \square \\ (x^3)^3 - \tfrac{3}{4}(y^2)^2 = \square' \end{cases}$$

The solutions of these problems involve mentally conducted reductions to other problems, namely to Problems II.9 and II.10. The table below shows these reductions, giving: (1) the pair of forthcoming equations which result in the course of the resolutory procedure in each case;[43] (2) the assignments adopted; and (3) the problem from Book II from which the assignments are found.

43. The unnamed squares indicated in the table by the symbols $\square$ and $\square'$ do not always coincide with the similar symbols in the list of the enunciations given above.

Pb	Forthcoming equations	Assignments	Subsidiary problem
34_1	$1C\ 4M = \square$, $1C\ \ell\ 4M = \square'$	Solved by double-equality	
34_2	$1C\ 4M = \square$, $1C\ \ell\ 4M = \square'$	$\square := 20\frac{1}{4}M$, $\square' := 12\frac{1}{4}M$	$m^2 - n^2 = 8$ (II.10)
35	$4M 1C\ = \square$, $4M\ \ell\ 1C = \square'$	$\square := 7\frac{21}{25}M$, $\square' := \frac{4}{25}M$	$2^2 + 2^2 = m^2 + n^2$ (II.9)
36	$1C\ 4M = \square, 1C\ \ell\ 5M = \square'$	$\square := 25M, \square' := 16M$	$m^2 - n^2 = 9$ (II.10)
37	$1C\ 5M = \square$, $1C\ 10M = \square'$	$\square := 53\frac{7}{9}M$, $\square' := 58\frac{7}{9}M$	$n^2 - m^2 = 5$ (II.10)
38	$1C\ \ell\ 5M = \square$, $1C\ \ell\ 10M = \square'$	$\square := 9M$, $\square' := 4M$	$\mathrm{n}^2 - m^2 = 5$ (II.10)
39	$7M\ \ell\ 1C\ = \square$, $3M\ \ell\ 1C = \square'$	$\square := 6\frac{1}{4}M$, $\square' := 2\frac{1}{4}M$	$m^2 - n^2 = 4$ (II.10)
40	$16MM\ 64C = \square$, $16MM\ \ell\ 64C = \square'$	$\square := 31\frac{9}{25}MM$, $\square' := \frac{16}{25}MM$	$4^2 + 4^2 = m^2 + n^2$ (II.9)
41	$64C\ 16MM = \square$, $64C\ \ell\ 16MM = \square'$	$\square := 36MM$, $\square' := 4MM$	$m^2 - n^2 = 32$ (II.10)
$42a_1$	$512CCC\ 256CCM = \square$, $512CCC\ \ell\ 256CCM = \square'$	Solved by double-equality	
$42a_2$	$512CCC\ 256CCM = \square$, $512CCC\ \ell\ 256CCM = \square'$	Not pursued	$m^2 - n^2 = 512$ (II.10)
$42a_3$	$32T\ 16u = \square$, $32T\ \ell\ 16u = \square'$	Not pursued	$m^2 - n^2 = 32$ (II.10)
42b	$256CCM\ 512CCC = \square$, $256CCM\ \ell\ 512CCC = \square'$	Not pursued	$512 = m^2 + n^2$ (II.9)
43	$1CCC\ 20CCM = \square$, $1CCC\ \ell\ 12CCM = \square'$	$\square := 36CCM$, $\square' := 4CCM$	$m^2 - n^2 = 32$ (II.10)

Two kinds of assignment are used in the solutions of the above problems, which might be characterized as "effective" and "virtual" (or "assignments in the indeterminate"). "Effective" is, for example, the initial assignment in Problem IV^{a}.37, which is introduced by the sentence "We assign the cube to be one Cube". "Virtual" is the assignment, in the same problem, which is introduced by the conditional phrase "If we make a side of the square [...] be Things," that is, "[...] be [a multitude of] Things", the multitude being unspecified. Thus, we have in this problem six assignments, four of which are "effective" and two "virtual". The "effective" assignments are, 1) $x^3 := 1C$; 2) $x^2 := 1M$; 3) $\square := 7\frac{1}{3}T$; 4) $\square' := 7\frac{2}{3}T$, while the "virtual" assignments, which we give in quasi-modern notation, are, 5) $\square := mT$; 6) $\square' := nT$. The last two assignments may be considered as "assignments in the indeterminate", in the same sense that the solutions to the lemmas to Problems IV^{g}.34–36 are "solutions in the indeterminate" [ἐν τῷ ἀορίστῳ], whose role is to provide assignments to be used in the problems that follow.

Now, according to Klein, "the calculation ending 'in the indeterminate', which Diophantus uses only as an auxiliary procedure, must be understood as the true analogue to geometric ('problematical') analysis" [Klein 1968, 163]. Under such a perspective, the "virtual" assignments 5) and 6) in Problem IV^{a}.37 may be considered as belonging to the "transformation" part of an analytical reasoning, which ends with a known problem, namely the problem $n^2 - m^2 = 5$ (II.10). The "resolution" part of this analysis would be framed this way: Once a solution of the problem $n^2 - m^2 = 5$ is given, the multitude (m) of Things in the assignment of the side of $\square$, and the multitude (n) of Things in the assignment of the side of $\square'$ are also given. Of course such "resolution" does not exist in the text. Always under this perspective, the "construction" part of the procedure would be the production of the "effective" assignments 3) and 4) from the "virtual" assignments 5) and 6).

If we adopt this explanation for the word "analysis" in the text of the three problems, then we must admit that the analytical reasoning refers not to the whole solution but only to a task pertaining to a specific stage of it, that of finding assignments for the two unnamed squares. In this sense, analysis would be a heuristic tool to carry out only this task. However, textual evidence does not support this interpretation. For in Problems 42a and 43, just after the finding of the numerical value of the algebraic unknown (the "Thing"), and before the next stage, which is the calculation of the numerical values of the sought-after numbers, there is a sentence which marks the transition from one stage to the next. In Problem 42a, for which the text offers three solutions, the sentence in the first solution is "After knowing the Thing, we can synthesize everything in the problem"; in the second solution is "Then we return to perform the synthesis of the problem"; and in the third solution is "Once we know it [i.e., the numerical value of the "Thing"], we return to synthesize the problem according to the way we set it up it in the analysis". In Problem 43 the sentence is, "We will now perform the synthesis of the problem in the way we did the analysis". These phrases seem to imply that the word "analysis" refers to the whole series of assignments, and not only to the assignments for the two unnamed squares. Indeed, only in this manner is the allusion to "the synthesis of the problem" consistent with the calculation of all numbers for which the finding the enunciation of the problem calls.[44]

Let us recapitulate: Problems 37, 42a, and 43 belong to a group of ten problems of the Arabic Book IV of the *Arithmetica*, in which a mental process is employed to reduce the task involved in a specific step of the resolutory procedure into a known problem from Book II. The words "analysis" and "synthesis"/ "synthesize" occur only in these three problems of the group. With the exception of the first occurrence of the word "analysis" in Problem 37, all other occurrences appear in sentences which mark a transition to the final stage of the solution, which is the calculation of the sought-after numbers. The table below shows the wording of the transition in the ten problems of the group:

Pb	Without sentence marking the transition	With sentence marking the transition
34_1	Let us then divide all of that by a *Māl*, to get one Thing Equals five units. Therefore a side of the cube is five units, and the cube is one hundred twenty-five...	
34_2	Therefore, the one Thing Equals sixteen units and a fourth of a unit. Since we assigned a side of the cube to be one Thing, a side of the cube is sixteen and a fourth...	
35	[...] it gives three and four fifths and a fifth of a fifth of one Equal one Thing. Since we assigned the cube to be from a side of one Thing, a side of the cube is ninety-six parts of twenty-five parts...	
36	[...] to get one Thing Equals twenty-one. Since we assigned a side of the cube to be one Thing, a side of the cube is twenty-one...	

44. What in the aforesaid problems from the Arabic Book IV is described by the expressions "synthesis of the problem" or "synthesize the problem" pertains to the textual unit which in the Greek books is headed by the clause "To the hypostases" [Ἐπὶ τὰς ὑποστάσεις]. For the meaning of this clause, see [Christianidis 2015].

37	[...] it gives one Thing Equals forty-eight units and seven ninths of a unit. And since we assigned a side of the cube to be one Thing, its side is four hundred thirty-nine ninths...	
38	[...] and the one Thing Equals fourteen units. And since we assigned a side of the cube to be one Thing, its side is fourteen...	
39	Therefore the Thing is three fourths of one. The Cube is twenty-seven eighths of an eighth, and a square of a side of the Cube is thirty-six eighths of an eighth.	
40	Therefore the one Thing is what results from dividing one thousand six hundred by three hundred eighty-four, which is four units and a sixth of a unit. Since we assigned a side of the square to be two Things, a side of the square is eight units and a third of a unit...	
41	So the one Thing is three units and a fifth of a unit. Since we assigned the square to be from a side of two Things, <its side> is six units and two fifths of a unit...	
$42a_1$		And once the Thing is found, we can return to the hypostases we established. After knowing the Thing, we can synthesize everything in the problem.
$42a_2$		[...] and from that we can find the Thing whose value we are looking for. Then we return to perform the synthesis of the problem.
$42a_3$		so what results from the division is the Thing. Once we know it, we return to synthesize the problem according to the way we set it up in the analysis.

42b	Therefore, the one Thing is twelve parts of twenty-five. And since we assigned a side of the cube to be two Things, a side of the cube is twenty-four parts of twenty-five parts of a unit...	
43		We will now perform the synthesis of the problem in the way we did the analysis.

The only occurrence of the word “analysis” in a non-transitional sentence is found in Problem 37. Referring to the second equation of the pair of forthcoming equations:

$$\begin{cases} 1C\ 5M = \square \\ 1C\ 10M = \square' \end{cases}$$

the text has the phrase “the assigned number in this analysis is a Thing equal to the number of remaining $M\bar{a}ls$”. However, a few lines above, referring to the first forthcoming equation, the phrase has “problem” instead of “analysis”: “the number assigned in this problem to be a Thing is equal to the number of the remaining $M\bar{a}ls$”. It seems, therefore, that the use of word “analysis” is due to a scribal mistake. This is corroborated by the fact that all other problems of the group 37–43 which contain similar phrases, have “problem”, as shown in the table below:

Pb	Forthcoming equations	
34_2	$1C\ 4M = \square$	“the number that was assigned in the *problem* to be one Thing...”
	$1C\ \ell\ 4M = \square'$	“the number that was assigned in the *problem* to be a Thing...”
35	$4M\ 1C = \square$	“the number that was assigned in the *problem* as <a Thing>...”
	$4M\ \ell\ 1C = \square'$	“the number assigned in the *problem* to be a Thing...”
37	$1C\ 5M = \square$	“the number assigned in this *problem* to be a Thing...”
	$1C\ 10M = \square'$	“the assigned number in this *analysis* is a Thing...”
38	$1C\ \ell\ 5M = \square$	“the number taken to be Things in the *problem*”
	$1C\ \ell\ 10M = \square'$	“the number taken to be Things in the *problem*”

As for the transitional sentences in Problems 42a–43 which contain the words “analysis” and “synthesis”/ “synthesize,” they are in all probability later additions. The extreme case that the problems as a whole are not genuine cannot be excluded, especially if one takes into account that in the *Fahrī* of al-Karajī, which borrows heavily from Diophantus, the last three problems of the Arabic Book IV are omitted [Sesiano 1982, 60].

5 Conclusion

Let us provide a brief summary of what we discussed in this paper. In Section I we highlighted the unsuitability of two schemes which have been proposed for describing the structure of the propositions in *Arithmetica*, the Proclean and the analytical. A weakness that both schemes share in common is that they do not take into account that Diophantus's solutions are solutions by premodern algebra. In Section II we investigated in particular some discrepancies between the analytical style of reasoning and Diophantus's presentation. In Section III we discussed the only occurrence of an analytical argument in the preserved *Arithmetica*, namely the argument by "givens" in Problem 10 of the Greek Book V, and we showed that its function is to reduce the problem into another, and not to solve it. Lastly, in Section IV we investigated the arguments referred to as "analyses" and "syntheses" in three problems from the Arabic Book IV, and we concluded by questioning the genuineness of the relevant passages.

The basic thesis that recurs like a leitmotif throughout this paper is that *Arithmetica* is a work of premodern algebra, and so the solutions it contains not only exhibit the technical vocabulary of Diophantus's algebra but also are structured according to the norms of the premodern algebraic problem solving.

Bibliography

Acerbi, Fabio [2011], The language of the Givens: Its forms and its use as a deductive tool in Greek mathematics, *Archive for History of Exact Sciences*, 65(2), 119–153, doi: 10.1007/s00407-010-0072-z.

Berggren, Lennart J. & Van Brummelen, Glen [2000], The role and development of geometric analysis and synthesis in Ancient Greece and Medieval Islam, in: *Ancient & Medieval Traditions in the Exact Sciences: Essays in Memory of Wilbur Knorr*, edited by P. Suppes, J. M. Moravcsik, & H. Mendell, Stanford, CA: CSLI Publications, 1–31.

Christianidis, Jean [2015], The meaning of hypostasis in Diophantus' *Arithmetica*, in: *Relocating the History of Science: Essays in Honor of Kostas Gavroglu*, edited by Th. Arabatzis, J. Renn, & A. Simões, Cham: Springer, 315–327, doi: 10.1007/978-3-319-14553-2_21.

—— [2018a], Diophantus and premodern algebra: New light on an old image, in: *Revolutions and Continuity in Greek Mathematics*, edited by M. Sialaros, Berlin; Boston: Walter de Gruyter, 35–66, doi: 10.1515/9783110565959-003.

—— [2018b], La démarche de Diophante démystifiée: L'algèbre prémoderne au service de la résolution de problèmes, in: *Actes du 12e colloque maghrébin d'histoire des mathématiques arabes (Marrakech 26-28 mai 2016)*, edited by E. Laabid, Marrakech: École normale supérieure, 41–69.

Christianidis, Jean & Megremi, Athanasia [2019], Tracing the early history of algebra: Testimonies on Diophantus in the Greek-speaking world (4th-7th century CE), *Historia Mathematica*, 47, 16–38, doi: 10.1016/j.hm.2019.02.002.

Christianidis, Jean & Oaks, Jeffrey [2013], Practicing algebra in late Antiquity: The problem-solving of Diophantus of Alexandria, *Historia Mathematica*, 40(2), 127–163, doi: 10.1016/j.hm.2012.09.001.

—— [2021], *The Arithmetica of Diophantus. A Complete Translation and Commentary*, Abingdon: Routledge.

Christianidis, Jean & Skoura, Ioanna [2013], Solving problems by algebra in Late Antiquity: New evidence from an unpublished fragment of Theon's commentary on the *Almagest*, *Sciamus: Sources and commentaries in exact sciences*, 14, 41–57.

Diofanto [2011], *De Polygonis Numeris*, Pisa; Roma: Fabrizio Serra Editore, Introduzione, testo critico, traduzione Italiana e commento di Fabio Acerbi.

Diophante [1984], *Les Arithmétiques*, vol. 4: *Livres V–VII*, Paris: Les Belles Lettres, texte établi et traduit par R. Rashed.

Diophantus [1893-1895], *Diophanti Alexandrini opera omnia cum Graeciis commentarii*, Leipzig: Teubner, edidit et latine interpretatus est P. Tannery.

Euclid [1896], *Euclidis Data, cum commentario Marini et scholiis antiquis*, Leipzig: Teubner, ed. by H. Menge.

Fournarakis, Philippos & Christianidis, Jean [2006], Greek geometrical analysis: A new interpretation through the "givens"-terminology, *Bollettino di Storia delle Scienze Matematiche*, 26(1), 33–56.

Hankel, Hermann [1874], *Zur Geschichte der Mathematik in Alterthum und Mittelalter*, Leipzig: Teubner.

Heron [1912], *Heronis Definitiones cum variis collectionibus. Heronis Quaeferuntur Geometrica*, Leipzig: Teubner, ed. by J. L. Heiberg.

HINTIKKA, Jaakko & REMES, Unto (eds.) [1974], *The Method of Analysis: Its Geometrical Origins and Its General Significance*, *Boston Studies in the Philosophy of Science*, vol. XXV, Dordrecht; Boston: Reidel.

IWATA, Naoya [2016], Plato's hypothetical inquiry in the *Meno*, *British Journal for the History of Philosophy*, 24(2), 194–214, doi: 10.1080/09608788.2015.1136260.

KLEIN, Jacob [1968], *Greek Mathematical Thought and the Origin of Algebra*, Cambridge, Mass.: MIT Press, translated by E. Brann.

MESKENS, Ad [2010], *Travelling Mathematics – The Fate of Diophantos' Arithmetic*, Basel: Birkhäuser.

NETZ, Reviel [1999], Proclus' division of the mathematical proposition into parts: How and why was it formulated?, *The Classical Quarterly*, 49(1), 282–303, doi: 10.1093/cq/49.1.282.

—— [2012], Reasoning and symbolism in Diophantus: Preliminary observations, in: *The History of Mathematical Proof in Ancient Traditions*, edited by K. Chemla, Cambridge: Cambridge University Press, 327–361.

OAKS, Jeffrey A. [2009], Polynomials and equations in Arabic algebra, *Archive for History of Exact Sciences*, 63(2), 169–203, doi: 10.1007/s00407-008-0037-7.

—— [2010a], Equations and equating in Arabic mathematics, *Archives Internationales d'Histoire des Sciences*, 60(165), 265–298, doi: 10.1484/J.ARIHS.5.101537.

—— [2010b], Polynomials and equations in medieval Italian algebra, *Bollettino di Storia delle Scienze Matematiche*, 30, 23–60, doi: 10.1400/143289.

OAKS, Jeffrey A. & ALKHATEEB, Haitham M. [2005], *Māl*, enunciations, and the prehistory of Arabic algebra, *Historia Mathematica*, 32(4), 400–425, doi: 10.1016/j.hm.2005.03.002.

—— [2007], Simplifying equations in Arabic algebra, *Historia Mathematica*, 34(1), 45–61, doi: 10.1016/j.hm.2006.02.006.

PROCLUS [1873], *Procli Diadochi in primum Euclidis Elementorum librum commentarii*, Leipzig: Teubner, ed. by G. Friedlein.

RASHED, Roshdi & HOUZEL, Christian [2013], *Les "Arithmétiques" de Diophante. Lecture historique et mathématique*, Berlin; Boston: Walter de Gruyter.

SAITO, Ken & SIDOLI, Nathan [2010], The function of diorism in ancient Greek analysis, *Historia Mathematica*, 37(4), 579–614, doi: 10.1016/j.hm.2009.12.003.

SESIANO, Jacques [1982], *Books IV to VII of Diophantus' "Arithmetica" in the Arabic Translation Attributed to Qusṭā Ibn Lūqā*, New York: Springer.

SIALAROS, Michalis & CHRISTIANIDIS, Jean [2016], Situating the debate on "Geometrical Algebra" within the framework of premodern algebra, *Science in Context*, 29(2), 129–150, doi: 10.1017/S0269889715000411.

SIALAROS, Michalis, MATERA, Rosa, *et al.* [2019], Searching for definitions: Marinus' "Introduction to Euclid's *Data*", *Sciamus: Sources and commentaries in exact sciences*, 20, 119–155.

SIDOLI, Nathan [2004], *Ptolemy's Mathematical Approach. Applied Mathematics in the Second Century*, Ph.D. thesis, University of Toronto.

—— [2018a], The concept of given in Greek mathematics, *Archive for History of Exact Sciences*, 72(4), 353–402, doi: 10.1007/s00407-018-0211-5.

—— [2018b], Uses of construction in problems and theorems in Euclid's *Elements* I–VI, *Archive for History of Exact Sciences*, 72(4), 403–452, doi: 10.1007/s00407-018-0212-4.

VITRAC, Bernard [2005], Peut-on parler d'algèbre dans les mathématiques grecques anciennes, *Ayene-ye Miras*, 3, 1–44.

Entre l'« analyse des Anciens » et l'« algèbre des Modernes » : Y a-t-il une place pour Pierre de La Ramée ?

François Loget
Centre d'études supérieures de la Renaissance – UMR 7323,
Université de Tours
Université de Limoges (France)

Résumé : Dans cet article, j'étudie la façon dont Pierre de La Ramée aborde la question de l'analyse mathématique, d'abord dans ses écrits de logicien, puis dans ses traités mathématiques. Dans les *Scholae mathematicae* (1569), en reprenant un argumentaire qui lui avait servi dans les controverses des années 1550 concernant la « méthode unique », il est conduit à la conclusion que l'analyse n'a aucune valeur démonstrative. Ses recherches sur les significations diverses du mot *analysis* et sur la nature de l'analyse dans les mathématiques grecques m'apparaissent pourtant comme une condition préalable pour que soit reconnue au XVIIe siècle la fécondité de la méthode analytique en géométrie.

Abstract: In this paper, I study Pierre de La Ramée's approach to mathematical analysis, both in his writings as a logician and in his mathematical treatises. In the Scholae mathematicae (1569), by taking up an argument that had served him in the controversies of the 1550s concerning the "unique method", he was led to the conclusion that analysis has no demonstrative value. According to me, his research on the various meanings of the word analysis and on the nature of analysis in Greek mathematics is, however, a prerequisite for the recognition of the fruitfulness of the analytical method in geometry in the 17th century.

1 Introduction

Lorsque Jean-Étienne Montucla présente au milieu du XVIIIe siècle le développement de l'analyse comme la cause des progrès de la géométrie, il ne fait pas

Philosophia Scientiæ, 25(3), 2021, 131–154.

que rappeler la rupture introduite par Viète et les développements apportés par Oughtred, Harriot, Descartes, etc. Il décrit aussi les « insuffisances » qui rendaient nécessaire qu'on donnât à l'analyse la « forme nouvelle » qui permit à ces auteurs de parvenir à leurs résultats [Montucla 1758, vol. IV, livre II, 74–75][1]. Il reconnaît ainsi une parenté, mais aussi une distance, entre l'« analyse des Anciens » et celle des « Modernes ». Tout le problème, pour les mathématiciens et historiens des mathématiques est, depuis lors et jusqu'aux études classiques de la fin du XXe siècle, d'établir cette parenté et de mesurer cette distance – et de faire face à l'ambiguïté du jugement porté sur l'« analyse des Anciens » : notoirement limitée, on y voit cependant le germe de développements futurs.

La parenté entre l'« analyse des Anciens » et l'« algèbre des Modernes » a été reconnue à la Renaissance, grâce à la circulation des manuscrits et à l'impression des traductions et commentaires des mathématiciens grecs, permettant l'examen des démonstrations par analyse d'Euclide[2], de Pappus ou d'Archimède. Il n'est pas difficile d'imaginer les étapes qui ont conduit de là à l'appréciation ambiguë portée sur l'analyse par Montucla et d'autres historiens à sa suite. Il fallait d'abord qu'un sens spécifique du mot *analysis* en géométrie, distinct des sens que ce mot avait dans une culture dominée par la philosophie d'Aristote, et désignant une forme de raisonnement dont avaient usé les géomètres de l'Antiquité, soit distingué. Une fois cette signification dégagée, il devenait possible de juger de la puissance de la démarche analytique par rapport à la voie synthétique et d'apprécier sa proximité avec d'autres démarches comme le raisonnement par l'absurde. Et simultanément, la comparaison de l'« analyse des Anciens » avec les procédures de l'« algèbre des Modernes » permettait de rendre visible le bénéfice apporté par l'adoption d'une langue formelle. On allait en somme louer la fécondité heuristique et apodictique de l'analyse pratiquée par les Grecs tout en affirmant l'incontestable supériorité de la « nouvelle forme » que l'analyse avait prise chez les Modernes. On actait ainsi une transformation – transition lente ou franche rupture –, marquée dans l'histoire par les œuvres de quelques auteurs, ceux-là même que mentionne Montucla.

---

1. « La forme nouvelle qu'a prise l'analyse entre les mains des géomètres [du XVIIe siècle] est l'une des causes principales des rapides progrès qui ont mené la géométrie au point où elle est aujourd'hui. Tant que les rapports dont la recherche occupa les géomètres ne furent pas trop compliqués, les méthodes anciennes purent les aider à les démêler. [...] Ils pénétrèrent aussi avant que les instruments [...] dont ils étaient en possession leur purent servir, et ils en tirèrent un parti que ne soupçonneront pas ceux qui ne connaissent que la nouvelle géométrie. Mais enfin il était de la nature de ces instruments de ne pouvoir les aider que jusqu'à un certain point, et lorsqu'après avoir épuisé les recherches qui étaient à leur portée, ils voulurent s'élever à des spéculations plus difficiles, ils échouèrent devant des difficultés qu'une analyse moins savante, mais plus commode, surmonte aujourd'hui sans peine. »

2. Démonstrations attribuées à Euclide, pour les propositions II, 2-10, dont on sait qu'elles sont en fait l'œuvre d'Héron d'Alexandrie.

Les historiens contemporains qui se sont penchés sur cette transition ont relevé les singularités qui caractérisent la France de la Renaissance et du début de l'Âge classique. Des travaux récents portant sur les mathématiques françaises de la Renaissance ont permis d'apporter des éléments de réponse substantiels à la question posée à la fin des années 1980 par Warren Van Egmond sur l'origine du développement de l'algèbre dans une France qu'on supposait moins bien « équipée » que l'Italie ou les pays du nord de l'Europe pour que s'y implante une algèbre nouvelle [Van Egmond 1988][3]. D'autres auteurs, s'intéressant à la dimension « symbolique » ou « scripturaire » de ce changement[4], ont parfois été amenés à interroger la référence à l'« analyse des Anciens » dans les œuvres de Viète et Descartes[5]. Enfin, l'articulation entre le thème spécifique de l'analyse mathématique et celui de la méthode a conduit historiens et philosophes à rechercher le « chaînon manquant » qui assura la continuité entre l'analytique d'Aristote et la méthode canonique de raisonnement fondée sur l'analyse géométrique que propose Descartes.

Auteur d'un modeste traité d'algèbre, mais surtout promoteur de la « méthode unique », Pierre de La Ramée est apparu comme le candidat idéal pour assurer cette position[6]. L'ambition de cet article, limitée, est d'abord de préciser le sens que prend la notion d'analyse chez La Ramée, en lien avec sa

---

3. Giovana Cifoletti a ouvert la voie aux études sur l'algèbre française de la Renaissance [Cifoletti 1992]. Parmi les travaux les plus récents sur les mathématiques et l'algèbre dans la France de la Renaissance, on pourra consulter notamment [Kouteynikoff 2016], [Axworthy 2016] et les articles consacrés au domaine français dans [Rommevaux, Spiesser *et al.* 2012].

4. Voir par exemple [Heeffer & Van Dyck 2010], [Heeffer & Esteve 2012], [Serfati 2005]. Dans cette catégorie, l'ouvrage de Jean-Louis Gardies est à classer à part, tant son ambition et son propos sont spécifiques [Gardies 2001]. Enfin Panza offre une belle analyse en contrepoint de la « révolution symbolique » en s'efforçant de montrer que la rupture entre l'« analyse des Anciens » et l'algèbre des Modernes ne tient pas tant à l'introduction d'une langue nouvelle qu'au passage d'une analyse dite « intra-configurationnelle » à une analyse « trans-configurationnelle », dont il trouve des exemples chez Omar al-Khayyâm, puis chez François Viète [Panza 2007].

5. Dans la préface du traité *In artem analyticem isagoge* (1591, 1r–1v), Viète présente le traité en question comme le premier d'un ensemble de dix traités dont le titre générique, *Opus restitutae mathematicae analyseos, seu Algebra nova*, indique que le savant vendéen prétend s'inscrire dans la dynamique d'une « restauration » de l'analyse des Anciens qui constituerait la matrice d'une « algèbre nouvelle ». Descartes [*Regulae*, AT, X, 374] évoque les anciens géomètres qui utilisaient « quelque analyse » qu'ils avaient « cachée à leurs neveux » pour éviter qu'elle ne se perde en étant divulguée, jugement qui l'autorise à développer une forme d'analyse qui ne soit pas la simple « restauration » de l'analyse des Anciens, et à montrer sa capacité à le faire en abordant le problème de Pappus.

6. La thèse d'un « axe La Ramée/Descartes » défendue par André Robinet [Robinet 1996] a été contestée [de Buzon 2005]. Parmi les auteurs qui ont cherché à mettre en évidence les liens et différences entre les conceptions raméenne et cartésienne de la méthode, un article récent de P. Hamou [Hamou 2014] est d'une lecture stimulante, j'y reviendrai. Mais je me référerai aussi à [Dubouclez 2013] et [Mahoney 1994].

réflexion sur la méthode et dans le cadre des polémiques qu'il conduit avec les « aristotéliciens ». Je m'efforcerai ensuite de dégager le sens spécifique qu'il donne à l'analyse géométrique. Pour cela, j'examinerai les quelques passages qu'il a consacrés, dans ses écrits philosophiques, à la question de l'analyse et, dans ses traités mathématiques, à la forme géométrique de l'analyse. À l'issue de cette enquête, je tenterai de répondre à la question de savoir si l'on peut attribuer à La Ramée, à travers la réflexion qu'il a conduite sur le sujet de l'analyse, un rôle dans la transition vers l'« algèbre des Modernes ».

2 Méthode unique et critique de l'analyse/synthèse dans la *Dialectica*[7]

Chez Pierre de La Ramée, comme sans doute chez nombre de ses contemporains, la réflexion sur l'analyse ne s'inscrit au premier abord pas dans le champ des mathématiques. C'est dans des discussions qui relèvent de la théorie générale de la connaissance, impliquant l'interprétation des œuvres de référence pour l'enseignement à l'université de Paris, qu'il aborde d'abord cette question, au moment même où il élabore le thème de la « méthode unique ».

2.1 La mise en place du couple analyse/genèse

À l'origine de l'interrogation de La Ramée sur l'analyse, il y a les polémiques dans lesquelles il est impliqué au sujet de cette « méthode unique ». Lorsque, dans ses premiers écrits de 1543[8], La Ramée attaque Aristote et les aristotéliciens, les accusant de n'avoir pas traité de la méthode, ses premiers opposants, Antoine de Gouvea et Joachim Périon, lui répondent qu'il en a traité, non pas dans le sens d'une unicité de la méthode, mais d'une méthode multiple, comme c'est aussi le cas chez Galien. Ainsi, Périon[9] oppose à la méthode unique les trois voies décrites par Galien *(synthesis, analysis, diairesis)*, auxquelles il ajoute une quatrième voie *(apodeixis)* décrite par Eustrate. Il y aurait donc, aux yeux de Périon, non pas une, mais quatre voies pour l'établissement et

7. Je m'appuie pour cette première partie sur l'irremplaçable étude de Nelly Bruyère [Bruyère 1984, chap. III–V].

8. Les premiers textes de La Ramée, parus en 1543 sont les deux versions des *Dialecticae Partitiones* [La Ramée 1543a,d], l'une manuscrite, l'autre imprimée, qui prennent dès leur première réimpression le nom d'*Institutiones* [La Ramée 1543c]. L'année suivante, il fait paraître les *Aristotelicae Animadversiones* [La Ramée 1543b], où il s'en prend à la logique d'Aristote. Les deux premiers imprimés sont mal accueillis. Antoine de Gouvéa, un théologien de la Sorbonne, conduit devant l'université de Paris un procès à l'issue duquel La Ramée est condamné, par un décret de François Ier du 10 mars 1544, à ne plus enseigner la philosophie. Cette interdiction est levée en 1551.

9. Cf. « Oratio I », in [Périon 1554].

l'enseignement des arts. L'analyse serait l'une d'elle, l'un des embranchements de la méthode.

Dans l'édition de 1548 des *Animadversiones* [La Ramée 1548], La Ramée leur répond. Intitulé « De Methodo », le livre XIX est entièrement consacré à la question de la méthode selon Aristote, puis selon Galien. Aristote et les aristotéliciens, dit-il, n'ont jamais défini ce qu'est la méthode universelle. Au contraire, ils distinguent les deux voies inverses de l'analyse et de la genèse. L'analyse serait la voie où l'on commence par la fin, par les choses les plus grossières et composées, pour aller vers les plus simples, la genèse étant la voie inverse qui procède au contraire du simple au composé. Ce point de vue d'Aristote sur la méthode est d'autant plus confus, explique La Ramée, qu'il doit être combiné avec ce qu'il enseigne par ailleurs sur le syllogisme, ses différents genres (démonstratif, dialectique, sophistique), ses composants (noms et verbes, prédicaments et prédicats, termes simples), qui seraient autant de degrés de la méthode. La critique d'Aristote est ici couplée avec celle de Galien, auquel La Ramée fait le même reproche qu'aux aristotéliciens : il ne donnerait pas une définition ferme et constante de la méthode.

En somme, dès les années 1540, l'argumentation en faveur de la méthode unique, qui s'appuie sur la critique d'Aristote et des aristotéliciens d'une part, de Galien et des médecins d'autre part, conduit à une réflexion sur les méthodes d'analyse et de genèse : ce dédoublement des voies « contraires » est inutile, mais aussi confusionnel, comme le montrent les multiples usages et acceptions distinctes du terme « analyse » chez Aristote.

Au milieu de la décennie 1550, c'est aux arguments de Jacques Charpentier contre l'idée d'une méthode unique que La Ramée doit s'opposer [Charpentier 1554]. Charpentier discute l'idée de la double voie analyse/genèse chez Platon et Aristote. Dans des traités qui ne relèvent pas de l'*Organon*, comme la *Physique* ou l'*Éthique*, Aristote descend « analytiquement » des choses générales aux choses spéciales, mais il suit aussi fréquemment la démarche inverse. Là où La Ramée ne voyait que de la confusion, son adversaire se range à l'opinion des commentateurs : il y a bien, chez Aristote comme chez Platon avant lui, une double voie d'accès à la connaissance.

2.2 L'argumentaire du *Quod sit unica methodus*

Les attaques de Charpentier portaient sur l'édition de 1550 de la *Dialectica* et l'édition séparée des livres IX et X (1554[10]). Dans ces textes, La Ramée renouvelle sa discussion sur la méthode chez Aristote et Galien en atténuant sa critique envers le premier et en faisant porter ses griefs avant tout contre les aristotéliciens. Ce sont eux qui auraient distingué deux voies : la première,

10. Ces deux livres, parus séparément au début de l'année 1554, prennent dans la réédition de 1557 un titre à valeur de proclamation : *Quod sit unica doctrinae instituendae methodus.* Je me réfère ici à cette édition [La Ramée 1557] et dans les paragraphes qui suivent, je résume le contenu des pages qui touche à notre sujet.

descendante, appelée *analysis* par Porphyre, Ammonius ou Philopon, *theoria* par Simplicius, qui part de la fin et progresse par degrés en s'en éloignant. Cette voie, clairement identifiée dans les écrits d'Aristote, a la faveur de La Ramée, qui la rapproche de la voie « universelle » qui va du composé au simple et des choses les plus connues à celles qui le sont moins. La seconde voie que prétendent repérer chez Aristote ses commentateurs, inverse de la précédente, est la voie ascendante de la genèse (appelée *praxis* par Simplicius).

Pour La Ramée, plusieurs graves erreurs entachent l'interprétation par les aristotéliciens de la logique d'Aristote. En particulier, l'opposition entre les deux voies d'analyse et genèse est confusionnelle : si la méthode d'Aristote est celle qui procède du général au particulier et du plus connu au moins connu – laquelle méthode est baptisée « analyse » ou « théorie » par les aristotéliciens –, comment pourrait-on procéder par la voie inverse, baptisée genèse ou *praxis* ? La voie descendante, baptisée analyse par les commentateurs, la seule valable en fait, devrait être appelée genèse [La Ramée 1557, 9r–10r].

Il est caractéristique des écrits des années 1550 que La Ramée incrimine, plutôt qu'Aristote lui-même, ses commentateurs, accusés d'avoir rendu la logique d'Aristote, déjà peu claire par elle-même, plus obscure encore. Au final, l'argumentation de La Ramée tient en une thèse : il n'y a qu'une méthode, connue d'Aristote mais mal exposée par lui ; cette méthode, les commentateurs d'Aristote l'ont encore obscurcie ; concernant le couple analyse/genèse, ils donnent à tort le premier rang à l'analyse, alors que c'est à la genèse que revient ce premier rang. On voit que ces critiques convergent vers une disqualification de l'analyse : la méthode unique a pour nom genèse et l'analyse, voie inverse de la genèse, est de trop, puisqu'il n'y a qu'une voie d'accès à la connaissance.

2.3 Du couple analyse/genèse au couple analyse/synthèse

Dans la deuxième partie du traité, La Ramée répond à ceux qui prétendent qu'il y aurait plusieurs méthodes chez Galien. Le médecin latin, explique-t-il, a usé de bien des noms pour désigner la méthode. Dans le *De placitis Hippocratis et Platonis*, il distingue par exemple la voie divisive [*diairetikê*], aussi nommée *odos*, et la voie synthétique [*synthetikê*] ou *anodos*. On reconnaît ici, dit La Ramée, le couple introduit par les aristotéliciens et baptisé par Simplicius *analysis* et *genesis*. Et ce couple est tout aussi factice : Galien s'est laissé abuser par une lecture erronée du *Phèdre* de Platon[11], lorsqu'il affirme que le philosophe appréciait les deux méthodes contraires, division et synthèse, alors qu'il y défend au contraire la voie unique que défend La Ramée lui-même. Nulle part Platon ne professe la synthèse ou voie regressive [*anodos*].

11. Nelly Bruyère a identifié le passage de Platon auquel renvoie Galien et que réinterprète La Ramée : Platon, *Phèdre*, 265d-e [Bruyère 1984, 154, n. 1].

Un autre passage fameux dans lequel Galien traite de la méthode est le début de l'*Art médical* où il définit trois modes d'enseignement de la médecine[12]. La Ramée cite le texte grec de Galien avant de traduire et de le commenter. Le médecin évoque trois voies : la première, « qui part de l'intelligence et de la notion de la fin, opère par résolution » ; la seconde qui procède par la « composition de ce qui ce qui avait été découvert par résolution » ; la troisième, « suivant la décomposition de la définition [La Ramée 1557, 16r] ». Le propos est ici tout à fait obscur, juge La Ramée. La troisième méthode doit être rejetée : ce n'est en rien une méthode. Les deux premières, décrites comme inverses l'une de l'autre, correspondent au couple analyse/genèse de Simplicius, à ceci près que le second terme est remplacé par celui de synthèse et que la priorité est inversée. Or, la voie ici baptisée « synthèse » est absurde : aucun art ne procède à partir du plus éloigné par nature et du moins connu ; en géométrie, cela reviendrait à commencer par l'étude du livre XV des *Éléments* avant de remonter progressivement au premier [La Ramée 1557, 19v]. Au contraire toute science procède des choses générales aux spéciales. Ce que Galien appelle ici « analyse » correspond à la voie divisive du *De placitis Hippocratis et Platonis*. Finalement, on ne trouve chez Galien qu'une seule méthode, identique à celle, également unique, que l'on trouve chez Aristote, et cette méthode est celle qui convient à tous les arts.

2.4 Valeur de l'analyse

Tout au long des décennies 1550-1560, la réflexion de La Ramée a été nourrie par les controverses sur la méthode unique. La nécessité de répondre aux objections de ses adversaires l'a conduit à reprendre et enrichir ses arguments, notamment en interprétant des passages de plus en plus nombreux tirés des écrits d'Aristote. L'enjeu est alors de montrer que, partout où ses adversaires voient des méthodes multiples, il n'y en a en fait aucune autre que celle qui procède du général au particulier. En somme, La Ramée réduit la pluralité des doctrines qu'il observe chez les auteurs de l'Antiquité à une seule, laquelle constitue la *prisca philosophia*, l'unique philosophie antique, pervertie par la négligence des auteurs en question et par les injures du temps. En défendant la méthode unique, c'est un projet de restauration des savoirs de l'Antiquité qu'entend accomplir La Ramée.

La réflexion sur la méthode unique, rendue assez formelle par les développements polémiques dans lesquels il s'inscrit, conduit donc La Ramée à rejeter

12. [Galien 1821-1833, I, 305–306] et [Galien 2000]. Le médecin distingue l'« analyse », la « synthèse » et la « décomposition de la définition ». C'est ce troisième mode d'enseignement qui est illustré dans *l'Art médical*, mais il est « inférieur » à l'analyse, mode dont Galien dit qu'il est le premier à l'avoir utilisé. Galien dit encore dans ce passage que certains médecins ont nommé la « décomposition de la définition » autrement : « développement », « analyse », « division », « explication », « exposition ». L'exposé est, on le voit, assez sybillin et laisse le champ libre à La Ramée pour dénoncer la confusion du propos de Galien.

les divers points de vue tendant à affirmer que l'analyse constitue une méthode. Est-elle pour autant privée de toute valeur ? Non. Si elle est rejetée hors du champ de l'apodictique, elle trouve néanmoins place dans le processus qui rend possible l'exercice de la méthode. Pour le comprendre, il faut se souvenir que, dans les premiers écrits de La Ramée, le concept de méthode s'enracine dans celui de *jugement*, lequel s'articule avec celui d'*invention*. Le *jugement* consiste à agencer des arguments ou des exemples préalablement sélectionnés et évalués lors du processus d'*invention*[13]. Ce processus consiste donc à recueillir, dans les savoirs constitués, les éléments susceptibles de fournir les matériaux de nouveaux discours. Les arguments ou exemples d'où le jugement méthodique tire sa force sont donc extérieurs ou étrangers au jugement méthodique lui-même. Matériaux empruntés aux savoirs constitués, ils sont recyclés en vue de la composition de nouveaux discours.

C'est au champ de l'*invention* qu'appartient l'analyse. De manière significative, La Ramée emploie, pour décrire son office propre, le verbe *retexere* (« détisser[14] ») : par analyse, on détisse les œuvres constituées pour pouvoir en inspecter et évaluer les arguments qui entreront en composition dans les œuvres nouvelles. L'analyse a donc bien une valeur positive, en partie masquée par le contexte polémique dans lequel la réflexion sur l'analyse est conduite, visant à défendre l'unicité de la méthode en condamnant tout ce qui peut y faire ombrage. Dans son versant positif, l'analyse, relevant de l'*invention*, intervient avant la mise en œuvre du jugement méthodique et cette antériorité justifie son rejet hors du champ de l'apodictique. Il faut garder en mémoire cette caractéristique lorsque l'on aborde les traités qu'il publie à Bâle en 1569, où l'on trouve les passages concernant une forme spécifique d'analyse : l'analyse géométrique.

3 La critique de l'analyse géométrique dans les *Scholae mathematicae*

L'état final de sa réflexion sur la question de l'analyse/synthèse se trouve dans ses publications de l'année 1569. Résidant alors à Bâle, il publie notamment une nouvelle version des *Praelectiones* et les *Scholae in liberales artes* [La Ramée 1569b,c]. Dans les *Praelectiones* de 1569, le rôle de Galien est à nouveau examiné. La Ramée aboutit aux mêmes conclusions qu'en 1557, mais pour la première fois, il distingue nettement l'analyse/genèse des philosophes

13. Andreas Blank montre qu'en cela, La Ramée rompt avec la conception traditionnelle du syllogisme comme combinatoire de concepts, au profit d'une conception qu'il appelle « pragmatique », consistant à évaluer [*weighing*] les arguments qui entrent en composition dans le syllogisme [Blank 2008]. Ce qui vaut pour la forme syllogistique vaut pour les autres formes de jugement.

14. Cf. à ce sujet [Dubouclez 2013, 168 *ff.*].

de celles que pratiquent les géomètres. Il donne une définition de l'analyse géométrique, empruntée à Pappus et Proclus, et signale également un autre sens du mot « analyse », en algèbre, pour désigner l'opération consistant à calculer la racine d'un binôme[15]. Cet ajout doit être mis en rapport avec la parution des éditions bâloises des traités mathématiques : les *Scholae mathematicae* [La Ramée 1569d], qui complètent les *Scholae in liberales artes* [La Ramée 1569c], et les dernières versions de l'*Arithmétique* et de la *Géométrie*, associées dans un volume unique [La Ramée 1569a]. La confrontation entre une forme spécifique d'analyse, définie par Pappus et illustrée dans le livre XIII des *Éléments*, et l'analyse comme telle, lui impose une révision de ses conceptions. L'examen de ces traités permettra de saisir l'évolution de sa réflexion.

3.1 Qu'est-ce que l'analyse géométrique ?

La Ramée aborde la question de l'analyse géométrique dès le livre III des *Scholae mathematicae*. Il en donne alors une définition avant de porter un premier jugement à son sujet :

> L'analyse est une certaine inversion de la démonstration, concluant la cause par l'effet, comme le dit ici justement Proclus ; et il dit que ladite analyse est souvent employée et mise en œuvre dans tous les *Éléments*. Théon n'a pas approuvé Euclide sur ce point [car] il utilise l'analyse dans cinq propositions seulement, à savoir [les propositions] 1, 2, 3, 4, 5 du livre XIII. Au second de la *Sphère*, Archimède l'utilise dans quelques propositions. Pappus [l'utilise] au début du livre VII. Je n'ai remarqué l'analyse nulle part ailleurs chez tous les mathématiciens et la véritable analyse est avant tout utile pour les côtés du carré et du cube et souvent il est utile de chercher par analyse complète la cause de l'œuvre. Mais ces démonstrations par analyse (telles celles en tous cas qui sont dans les *Éléments*) sont sophistiques et faire deux doctrines de la même chose, l'une apodictique, et l'autre analytique, comme le font en l'occurrence Théon, Archimède et Pappus, est un sophisme. Car si tu as démontré la chose avec discernement et clairement en partant de la cause, tu le démontreras sans discernement et obscurément par l'effet[16]. [La Ramée 1569d, 99]

15. N'ayant pu consulter les *Praelectiones* de 1569, je m'appuie ici exclusivement sur ce qu'en dit Nelly Bruyère [Bruyère 1984, 179].

16. « Analysis est quædam inversio *apodeixeôs* ex effectis nempe caussam concludens, qualem significat Proclus in totis elementis ab Euclide frequenter adhibitam & tractatam esse. Theon Euclidem hac in re non probavit, in quinque tantúm propositionibus reliquit, nempe in 1, 2, 3, 4, 5 p. 13. Archimedes secundo de sphaera in aliquot propositionibus usurpavit : Pappus initio libri 7. alibi in totis mathematicis *analysin* nullam animadverti : vera est analysis et quadrati et cubici lateris, et imprimis utilis : et saepe prodest absoluti operis caussam analysi investigare :

Pour comprendre ce passage, on doit le situer dans l'ensemble formé par les trois premiers livres des *Scholae mathematicae.* La Ramée reprend là les trois livres de son *Prooemium mathematicum* [La Ramée 1567], ouvrage dans lequel il a entrepris de dresser un vaste panorama de l'histoire des mathématiques, puis de défendre leur « utilité », enfin de détailler les défauts qui entachent selon lui l'œuvre d'Euclide. Sans négliger l'importance du second livre, il faut insister sur le fait que la reconstruction historique que propose La Ramée dans le livre I du Proème lui offre la justification des critiques qu'il formule dans le livre III et des réformes qu'il juge nécessaire d'apporter à la somme euclidienne[17]. Ces réformes sont expliquées dans les livres suivants des *Scholae mathematicae* et mises en œuvre dans le volume associant l'arithmétique et la géométrie [La Ramée 1569a].

Tant pour son histoire des mathématiques que pour sa critique d'Euclide, La Ramée s'appuie principalement sur une source : Le *Commentaire au premier livre des Éléments d'Euclide* de Proclus. Mais si cet ouvrage est une source d'information, son auteur est par ailleurs un acteur singulier de l'histoire des mathématiques de La Ramée : son commentaire offrirait le meilleur témoignage sur les *Éléments* tels qu'ils ont été rédigés par Euclide, avant que le texte nous en soit transmis sous une forme dégradée et avec des démonstrations rédigées par Théon[18]. Aussi Proclus est-il convoqué par La Ramée dans son plaidoyer contre l'Alexandrin : c'est à lui qu'il se réfère lorsqu'il entreprend de mettre en évidence les défauts qui entachent les *Éléments*, à la fois dans leur structure et dans le détail des démonstrations. Mais en même temps, il fait figure d'accusé et partage avec Euclide la responsabilité de ces défauts.

Le Diadoque, explique La Ramée, fait l'éloge de la « logique » suivie par Euclide dans les *Éléments.* C'est à Euclide que reviendrait notamment un double mérite : celui d'avoir « sélectionné » les éléments et de les avoir « mis en ordre » [La Ramée 1569d, 97–98][19], justifiant ainsi sa réponse à l'interrogation du roi Ptolémée : il n'y a pas de « voie royale », pas d'autre voie possible pour l'enseignement de la géométrie que celle qu'il a proposée

at tales analyticae demonstrationes, (quales illae sunt in elementis plané) sunt sophisticae, duasque ejusdem rei doctrinas, alteram analyticam facere, ut illic Theon & Archimedes & Pappus faciunt, sophisma est. » [Sauf mention explicite, toutes les traductions de Pierre de La Ramée sont miennes.]

17. Sur l'histoire des mathématiques de La Ramée, voir [Goulding 2012, 131–138], ainsi que [Loget 2004].

18. À la suite de Zamberti, et comme d'autres parmi ses contemporains, La Ramée considère Théon comme l'auteur des démonstrations des *Éléments* transmises à la postérité. Par la suite, je mettrai le nom de Théon entre guillemets pour indiquer cette qualité. Plus étrange est la chronologie qu'adopte La Ramée, qui fait de Proclus (412-486) un auteur du Ier siècle, antérieur donc à Théon (situé à juste titre au Ve siècle). Cette inversion est indispensable, tant pour faire de Proclus le meilleur témoin de la mathématique euclidienne que pour transférer à Théon, dernier des « compositeurs d'Éléments » la responsabilité de la rédaction transmise à la postérité. Cf. à ce sujet [Goulding 2012, 159–161].

19. La Ramée résume et commente ici Proclus, *Commentaires*, II, 5.

dans les *Éléments.* Tout au long du livre III du Proème, La Ramée reprend à son compte la question de Ptolémée et s'attache à montrer que les mérites que Proclus attribue à Euclide sont usurpés. La sélection de propositions qu'il a faite convient-elle aux débutants ? L'ordre qu'il a choisi et les modes de démonstrations qu'il a utilisés sont-ils les meilleurs ? À chacune de ces questions, La Ramée répond négativement.

Que le choix effectué par Euclide ne soit pas le bon, il le montre en dénonçant le nombre considérable de « redondances », c'est-à-dire de propositions inutiles, que l'on trouve dans les *Éléments*, dont il établit le nombre à 222 [La Ramée 1569d, 91] ! Poussant plus loin son enquête, La Ramée observe : Proclus a admis que la méthode démonstrative (apodictique) va des principes à ce qui est cherché, mais il discute longuement du raisonnement par l'absurde ou des diverses méthodes de conversion. Se pourrait-il alors qu'on puisse démontrer par une autre voie, inductive, qui remonte à partir d'un exemple singulier ? Tous ces procédés, conclut finalement La Ramée, sont à rejeter : si les propositions « non démontrables », ou principes, sont connues par induction, ce n'est pas le cas des propositions démontrables ; comme l'a enseigné Aristote : supposer ce qui est demandé, c'est faire un sophisme et non démontrer [La Ramée 1569d, 95][20]. Ces méthodes sont donc à compter parmi les redondances qui entachent les *Éléments.*

Pour ce qui est de la deuxième question, La Ramée fait l'examen des passages où Proclus évoque les « méthodes » d'Euclide et la « logique » qu'il a suivie dans ses démonstrations. L'Alexandrin, résume-t-il, a utilisé toutes les « méthodes dialectiques » : méthode de division, de définition, les diverses méthodes de conversion, ainsi que les deux voies contraires de l'apodictique – qui part des principes pour atteindre ce qui est cherché –, et de l'analyse – qui remonte de ce qui est cherché aux principes[21].

C'est ici que se situe le passage cité plus haut. Comment l'interpréter ? La Ramée retient une caractéristique de l'analyse, soulignée par Proclus : c'est une voie « rétrograde », qui remonte des effets à la cause. Il adresse ensuite une première objection : si, comme le prétend le Diadoque, l'analyse était une méthode courante chez Euclide, elle ne l'a pas été chez ses successeurs : « Théon » ne l'a utilisée dans ses démonstrations des éléments qu'au début du livre XIII ; et hormis Archimède et Pappus occasionnellement, aucun autre

20. « Sophisma enim hic est Aristoteli [...] petere propositum, non demonstrare. »
21. Cf Proclus, *Comm.*, prologue II, chap. 2 et 5. Sur les méthodes de conversion, propositions, II, 409, 1–6.

auteur n'y a eu recours pendant l'Antiquité[22]. Cette remarque sur la rareté des recours à l'analyse annonce une condamnation de la voie de l'analyse qui est effectivement formulée à la fin du passage cité.

Ce rejet n'est pas inattendu. La Ramée l'a réaffirmé dès le début du livre III : il n'y a qu'une méthode pour l'enseignement des arts ; cette méthode unique, qu'Aristote suivait, mais qu'il avait exposée de façon confuse avant que ses commentateurs la rendent plus obscure encore, est aussi celle que suit Euclide, mais lui-même l'a obscurcie et elle a aussi été dégradée par Proclus. Toute démonstration part des causes et procède du plus connu au moins connu. La voie inverse de l'analyse n'est donc pas démonstrative, mais « sophistique ». On le voit : l'argument qui conduit au rejet de l'analyse en mathématique est le même que celui qui conduit au rejet des doubles voies (analyse/genèse) de Simplicius et Galien. Ici, c'est le primat de la voie descendante – disons de la synthèse – qui rend inutile une hypothétique voie inverse de l'analyse.

Pourtant, La Ramée mentionne, comme en passant, une autre acception, positive cette fois, du mot « analyse » : la « véritable analyse est utile, remarque-t-il, pour les côtés du carré et du cube[23] ». On voit se dessiner ici un schéma symétrique, pour l'analyse géométrique, à celui qui prévaut pour l'analyse comme telle : La Ramée rejette l'analyse géométrique hors du champ de la méthode, mais lui reconnaît une « utilité ». De quelle nature est cette utilité ? Officie-t-elle avant la mise en œuvre de la démonstration pour offrir les ressources utiles à la conduite de celle-ci ? Je réserve à un développement ultérieur mes remarques sur cette question de la « véritable analyse ».

3.2 Il n'y a pas de voie rétrograde en géométrie

La dernière mention de l'analyse dans les *Scholae mathematicae* se trouve, sans surprise, au début du livre XXIX, dans un préambule où La Ramée donne une première appréciation du livre XIII des *Éléments*, avant d'entamer l'examen des propositions :

22. La Ramée oublie de mentionner Apollonius parmi les utilisateurs de l'analyse. Son nom apparaît bien dans le premier livre du Proème et il souligne ailleurs dans le livre III qu'il a poussé plus loin qu'Euclide l'étude des coniques... Mais il est probable qu'il n'a pas lu l'œuvre d'Apollonius, dont il ne mentionne pas la traduction des livres I-IV des *Coniques* publiée en 1566 par Federico Commandino. Plus étonnant, La Ramée, bien qu'il se réfère à Pappus, ne relève pas que celui-ci fait de l'analyse une méthode pratiquée par Euclide ailleurs que dans les *Éléments* et par d'autres auteurs, Apollonius, Aristée, Eratosthène. On sait par son biographe Nicolas de Nancel [Nancel 1599, 202–203] que La Ramée a possédé une copie manuscrite de la *Collection mathématique* et il ne pouvait donc ignorer la mention par celui-ci de la « Collection analytique » des Anciens, qu'il mentionne d'ailleurs lorsqu'il commente le livre XIII, comme on va le voir bientôt.

23. Relevons que cette remarque est absente de la première version du Proème [La Ramée 1567, 433–434] et est donc insérée en 1569, au moment de la rédaction des *Scholae*.

> Ici Théon ajoute en outre, comme des choses nouvelles, *synthesis et analysis, composition et résolution*, des cinq premières. La *synthesis* est la position de ce qui est connu [pour parvenir] par voie de conséquence à la fin et à la compréhension de ce qui est cherché ; l'*analysis* est la position de ce qui est cherché comme connu [pour parvenir] par voie de conséquence à ce qui est admis pour vrai. Telles sont les définitions de Théon, et elles concordent avec celles qu'a proposées Proclus au premier livre des *Éléments* : les preuves mathématiques sont soit à partir des principes soit vers les principes ; à partir des principes connus par eux-mêmes ou démontrés d'une autre façon ; ou bien vers les principes, et ce sont *résolutions* et *déductions*. Les *résolutions* [ou analyses], qui ont le pouvoir de poser des principes, auxquelles sont opposées les *compositions* [ou synthèses], puisqu'on [y] procède des principes à ce qui est cherché. Les déductions par l'impossible tirent leur puissance de ce qu'elles démentent : ainsi, ce que propose Pappus au début du VIIe livre, selon qui l'*analysis* serait *anapalin lysis* [décomposition rétrograde] et celle-ci double *synthetike* et *poristike*, et bien plus : il parle de 32 livres *ton analuomenon* de trois auteurs, Euclide, Apollonius, Aristée[24]. [La Ramée 1569d, 306]

« Théon », dit d'abord La Ramée, a ajouté les démonstrations des cinq premières propositions par *synthesis* et *analysis* (il utilise ici, pour traduire le grec, les mots *compositio* et *resolutio*, qui figurent dans les éditions latines de la Renaissance) et les a présentées comme une nouveauté. Il rapporte ensuite les définitions de la synthèse et de l'analyse qui accompagnent ces démonstrations[25] et note qu'elles concordent avec celles de Proclus : celui-ci dit en effet que les preuves mathématiques, soit descendent des principes, soit remontent vers les principes, et distingue parmi ces dernières les *résolutions* (analyses) et les *déductions* ou raisonnements par l'absurde. Lorsque

24. « Theon hic adhibet praterea *synthesin kai analysin* compositionem & resolutionem quinque primarum, tanquam res aliquas novas. *synthesis* est assumptio concessi per consequentia ad quaesiti finem et comprehensionem, *analysis* est assumptio quaesiti tanquam concessi per consequentia ad verum concessum. Hae sunt definitiones Theonis, quibus consentanea sunt illa, quae Proclus primo libro elementorum protulit, mathematicas probationes esse à principiis vel ad principia, à principiis per se notis vel aliunde demonstratis, ad principia esse resolutiones et deductiones. Resolutiones quae ponendorum principiorum vim habent, quibus compositiones opponuntur, cum a principiis ad quaesitum ordine progredimur. Deductiones ad impossibile habent vim destruendi : similiaque iis Pappus affert initio septimi libri, velut analysis sit *anapalin lusis*, eaque duplex *zetetike* et *poristike*, quin libros *ton analuomenon* narrat 32 à tribus authoribus Euclide, Apollonio, Aristeo. »

25. Les définitions en question sont placées, dans les éditions de la Renaissance comme dans la plupart des manuscrits, après la démonstration de XIII, 5, en préambule des doubles démonstrations par analyse et synthèse. Que cet ensemble soit interpolé ne fait guère de doute.

Pappus présente l'analyse comme voie inverse de la synthèse et distingue les deux formes d'analyse, *zététique* et *poristique*, il est aussi en accord avec ce que dit Proclus.

La Ramée affirme donc que trois auteurs, Proclus, Théon et Pappus – auxquels il faut associer les autres auteurs de la « collection analytique », dont il mentionne le nom : Euclide, Apollonius, Aristée – ont partagé une même conception de l'analyse. Un examen plus attentif pourrait sans doute l'obliger à admettre que les définitions, telles qu'elles sont formulées dans le livre XIII d'Euclide et le livre VII de Pappus, ne sont pas strictement équivalentes, mais il n'entreprend pas cet examen. Ce qui lui importe est d'affirmer l'unité des conceptions des Anciens pour pouvoir porter ensuite sur l'analyse le jugement que voici[26] :

> Cette doctrine de Proclus et de Pappus s'accorde, dis-je, avec celle de Théon et tout ce genre de doctrine « rétrograde », comme dit Campanus, est une fiction tout à fait vaine. Ici en effet, Théon, de cinq propositions en fait quinze : les cinq premières sont démontrées séparément, ensuite deux autres démonstrations en sont faites, la première par résolution, la seconde par composition. Cette analyse ainsi définie par Théon est utile certes pour inventer des choses, et on a dit que cette façon de découvrir la vérité en mathématiques a été découverte par Platon. Mais le même Platon prévient qu'il faut ajouter la voie contraire de la genèse en composant et démontrant les choses inventées. Cette *analysis*, dis-je, est l'observation et l'expérience première, et ne sert pas à ordonner l'art et la doctrine. Les choses singulières sont d'abord inventées et les genres rassemblés ; elles sont enseignées après qu'elles ont été inventées, à savoir en commençant par les genres et en descendant vers les espèces[27]. [La Ramée 1569d, 306]

---

26. Olivier Dubouclez fait de ce passage un commentaire dont la teneur est assez semblable à ce que j'en dis ici [Dubouclez 2013, 174–176]. Je commenterai plus loin l'argument crucial qu'il développe à partir d'un passage de la *Geometria*. Dubouclez s'appuie sur une édition par Lazare Schöner datant de 1627, ce qui explique la non-concordance entre la pagination que j'indique ici et celle que l'on trouve dans son ouvrage.

27. « Haec (inquam) Procli & Pappi, consentiunt cum Theonis ista doctrina, totumque genus hujus retrogradae (ut loquitur Campanus) doctrinae commentitium est, & valde nugatorium. Hic enim pro quinque demonstrationibus factae sunt à Theone quindecim : Primo quinque propositiones demontrantur separatim deinde duae cujusque demonstrationes aliae factae, prima per resolutionem, secunda per compositionem. Analysis vero ista et sic à Theone definita rebus inveniendis utilis quidem est, eamque Plato veritatis inquirendae viam in mathematicis invenisse dicitur. At in componendis et demonstrandis rebus inventis contrariam geneseos viam adhibendam esse Plato idem admonet : *analysis* (inquam) ista est primae observationis et experientiae, artis et doctrinae ordinandae non est : aliter res singulares primo inveniuntur, deinde genera colliguntur : aliter docendae posteaquam inventae sunt, à generalibus nempe incipiendo, & descendendo ad species. »

La Ramée rejette donc une nouvelle fois la double voie analyse/synthèse en géométrie et tous les auteurs qui l'ont défendue. Mais il détaille cette fois les raisons de son rejet. D'abord, Théon a donné trois démonstrations des premières propositions du livre XIII quand une seule suffit. Les démonstrations par la voie analytique doivent donc être mises au nombre des multiples « redondances » présentes dans les *Éléments.* En second lieu, elles relèvent de l'« hystérologie » : la démarche analytique renverse l'ordre naturel de la démonstration, qui va du plus connu au moins connu. Le point de vue adopté par La Ramée ici pour l'analyse géométrique est bien calqué sur celui qu'il défendait pour l'analyse comme telle. En géométrie comme en général, l'analyse ne relève pas de la démonstration, mais de l'invention. Par l'analyse, écrit-il à la fin du passage cité, on collecte les « choses singulières » ou « genre » qui entrent en jeu dans la démonstration, c'est-à-dire dans l'enseignement, conduits dans un second temps.

La Ramée reproduit donc, dans sa critique de l'analyse en géométrie, l'argumentaire qu'il avait utilisé contre les interprètes d'Aristote et Galien pour défendre la méthode unique et critiquer la double voie analyse/genèse. C'est d'ailleurs contre eux qu'il est le plus virulent ensuite [La Ramée 1569d, 306–307] : que l'analyse soit inutile en géométrie, dit-il, Euclide et Théon le montrent eux-mêmes, puisqu'ils ne l'utilisent jamais qu'au début du livre XIII. Mais les commentateurs d'Aristote et de Galien ont eu un tort bien plus grand : ils ont imaginé une « méthode double » et prétendu que tous les arts pouvaient être exposés suivant cette méthode. Et La Ramée renvoie finalement à sa *Dialectique*, où, dans le chapitre consacré à la méthode, cette question est traitée plus longuement. Tout montre ici que La Ramée maintient, dans son appréciation de l'analyse géométrique, la position qu'il a toujours maintenue pour l'analyse en général : l'analyse relève de l'invention et non du jugement. Comme telle, son office est antérieur, mais aussi indispensable à la mise en œuvre du jugement méthodique.

Pour La Ramée, le sujet de l'analyse est clos. Il peut dès lors commencer la présentation des premières propositions du livre XIII, mais sans se donner la peine d'examiner les démonstrations « ajoutées par Théon ». Les démonstrations par analyse et synthèse sont simplement rejetées.

3.3 La question de la *vera analysis* : des *Scholae* à la *Geometria*

Dans les passages des *Scholae* que nous avons examinés, La Ramée condamne l'analyse géométrique, tout en défendant, sans grande précision, l'idée qu'une « véritable analyse », relevant de l'invention, serait utile à la conduite de la démonstration géométrique.

Revenons d'abord sur la remarque qu'il fait au sujet de la « véritable analyse » dans le livre III. La Ramée renvoie ici à une technique opératoire : l'invention du « côté » des carrés ou cubes, c'est-à-dire l'extraction de leur racine ; et, renchérit-il, l'analyse peut être utile pour accéder à la connaissance des causes. La Ramée évoque à deux autres reprises cette technique, qu'il désigne alors comme *vera analysis*, dans les *Scholae mathematicae.* La première fois, brièvement, au livre XXV, alors qu'il commente le livre X des *Éléments.* Il s'agit alors d'extraire – il emploie ici encore le verbe *retexere* – la racine d'une entité algébrique, une ligne irrationnelle de la catégorie « binôme » $(23+\sqrt{448})$. La Ramée ajoute que les propositions II, 4 et II, 5 des *Éléments* enseignent, la première par genèse, la seconde par analyse, l'invention du « côté » des binômes. Il reproduit les figures des deux propositions, sans la démonstration qui les accompagne et, sur la première, associe à ses divers éléments (côtés, carrés, rectangles) les valeurs numériques correspondant à l'exemple qu'il vient de traiter. Il ajoute enfin que la voie de la genèse est plus brève [La Ramée 1569d, 282]. L'algorithme qu'il emploie ici pour extraire la racine d'un binôme avait été décrit dans le traité d'algèbre de 1560, ou le terme *analysis* était déjà employé pour désigner l'opération consistant à trouver [*retexere*] le « côté » de ces lignes irrationnelles que sont binômes et résidus[28].

On voit ici que la forme spécifiquement géométrique de l'analyse reste associée, dans l'*Algebra*, comme dans les *Scholae*, à l'acte de détissage associé à l'analyse comme telle. On peut donc penser que, pour La Ramée, l'extraction de racine est, dans le champ des mathématiques, le procédé qui correspond au « détissage » analytique tel que pratiqué dans le cadre de l'*invention.* Toutefois, alors que, dans les textes précédemment examinés, La Ramée utilisait ce verbe pour décrire un acte mental spécifique, indépendant et antérieur au jugement méthodique, ici la symétrie entre les deux démarches, analyse et genèse (l'une étant posée comme inverse de l'autre dans les définitions que La Ramée emprunte à Proclus et Pappus), est maintenue. En somme, sans admettre que l'analyse est une « seconde méthode », La Ramée laisse transparaître l'idée d'une complémentarité, et non la simple antériorité de l'analyse par rapport à la genèse.

En 1569, dans les *Scholae mathematicae*, la considération de l'analyse géométrique semble conduire La Ramée à faire un pas de côté par rapport à la position qu'il défendait dans ses écrits antérieurs et encore dans ses écrits philosophiques de 1569. Cette évolution est confirmée lorsque l'on se tourne vers les traités « techniques » que sont l'*Arithmetica* et la *Geometria.* Dans l'« élément » XI, 8 de la *Geometria* [La Ramée 1569a, 87–90], La Ramée relève que l'égalité qu'exprime II, 4 entre le « grand carré » et ses composants (carrés et rectangles), exprimée au moyen de nombres, conduit à l'analyse, c'est-à-dire à l'extraction de la racine carrée. Pour le montrer, il considère l'exemple numérique suivant, dans lequel, aux côtés des « petits carrés » composant le « grand carré » sont assignées les valeurs 10 et 2, valeurs qui sont indiquées sur la figure qui accompagne la proposition :

28. C'est-à-dire des irrationnels de la forme (respectivement) $a+\sqrt{b}$ et $a-\sqrt{b}$, cf. [La Ramée 1560, 9r-v].

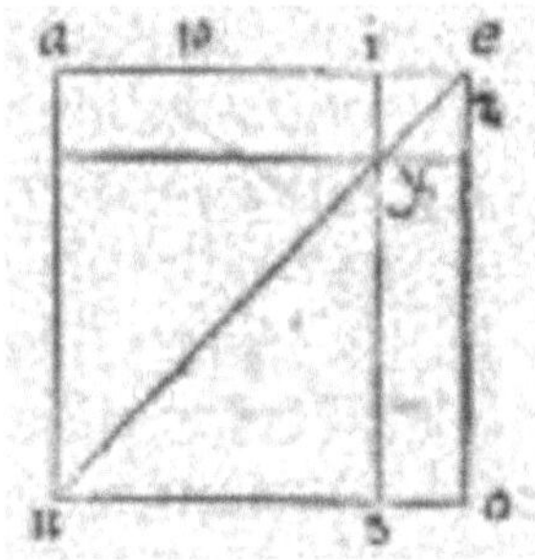

Mais on cherchera souvent le côté du [carré] proposé en nombre. Ainsi, par l'élément [XII, 8] qui précède et son corollaire, l'analyse du côté du carré est disposée [*instructa*]. Cherchons donc le côté du carré proposé et considérons-en d'abord la genèse, telle que tu la vois ici, dans les nombres mêmes, à partir de la multiplication des nombres :

	10	2
	10	2
	2	4
	2	0
1	0	0
1	4	4

Tel est le rapport du carré avec les rectangles et les carrés, d'où est tirée l'analyse du côté du carré explicable en nombre. Et du moment que c'est le même chemin qui conduit d'Athènes à Thèbes et de Thèbes à Athènes, l'usage de l'analyse géométrique demeure ici [*superest*], comme plus loin pour le cube, alors qu'elle ne se trouve nulle part dans tous les *Éléments*[29]. [La Ramée 1569a, 87–88]

La Ramée exprime, sur cet exemple numérique, la « genèse » du côté du grand carré, au moyen d'une multiplication présentée sous une forme inhabituelle. Procédant ainsi, son ambition est sans doute non seulement de

29. « Quadrati autem numero propositi latus saepe quaeritur. Itaque per proximum elementum, & ejus consectaria analysis quadrati lateris instructa est. Quaeratur igitur latus jam propositi quadrati, & genesis ante spectetur, qualem hic é numerorum multiplicatione in numeris ipsis vides. [...] Haec ratio est quadrati cum rectangulo & quadrato, unde habetur analysis quadrati lateris explicabilis numero. Eadem siquidem via est Thebis Athenas, qua Athenis Thebas : Et hic geometrica analyseos usus superest, ut postea in cubo, cum alius in totis elementis nullus sit. »

calculer la valeur du « grand carré » (144), mais aussi d'exhiber les relations entre ce grand carré et ses composants (les carrés de valeur 100 et 4, construits sur les côtés donnés 10 et 2, et les rectangles de valeur 20 produits par la multiplication desdits côtés). Le schéma d'opération qu'il propose n'est pas exempt de défauts, car s'il fait bien apparaître les deux carrés 4 et 100, les valeurs numériques des deux rectangles ne sont pas nettement distinguées (alors qu'un simple aménagement consistant à ajouter une ligne aurait pu faire apparaître les deux valeurs 20).

Ayant ainsi exposé la « genèse », La Ramée entreprend l'analyse sur le même exemple numérique. Celle-ci consiste en une simple opération arithmétique, l'extraction de la racine de 144, dont il détaille l'algorithme (classique au demeurant[30]). Comment interpréter ce passage à la lumière de ce qui précède ? Le contenu lexical du terme *analysis* ici mobilisé est le même que dans les *Scholae* : il désigne l'opération consistant à extraire la racine carrée d'un nombre. C'est ici un entier, dans les exemples examinés plus haut, il s'agissait d'entités algébriques (binôme), mais l'opération est la même et tout porte à croire qu'elle renvoie au même champ sémantique que celui porté par le verbe *retexere* : il s'agit de détisser le carré pour en faire apparaître les composants.

Au-delà de ces points communs, ce passage comporte des singularités remarquables. D'abord, par un curieux renversement, La Ramée propose la genèse avant l'analyse, au rebours de ce qu'exigerait l'antériorité de cette dernière, constamment affirmée par La Ramée dans ses autres écrits. Bien plus, la multiplication posée par La Ramée au titre de la genèse semble accomplir aussi les fonctions d'une analyse, puisqu'elle inventorie les « arguments » qui entrent en jeu dans le « jugement » que constitue le calcul lui-même. Ainsi, c'est à la fois l'ordre de priorité entre analyse et genèse et le sens portés par l'analyse qui paraissent pervertis ici. Au regard de ces remarques, la formule « Eadem siquidem via est Thebis Athenas, quae Athenis Thebas » prend une signification forte : elle ne sert pas seulement à indiquer la symétrie entre genèse et analyse, ni même à introduire la remarque sur l'intérêt de la seconde, mais sonne plutôt comme un aveu : La Ramée semble concéder qu'il a renversé l'ordre de priorité entre analyse et genèse et mélangé leurs fonctions[31]. Dans

30. Cet algorithme est exposé, dans la forme même que reprend La Ramée, dans tous les traités d'arithmétique de l'époque. Voir par exemple [Peletier 1549, livre III, chap. 1, 47v–51r].

31. Il revient à Olivier Dubouclez [Dubouclez 2013, 176–185] d'avoir saisi, après Michael Mahoney [Mahoney 1994, 32, n. 17] la portée de ce passage. Dans le commentaire qu'il lui consacre, il affirme que l'équivalence entre les deux mouvements analyse/synthèse est rendue possible par la conversion de la figure en « chose nombrée » renvoyant à une identité algébrique : la multiplication posée par La Ramée serait l'expression (masquée) d'une identité remarquable, une formule « proto-algébrique » [Dubouclez 2013, 180], exprimée dans un « langage dépourvu de toute obscurité » [Dubouclez 2013, 180]. Je suis réservé sur cette affirmation, que Dubouclez emprunte à Mahoney sans la mettre en question : peut-on vraiment dire qu'on retrouve dans la multiplication de La Ramée le développement de l'identité remarquable $(a+b)^2$ sur l'exemple numérique $(10+2)^2$?

la *Geometria*, La Ramée précise donc le sens qu'il faut donner à l'expression *vera analysis*[32]. Ce faisant, il offre une vision de l'analyse qui semble allégée des critiques qu'il lui avait constamment adressées dans ses autres traités. Et surtout, il semble, plus encore que dans ses autres écrits, admettre une forme de complémentarité de l'analyse et de la genèse, au point que la première peut apparaître comme une « voie » à part entière, un mode de démonstration au même titre que la seconde.

4 Conclusion

Dans le vaste panorama qu'il dresse de l'histoire des mathématiques, La Ramée ne laisse de côté aucune question. Celle de l'analyse géométrique, qu'il trouve posée dans le *Commentaire* de Proclus et les *Éléments* d'Euclide et qu'il sait avoir été évoquée par Pappus, ne lui est pas indifférente. Les auteurs auxquels il se réfère [La Ramée 1567, livre I, 12, 15, 17][33] lui ont appris que Platon a « inventé » l'analyse, qu'il en a transmis la connaissance à Léodamas, qu'Eudoxe l'a utilisée ainsi qu'Archimède dans *La Sphère et le Cylindre*. Un examen sommaire des définitions qu'en donnent Proclus et Pappus lui apprend par ailleurs qu'analyse et synthèse sont deux voies « inverses » et que la première procède à rebours. C'est sur la base de ces données qu'il livre son appréciation sur l'analyse géométrique : ce n'est pas une méthode de démonstration ; quant à la « véritable analyse », c'est une simple opération consistant à extraire une racine (carré ou cubique).

Cette appréciation est conditionnée par son parti pris en faveur d'une « méthode unique », qui lui interdit d'accepter aucune voie alternative. Toute démonstration procédant par voie de déduction, du plus connu au moins connu, du général au particulier, l'analyse qui procède « à rebours » ne peut être une voie d'accès à la connaissance. Pourtant, il attribue une valeur à la « véritable analyse » ; bien plus, à travers les maigres éléments qu'il livre à ce sujet, il suggère à son lecteur que celle-ci n'a pas pour seule fonction de permettre l'inventaire des « arguments » entrant en jeu dans la démonstration, mais qu'elle pourrait valoir comme « voie » démonstrative, complémentaire de la genèse.

L'ambiguïté de ce jugement peut faire comprendre l'appréciation, elle-même contrastée, des historiens, quant à la contribution de La Ramée à la transition vers l'« algèbre des Modernes ». La plupart d'entre eux la jugent sévèrement, sur la base d'un jugement rétrospectif porté sur les mathématiques de la fin du XVIe siècle. Deux décennies après La Ramée, Viète, s'appuyant

32. Je ne m'arrête pas sur un autre passage de la *Geometria* où il est question de l'analyse [La Ramée 1569a, 156–157] : dans son Élément XXIII, 5 (où il reprend la proposition VII, 19 des *Éléments*, sur VII, 19), La Ramée traite de l'analyse du cube et présente l'algorithme permettant l'extraction des racines cubiques.

33. La Ramée tire ces informations de Proclus, mais aussi de Diogène Laërce.

à son tour sur le livre XIII des *Éléments* et le livre VII de la *Collection mathématique*, et saisissant la parenté entre l'analyse des Anciens et l'algèbre des Modernes, rebaptisée par lui *Art analytique*, donnera sa pleine valeur à la démarche analytique [Viète 1591], [Viète 2004, chap. I, « De la définition et division de l'analyse et des auxiliaires de la Zététiques »]. Sur la base de ce constat, on peut imputer à La Ramée une forme de cécité : aveuglé par une obsession de logicien, il n'aurait pas su voir ce qu'il y avait de fécond dans l'analyse géométrique. À l'opposé, quelques historiens ont été tentés de faire valoir que La Ramée avait pu, en donnant à l'analyse la valeur d'une voie démonstrative, voire en l'assimilant à l'algèbre, inspirer Viète ou Descartes[34]. Entre ces points de vue opposés, quel parti prendre ?

Peut-être faut-il pour commencer poser la question des influences de façon plus fine. Pour un lecteur d'aujourd'hui, la « restauration » entreprise par La Ramée apparaît comme un bouleversement de la forme euclidienne, et pour les contemporains de La Ramée, elle devait sans doute apparaître comme plus radicale encore, puisqu'elle aboutissait à mettre en question, en le confrontant au modèle de la « méthode unique », tout l'héritage des Anciens. Cela pouvait discréditer La Ramée auprès de bien des mathématiciens, mais on peut supposer que le caractère très corrosif de sa critique a pu stimuler la curiosité de quelques-uns et les inciter à dégager le sens spécifique de l'analyse géométrique, à en examiner les démonstrations et les comparer avec celles que permettait l'algèbre symbolique. Ils pouvaient ainsi s'affranchir des limites que La Ramée s'était lui-même imposées et affirmer la puissance de l'algèbre des Modernes tout en revendiquant leur dette à l'égard de l'« analyse des Anciens ».

Il ne s'agit donc pas ici de rouvrir le débat, d'importance minime à mes yeux, concernant l'influence qu'a pu avoir La Ramée sur Viète ou Descartes. Il me suffit de noter que ces derniers ne pouvaient pas ignorer les positions de La Ramée, compte tenu de l'audience qu'il avait eue de son vivant, de la large diffusion de ses traités et du rayonnement après sa mort de sa pensée, véhiculée par ses nombreux épigones. C'est ce qui me permet d'hasarder une hypothèse : au XVIIe siècle, des mathématiciens, même hostiles à La Ramée, même ne l'ayant lu que superficiellement, ont pu être influencés par la pensée ramiste et incités à réagir à son entreprise corrosive. Par définition,

34. Avant Olivier Dubouclez, Michael Mahoney [Mahoney 1994, 32] a supposé que Viète avait pu emprunter à La Ramée l'idée d'identifier algèbre et analyse. À sa suite, Olivier Dubouclez affirme que La Ramée « a contribué à nourrir le mouvement par lequel l'analyse s'est ouverte à un nouveau champ d'objets » [Dubouclez 2013, 186]. Mahoney affirme même, de façon abusive, que La Ramée a fait lui-même cette identification dans l'*Algebra* [La Ramée 1560] en citant une phrase tirée du commentaire qu'en a donné son disciple Lazare Schöner [Schöner 1586]. Que ce soit un ramiste, sinon Ramus lui-même, qui fasse (pour la première fois ?) cette identification est une donnée qui autorise un questionnement : la contribution de La Ramée de la question de l'analyse, si rudimentaire soit-elle, a-t-elle permis à ses contemporains – et à ses partisans en premier lieu – de pousser plus loin la réflexion, pour permettre à l'analyse de muter vers la forme qu'elle a prise dans les mathématiques du XVIIe siècle ?

une telle hypothèse ne peut pas être confirmée : ce type d'influence est généralement invisible[35].

Pour aller plus loin encore, on peut adopter un point de vue surplombant et considérer la question, non pas simplement en termes d'influences, mais en termes de changement culturel. Dans son histoire des mathématiques, La Ramée développe une thèse : tout le savoir mathématique était connu des Anciens, mais ce savoir a été mal exposé par les savants de l'Antiquité, mal compris par les commentateurs, et encore dégradé à mesure qu'il a été transmis à travers les siècles pour parvenir dans le monde latin. Cette thèse justifie son projet d'une « restauration » du savoir mathématique des Anciens, à commencer par la pièce centrale de ce savoir, les *Éléments*. L'idée qu'il serait possible d'aller au-delà du savoir hérité des Anciens lui est étrangère, et tout comme sa méthode suppose la réutilisation d'arguments empruntés aux discours constitués, sa réécriture des *Éléments* n'a pas d'autre ambition que de réagencer le matériau euclidien pour l'exposer dans l'ordre conforme à la bonne méthode. C'est évidemment une tout autre ambition qui anime ceux qui, comme Viète et Descartes, ont promu après lui l'analyse mathématique. Assimilée par Descartes à la méthode, elle devient un art que chacun peut s'approprier (en ce sens, elle est générale ou universelle) et par lequel chacun peut s'instruire et instruire autrui. Changeant de visée, la méthode s'inscrit aussi dans un espace culturel profondément transformé, dans lequel le projet de restaurer les savoirs anciens a laissé place à l'ambition de produire des savoirs nouveaux, dans la dynamique qui est en train de naître autour de l'imaginaire du « progrès scientifique[36] ». À ce niveau, il ne s'agit plus de parler du rôle de La Ramée dans la transition de l'analyse des Anciens à l'algèbre des modernes, ni de ses éventuelles influences sur ses lecteurs et successeurs, mais de reconnaître qu'entre la génération de La Ramée et celle de Descartes s'est accompli un changement radical, une mutation culturelle

35. Je n'en n'ai trouvé aucune trace, si ce n'est quelques lignes du père Tacquet. Dans l'*Historica Narratio* qu'il place au début de son édition des *Éléments*, cet auteur reconnaît s'être appuyé sur le Proème, mais affirme immédiatement ensuite que La Ramée a été si excessif dans ses attaques contre Euclide qu'il ne pourra pas être écouté (« hic audiendus non erit ») [Tacquet 1654, 6v–7r].

36. Philippe Hamou met en évidence de façon lumineuse la différence entre méthodes raméenne et cartésienne, mais aussi le changement culturel en question : « La préoccupation essentielle n'est plus pour un Descartes ou un Bacon comment préserver le savoir face aux atteintes du temps et de la barbarie. Il ne s'agit plus essentiellement de se demander comment instruire autrui, lui communiquer un savoir déjà conquis par les anciens, mais dont la préservation serait précaire. Il s'agit d'abord et avant tout de se demander comment s'instruire soi, dans l'univers de la modernité, en un temps où tout concourt à montrer que l'édifice du savoir est loin d'avoir été achevé par les anciens, où la science se présente de nouveau comme un édifice à construire, une tâche ouverte pour les générations futures. Pour cette tâche, il semble qu'on ne puisse plus s'appuyer sur la tradition et l'autorité. Par la méthode bien entendue, il s'agit donc de se faire autodidacte, de s'instituer en maître de soi-même – c'est seulement à cette condition qu'on peut se rendre capable d'instruire autrui. » [Hamou 2014, 9–10]

que la simple recherche, si minutieuse soit-elle, des contributions individuelles ne peut permettre de comprendre pleinement – les acteurs de cette mutation n'étant eux-mêmes pas conscients qu'ils étaient en train de la rendre possible[37].

Bibliographie

AXWORTHY, Angela [2016], *Le Mathématicien renaissant et son savoir. Le statut des mathématiques selon Oronce Fine*, Paris : Garnier.

BLANK, Andreas [2008], Ramus and Leibniz on Analysis, dans *Leibniz : What Kind of Rationalist ?*, édité par M. Dascal, Dordrecht : Springer, 155–166, doi : 10.1007/978-1-4020-8668-7_10.

BRUYÈRE, Nelly [1984], *Méthode et dialectique dans l'œuvre de Pierre de La Ramée*, Paris : Vrin.

DE BUZON, Frédéric [2005], Mathématique et dialectique : Descartes ramiste ?, *Les Études philosophiques*, 75(4), 455–467, doi : 10.3917/leph.054.0455.

CHARPENTIER, Jacques [1554], *Animadversiones in libros tres dialecticarum institutionum Petri Rami*, Paris : T. Richard.

CIFOLETTI, Giovanna [1992], *Mathematics and Rhetoric : Jacques Peletier, Guillaume Gosselin and the French Algebraic Tradition*, Thèse de doctorat, Princeton University.

DUBOUCLEZ, Olivier [2013], *Descartes et la voie de l'analyse*, Paris : PUF.

GALIEN [1821-1833], *Galeni Opera omnia*, Leipzig : Knobloch, éd. par C. G. Kühn.

—— [2000], Art médical, dans *Œuvres*, édité par V. Boudon-Millot, Paris : Les Belles Lettres, t. II.

GARDIES, Jean-Louis [2001], *Qu'est-ce que et pourquoi l'analyse ? Essai de définition*, Paris : Vrin.

GOULDING, Robert [2012], *Defending Hypatia : Ramus, Savile and the Renaissance Rediscovery of Mathematical History*, Dordrecht ; Heidelberg ; London ; New-York : Springer.

37. Le moindre mérite de l'étude de Marco Panza n'est pas d'avoir justement mis en évidence la différence radicale entre l'analyse des Anciens et l'algèbre des Modernes et de montrer que pour la comprendre, il fallait situer l'analyse à un niveau théorique auquel les acteurs qu'il étudie ne pouvaient pas avoir accès [Panza 2007].

Hamou, Philippe [2014], Sur les origines du concept de méthode à l'âge classique : La Ramée, Bacon et Descartes, *Revue LISA/LISA e-journal*, XII(5), 1–15, doi : 10.4000/lisa.6249.

Heeffer, Albrecht & Esteve, Maria Rosa (éds.) [2012], *The Epistemic Functions of Algebraic Symbolism : Historical Case Studies*, *Philosophica*, t. 87, Gand : Ghent university.

Heeffer, Albrecht & Van Dyck, Maarten (éds.) [2010], *Philosophical Aspects of Symbolical Reasoning in Early Modern Mathematics*, Londres : College Publications.

Kouteynikoff, Odile [2016], *Guillaume Gosselin. De Arte Magna Libri Quatuor/ Traité d'algèbre suivi de Prælectio/ Leçon sur la mathématique. Étude introductive, traduction française, annotations*, Paris : Les Belles Lettres.

La Ramée, Pierre de [1543a], *Dialecticæ partitiones ad Franciscum Valesium Christianissimum Gallorum regem*, [Manuscrit], s. l.

—— [1543b], *Aristotelicæ animadversiones*, Paris : J. Bogard.

—— [1543c], *Dialecticæ institutiones, ad celeberrimam et illustrissimam Lutetiæ Parisiorum Academiam*, Paris : J. Bogard.

—— [1543d], *Dialecticæ partitiones, ad celeberrimam et illustrissimam Lutetiæ Parisiorum Academiam*, Paris : J. Bogard.

—— [1548], *P. Rami Aristotelicæ Animadversiones*, Paris : J. Bogard.

—— [1557], *Quod sit unica doctrinae instituendae methodus, Locus e IX animadversionum P. Rami*, Paris : A. Wechel.

—— [1560], *Algebra*, Paris : Wéchel.

—— [1567], *Prooemium mathematicum ad Catherinam Mediceam, reginam, matrem regis*, Paris : A. Wechel.

—— [1569a], *Arithmeticæ libri duo, geometriæ septem et viginti*, Bâle : Episcopius.

—— [1569b], *Praelectiones.*

—— [1569c], *Scholæ in liberales artes [...]*, Bâle : Episcopius.

—— [1569d], *Scholarum mathematicarum libri unus et triginta*, Bâle : Episcopius.

Loget, François [2004], La Ramée critique d'Euclide. Sur le *Prooemium mathematicum* (1567), *Archives Internationales d'Histoire des Sciences*, 54(153), 3–28, doi : 10.1484/J.ARIHS.5.101839.

MAHONEY, Michael S. [1994], *The Mathematical Career of Pierre de Fermat, 1601-1665*, Princeton : Princeton University Press, 2e éd.

MONTUCLA, Jean-Étienne [1758], *Histoire des mathématiques, dans laquelle on rend compte de leurs progrès depuis leur origine jusqu'à nos jours [...]*, Paris : Jombert, 4 vol., rééd. citée de la seconde édition (Paris, H. Agasse, 1799) : Paris, A. Blanchard, 1968.

NANCEL, Nicolas de [1599], *Petri Rami vita, edited with an English translation*, La Hague : Martinus Nijhoff ; Leuven University Press, edité par P. Sharratt, *Humanistica Lovaniensia – Journal of neo-latin studies*, 24, 1976.

PANZA, Marco [2007], Qu'est-ce qui est neuf et qu'est-ce qui est ancien dans l'*analysis restituta* et l'*algebra nova* de Viète et quelle en est leur provenance ? Quelques réflexions sur les relations entre l'algèbre et l'analyse avant Viète, *Revue d'histoire des mathématiques*, 13(1), 85–113, doi : 10.24033/rhm.48.

PELETIER, Jacques [1549], *L'Aritmetique de Jacques Peletier du Mans, departie en quatre Livres*, Poitiers : J. H. de Marnef.

PÉRION, Joachin [1554], *De Dialectica libri tres. Ejusdem Orationibus duae pro Aristotele, dialecticarum rerum cum primis refertae, in Petrum Ramum [...]*, Bâle : J. Oporinus.

ROBINET, André [1996], *Aux sources de l'esprit cartésien. L'axe La Ramée-Descartes, de la Dialectique de 1555 aux Regulæ*, Paris : Vrin.

ROMMEVAUX, Sabine, SPIESSER, Maryvonne *et al.* (éds.) [2012], *Pluralité de l'algèbre à la Renaissance*, Paris : Champion.

SCHÖNER, Lazare [1586], *Petri Rami Aritmetices libri duo, et Algebrae totidem : a Lazaro Schonero emendati & explicati Ejusdem Schoneri Libri duo : alter De Numeri figuratis ; alter De Logistica sexageneria*, Francfort : Wechel.

SERFATI, Michel [2005], *La Révolution symbolique : la constitution de l'écriture symbolique mathématique*, Paris : Pétra.

TACQUET, André [1654], *Elementa geometriæ planæ ac solidæ : Quibus accedunt selecta ex Archimedæ theoremata*, Anvers : J. Meursium.

VAN EGMOND, Warren [1988], How algebra came to France?, dans *Mathematics from Manuscript to Print (1300-1600)*, édité par C. Hay, Oxford : Clarendon Press, 127–144.

VIÈTE, François [1591], *In Artem analyticem Isagoge. Seorsim excussa ab Opere restitutae Mathematicae Analyseos, seu Algebra nova*, Mettayer.

—— [2004], Introduction à l'art analytique, *Cahiers François-Viète*, 7, en ligne.

Varia

Popper, Bohr et la contextualité de la mécanique quantique

Sébastien Poinat
Université Côte d'Azur, Centre de Recherches en Histoire des Idées (CRHI), Nice (France)

Résumé : Durant toute sa vie intellectuelle, Karl Popper a accusé Niels Bohr d'avoir défendu des thèses subjectivistes à propos de la mécanique quantique et d'avoir introduit le concept de sujet au sein de la physique. Or, cette accusation va à l'encontre des textes de Bohr. L'objectif de cet article est de montrer que, dans sa restitution même des positions de Bohr, Popper n'a pas pris au sérieux une thèse centrale défendue par Bohr, qu'on appelle « la contextualité des phénomènes quantiques », et qui a pour conséquence de modifier en profondeur l'acte de mesure et la constitution de l'objet en mécanique quantique. Nous essayons de montrer que c'est cette difficulté dans la restitution des positions de Bohr qui l'a amené à porter son accusation de subjectivisme à l'encontre de Bohr.

Abstract: During his intellectual life, Karl Popper blamed Niels Bohr for defending subjectivist theses about Quantum Mechanics and for introducing the concept of subject in physics. But Popper's accusation contradicts Bohr's texts. The goal of this article is to show that Popper did not take seriously a central point of Bohr's position: the contextuality of quantum phenomena. Quantum contextuality has strong consequences on the nature of measurement and on the constitution of the object in Quantum Mechanics. I try to show that this misunderstanding is the reason why Popper accused Bohr for being a subjectivist.

1 Introduction

Durant toute sa vie intellectuelle, Karl Popper a parlé de mécanique quantique, depuis [Popper 1934] jusqu'à [Popper 1990]. Il l'a toujours fait en s'opposant au

Philosophia Scientiæ, 25(3), 2021, 157–175.

point de vue de Niels Bohr, qu'il appelle « l'interprétation de Copenhague » et qu'il accuse, invariablement, de conduire à des positions subjectivistes dans un domaine, la physique, où elles n'ont pas leur place. Or, Bohr s'est explicitement défendu d'avoir adopté de telles positions subjectivistes et s'est toujours présenté, au contraire, comme animé par le souci de maintenir l'objectivité en physique, même si cette exigence rencontrait des difficultés nouvelles en mécanique quantique.

Plusieurs commentateurs, en particulier [Feyerabend 1969] et [Howard 2012], ont cherché à montrer que l'interprétation de Bohr ne conduit pas à de telles conséquences subjectivistes. Nous souscrivons à leurs conclusions mais nous pensons que le problème n'a pas été pris suffisamment à la racine : non seulement les arguments de Popper peinent à montrer que la position de Bohr conduit finalement à une position subjectiviste, mais l'établissement même des thèses de Bohr par Popper est, de notre point de vue, problématique.

Dans l'interprétation de Bohr, en effet, les phénomènes quantiques ne peuvent pas être définis sans faire mention de tout l'appareillage physique et la mesure ne peut plus être pensée comme un acte de pure observation d'une réalité physique déjà constituée. Cette contextualité des phénomènes quantiques a conduit Bohr à repenser les conditions de constitution de l'objet et l'exigence d'objectivité qui est inhérente à la physique. Or, comme nous tâcherons de le montrer dans notre article, Popper ne restitue pas la thèse de la contextualité défendue par Bohr et voit dans la position de Bohr l'intrusion du sujet et de la conscience humaine. De ce fait, il considère que Bohr a renoncé à l'exigence d'objectivité et a dû adopter une interprétation subjectiviste de la mécanique quantique. L'objectif de notre article est ainsi de montrer que la restitution par Popper des positions de Bohr manque systématiquement la thèse de la contextualité, et que cette omission le conduit à porter son accusation de subjectivisme à l'encontre de Bohr.

Une telle difficulté à restituer la position de Bohr a déjà été soulignée par [Peres 2002] sur un cas particulier. L'article porte sur une expérience de pensée proposée dans [Popper 1982] : il s'agit d'une variante de l'expérience EPR (voir section 4) fondée sur la production de faisceaux de particules intriquées qui s'éloignent dans des directions opposées (A et B). Chaque faisceau passe par une fente, puis vient déclencher des détecteurs. La question est de savoir si, en diminuant la largeur de la fente du côté A, on augmente la dispersion du faisceau du côté B. D'après Popper, alors même que prédire cette augmentation est absurde, c'est à une telle absurdité que conduirait l'interprétation de Copenhague. Au contraire, l'article de Peres vise à montrer que cette prédiction n'est pas conforme à l'interprétation de Copenhague, notamment parce qu'elle ne respecte pas le principe de complémentarité défendu par Bohr. Selon Peres, Popper commet donc une erreur dans la reconstruction du raisonnement de l'École de Copenhague. Nous proposons ici de faire le même type de travail que celui de Peres, mais appliqué à l'ensemble de la restitution par Popper des thèses de Bohr (et non pas seulement sur une expérience particulière).

Enfin, nous voudrions faire deux remarques destinées à prévenir de possibles malentendus. D'une part, seule la manière dont Popper restitue la pensée de Bohr nous intéresse ici. Ainsi, sauf exception, nous n'aborderons pas l'interprétation cohérente et originale de la mécanique quantique défendue par Popper[1], ni les critiques émises par d'autres auteurs que Popper à l'encontre de l'interprétation proposée par Bohr. Nos analyses ne visent pas à prendre parti pour une interprétation au détriment d'une autre. D'autre part, nous voudrions souligner que Popper a eu le mérite de proposer des objections aux thèses de Bohr, à une époque où il était souvent mal vu de s'opposer à l'interprétation dominante. En outre, les textes de Bohr sont souvent difficiles à comprendre. Aujourd'hui, la situation est différente : la discussion est plus ouverte et, surtout, de nombreux travaux ont été consacrés aux textes de Bohr, qui permettent de mieux comprendre sa pensée (voir ci-dessous, note 11). C'est cette situation nouvelle qui nous permet, aujourd'hui, de relire de manière critique les textes de Popper consacrés à Bohr.

2 L'interprétation de Copenhague selon Popper

Pour Popper, l'interprétation de Copenhague[2] peut être résumée par son adoption d'une forme de subjectivisme :

> En bref, [l'interprétation de Copenhague] dit que « la réalité objective s'est évaporée » et que la mécanique quantique ne décrit pas les particules, mais plutôt notre connaissance, nos observations, ou notre conscience, de celles-ci. [Popper 1982, 37]

Cette interprétation se serait fourvoyée en introduisant le sujet conscient et le « mysticisme » dans la physique[3].

D'après Popper, la première source du subjectivisme de Copenhague réside dans son interprétation des probabilités quantiques. De manière générale, les prédictions quantiques sont de nature probabiliste et la question est de savoir quel sens donner à ces probabilités. Popper distingue les interprétations objectivistes et subjectivistes : les premières considèrent les probabilités comme des propriétés des systèmes physiques, alors que les secondes en font des caractéristiques de notre connaissance (ou de notre manque de connaissance).

1. Sur l'intérêt suscité par les analyses de Popper chez plusieurs physiciens de premier plan, on pourra consulter [Shields 2012].

2. Parler d'« interprétation de Copenhague » est problématique car cela passe sous silence les importantes divergences entre Bohr et ses collaborateurs [voir Howard 2004]. Toutefois, c'est ainsi que Popper désigne et pense son adversaire, nous garderons donc cette expression dans cette section.

3. Sur les références au sujet et à la conscience, voir [Popper 1982, 37, 119, 123, 124, 176].

L'interprétation la plus courante en physique est objectiviste[4] : elle consiste à considérer que pour une expérience aléatoire ayant plusieurs résultats possibles, la probabilité d'un résultat particulier est le poids relatif de ce résultat par rapport à l'ensemble des résultats obtenus dans une série infinie de réalisation de cette même expérience. Cette interprétation est appelée l'interprétation fréquentiste.

Or, d'après Popper, ce n'est pas une telle interprétation que l'École de Copenhague a adoptée, mais plutôt une interprétation subjectiviste. Selon l'interprétation subjectiviste, la probabilité d'un résultat mesure le degré de croyance que nous avons dans sa réalisation. Dans cette interprétation, les probabilités renvoient donc à notre connaissance des événements possibles. D'après Popper, c'est une telle interprétation que l'École de Copenhague a principalement adoptée[5]. À l'appui de son allégation, [Popper 1982, 109–116] donne quelques citations extraites de [Born 1949], [von Neuman 1955] et [Pauli 1954]. Quoiqu'il ne s'appuie sur aucun texte de Bohr, Popper attribue aussi cette interprétation à ce dernier [Popper 1982, 117].

Par ailleurs, Popper considère que cette erreur trouve sa source dans un « préjugé déterministe inconscient » [Popper 1982, 99], que les partisans de l'interprétation de Copenhague auraient entretenu à propos de la physique classique : croyant que celle-ci est forcément déterministe, ils auraient adopté une lecture subjectiviste des probabilités de la thermodynamique et de la physique statistique. Quand il s'est agi d'interpréter les probabilités quantiques, ils leur auraient appliqué la même interprétation subjectiviste, alors même qu'ils ne croyaient plus au déterminisme pour ce qui concerne la mécanique quantique.

L'autre source majeure du subjectivisme de Copenhague selon Popper réside dans les relations de Heisenberg. Celles-ci portent sur des couples de grandeurs physiques qu'on avait coutume d'appeler, au début de la mécanique quantique, des « observables conjuguées » (par exemple la position et l'impulsion, ou le temps et l'énergie). Les relations de Heisenberg s'écrivent ainsi : $\Delta A \cdot \Delta B \geq \hbar$, où A et B sont deux variables conjuguées et où le symbole Δ représente l'écart quadratique moyen.

Dans [Heisenberg 1927], Heisenberg présente les relations qui portent son nom à partir d'une expérience utilisant un microscope. En observant un électron à l'aide d'un microscope, on peut établir sa position. Le résultat de l'expérience comporte une forme d'« imprécision » que l'on peut faire diminuer en réduisant la longueur d'onde du rayonnement interne au microscope. Or, le fait d'éclairer l'électron en l'observant à l'aide du microscope provoque une perturbation, incontrôlable, qui affecte l'impulsion de l'électron. En conséquence, si l'on cherche à établir la valeur finale de l'impulsion de l'électron, il

4. Dans le cadre de notre étude, nous n'exposons pas l'interprétation propensionniste défendue par Popper.

5. Plus précisément, selon Popper, les partisans de Copenhague alterneraient entre une position subjectiviste (principalement) et une position objectiviste (parfois).

faudra tenir compte d'une nouvelle « imprécision » qui affectera le résultat, imprécision qui, cette fois, est d'autant plus importante que la longueur d'onde du rayonnement est grande. Ainsi, selon la longueur d'onde utilisée, on peut diminuer l'imprécision concernant la position ou celle concernant l'impulsion, mais le produit des deux demeure constant et de l'ordre de h (la constante de Planck[6]).

Cet article ouvre la voie à deux manières différentes de comprendre ce qu'est cette « imprécision ». D'un côté, Heisenberg précise au début de l'article que des mots tels que « position d'un objet » ou « impulsion » ne peuvent trouver leur sens et leur définition que dans certaines expériences. Or, si les mots sont définis par les expériences, les grandeurs qu'ils désignent ne sont pas déterminées indépendamment de ces expériences et la latitude exprimée par les relations de Heisenberg est une forme d'indétermination des grandeurs physiques, et non pas seulement l'expression d'une imprécision irréductible de nos mesures.

Mais d'un autre côté, Heisenberg fait référence à plusieurs reprises à « la marge d'erreur » ou à « l'imprécision » liée au dispositif expérimental. Or, parler d'erreur ou d'imprécision suggère qu'il y a un écart entre la valeur obtenue et la valeur correcte. Dans cette perspective, la latitude exprimée par les relations de Heisenberg n'est pas une caractéristique des grandeurs physiques elles-mêmes, mais plutôt de notre connaissance de ces dernières. De même, les passages où il est question de la trajectoire des électrons (voir [Heisenberg 1927, 176]) suggèrent que les électrons ont bien à la fois une position et une impulsion, et que les relations de Heisenberg portent sur notre difficulté à les connaître[7].

Cette dualité des lectures possibles est soulignée par Popper, qui considère que, dans leur ensemble, les partisans de l'École de Copenhague ont hésité entre deux lectures, que Popper appelle « l'interprétation objective » et « l'interprétation subjective » des relations de Heisenberg [Popper 1934, 223–224]. Selon la première, « il est inadmissible, incorrect, ou métaphysique, d'attribuer à la particule quelque chose comme "une position-avec-un-moment", ou un "parcours", déterminé avec précision ». Selon la deuxième, au contraire, l'électron possède bien à la fois une position et une impulsion, mais en réalisant une mesure, le sujet introduit une perturbation qui affecte ces deux grandeurs. Ainsi, la connaissance des grandeurs conjuguées est irrémédiablement affectée d'une imprécision minimale et la mécanique quantique exprime une limite de notre connaissance de la matière.

Popper est surtout préoccupé par l'interprétation subjective [Popper 1982, 54] parce que, combinée à l'interprétation subjective des probabilités, elle rend

6. Heisenberg analyse d'autres expériences qui le conduisent à chaque fois aux mêmes relations.

7. Sur le vocabulaire utilisé par Heisenberg et par ses traducteurs pour caractériser ses relations (« indétermination », « imprécision », « incertitude »), voir [Lévy-Leblond & Balibar 1998].

possible plusieurs affirmations subjectivistes que l'École de Copenhague aurait défendues. D'une part, selon Popper, ses partisans ont accepté de parler d'une dualité de nature pour la lumière et les objets quantiques, qui seraient à la fois des ondes et des corpuscules. Bien sûr, aucune entité ne peut être réellement à la fois une onde et une particule, et prise en un sens objectiviste, la dualité de nature serait une contradiction dans les termes. Mais en adoptant une lecture subjectiviste des formules de la mécanique quantique, la dualité ne porte plus sur la matière mais sur notre connaissance et finit par exprimer les imperfections ou les limites de cette dernière.

D'autre part, les partisans de l'interprétation de Copenhague auraient également soutenu une thèse subjectiviste concernant « l'effondrement de la fonction d'onde » (ou du « paquet d'ondes ») [Popper 1982, section 8]. La « fonction d'onde » représente l'état du système. Son étalement avant la mesure correspond au fait que plusieurs résultats sont possibles. En revanche, après la mesure, l'état du système est égal à l'état propre correspondant à la valeur propre mesurée. L'étalement initial de la fonction d'onde a brutalement disparu : celle-ci s'est effondrée. Popper attribue à l'interprétation de Copenhague la thèse selon laquelle c'est l'intervention du sujet qui produit cet effondrement : en disposant un appareil de mesure, le sujet obligerait la nature à sélectionner une valeur parmi toutes celles qui sont possibles. Ce serait donc finalement l'accroissement de la connaissance du sujet qui produirait cette modification brutale de l'état du système : voilà, dit Popper, l'ultime conséquence du subjectivisme de Copenhague et des absurdités auxquelles il conduit ses partisans. À ses yeux, c'est même le statut de la physique comme science qui est menacé :

> Si l'on interprète les formules de Heisenberg dans un sens tout à fait subjectif, le statut de la physique comme science objective se trouve mis en péril. [...] Et c'est ainsi que toute la théorie subjectiviste de la probabilité envahit le royaume de la physique. [Popper 1934, 237]

3 La position de Bohr

Bohr s'est toujours défendu d'avoir adopté des thèses qui conduisent à une forme de subjectivisme, et la lecture de ses textes ne plaide pas en faveur de l'accusation portée par Popper. Pour ce qui est de l'interprétation des probabilités, Bohr exprime des positions qui relèvent de l'interprétation fréquentiste[8], que Popper lui-même considérait comme objective[9]. À plu-

8. Sur ce point, nous ne sommes pas d'accord avec [Howard 2012, 44] qui affirme que Bohr n'a jamais pris de position explicite concernant l'interprétation des probabilités.

9. Afin de demeurer dans le cadre de notre étude et parce que Popper lui-même considère que l'interprétation fréquentiste est objective, nous laissons de côté les critiques que l'on peut adresser à cette interprétation, y compris celle qui porte sur son objectivité.

sieurs reprises, Bohr fait ainsi référence au fait que la mécanique quantique résout des problèmes statistiques, ou qu'il faut comprendre les probabilités quantiques de manière statistique (voir [Bohr 1929, 26, 31, 88, 89, 100] et [Bohr 1991, 153, 163, 199, 200, 206, 234, 302]). Quand il doit donner un sens physique aux probabilités, il fait ainsi référence à des séries statistiques et à des poids relatifs. À propos de la probabilité de désintégration d'un atome de radium, il écrit :

> Si l'on considère un certain nombre d'atomes de radium, tout ce qu'on peut en dire, c'est qu'il y a une probabilité déterminée pour *qu'une certaine fraction de ce nombre se désintègre par seconde.* [Bohr 1929, 99, nous soulignons]

L'argumentation de Popper au sujet de l'interprétation des probabilités par Bohr peut surprendre. D'une part, aucune des citations données par Popper à l'appui de son affirmation n'est issue de textes de Bohr[10]. D'autre part, il choisit de fonder son analyse sur un « préjugé déterministe inconscient » au sujet de la physique classique [Popper 1982, 99], alors même que c'est contraire à ce que Bohr écrit explicitement. De ce fait, il nous semble que cet aspect de la critique de Popper est, globalement, le moins instructif.

Bohr n'a pas non plus soutenu une position subjectiviste concernant les relations de Heisenberg. Pour étayer notre affirmation, il faut repartir de ce que Bohr considère comme le point de départ de son interprétation : le postulat quantique[11]. Ce postulat, qui exprime selon Bohr « l'essence de la théorie », consiste en ceci que « tout processus atomique présente un caractère de discontinuité, ou plutôt d'individualité, complètement étranger aux théories classiques, et caractérisé par le quantum d'action de Planck » [Bohr 1929, 50].

La « discontinuité » renvoie à ce qui a été découvert grâce aux travaux de Planck sur le corps noir, puis à ceux d'Einstein sur les photons, à savoir que les échanges d'énergie sont des multiples d'une grandeur minimale, appelée le « quantum d'action » et qui est de l'ordre de la constante de Planck. Contrairement à la mécanique classique, les processus quantiques ne peuvent donc pas être décrits par des fonctions continues, dont la valeur pourrait être aussi proche de zéro que l'on veut. Par ailleurs, ces échanges sont « incontrôlables », au sens où ils comportent une part d'indétermination (par exemple le moment précis où ils ont lieu).

L'« individualité » renvoie à l'idée que les éléments qui interagissent de façon élémentaire au niveau atomique finissent par former un tout inanalysable. Lors d'un échange élémentaire d'énergie, on peut caractériser la situation initiale et la situation finale, mais pas les situations intermédiaires car celles-ci

10. De surcroît, ces citations ne portent pas sur la mécanique quantique.

11. Notre restitution de la position de Bohr se limitera aux aspects utiles pour notre étude. Pour une restitution plus complète, on pourra se référer à [Chevalley 1991], [Faye 1991], [Bitbol 1996], [Poinat 2014, Partie I]. Par ailleurs, nous laisserons de côté les premières thèses de Bohr, celles défendues avant 1925.

correspondent aux valeurs interdites du fait de la discontinuité des processus atomiques. Si les états intermédiaires ne peuvent pas être décrits, alors les composants forment un tout indivisible pendant l'interaction.

Bohr considère par ailleurs que le postulat quantique s'applique aux mesures quantiques. Par conséquent, la discontinuité et l'individualité associées au postulat quantique se manifestent aussi lors d'une mesure quantique. Le caractère d'individualité du postulat quantique appliqué à la mesure signifie que, pendant le processus de la mesure, le système mesuré et l'appareil de mesure forment un tout indivisible. Bohr écrit ainsi : « on ne peut pas [...] attribuer ni au phénomène ni à l'instrument d'observation une réalité physique autonome » [Bohr 1929, 51]. Ici, Bohr applique ce qu'il a dit de façon plus générale à propos de l'individualité associée au postulat quantique. Pendant une mesure, la seule réalité est globale, inanalysable :

> il est impossible de séparer nettement un comportement indépendant des objets, de leur interaction avec les instruments de mesure définissant le système de référence. [Bohr 1991, 225]

Les phénomènes quantiques dépendent des appareils de mesure pour leur apparition et leur définition, et on ne peut pas parler d'eux indépendamment des appareils de mesure. Le postulat quantique implique donc, selon Bohr, la thèse de la contextualité : les grandeurs physiques que l'on mesure ne peuvent pas être détachées du contexte global et attribuées à un objet supposé exister par lui-même.

D'autre part, la discontinuité associée au postulat quantique conduit à considérer que toute mesure provoque un échange d'énergie au moins égal à la constante de Planck. Or, à l'échelle atomique, un tel échange n'est pas négligeable et il faut donc renoncer à une supposition que nous pouvions faire en mécanique classique, à savoir que « l'observation d'un phénomène ne lui causait aucune perturbation essentielle » [Bohr 1929, 50]. La prise en compte de l'échange d'énergie lors de la mesure conduit Bohr à opposer deux types de description d'un système quantique : d'un côté, l'application des lois de conservation de l'énergie et de l'impulsion aux systèmes quantiques correspond à ce que Bohr appelle la « description causale » (ou « principe de causalité ») ; de l'autre, la localisation du système dans l'espace et dans le temps est la « représentation spatio-temporelle » des systèmes quantiques. Si on veut établir la description causale d'un système, il faut empêcher toute modification (d'origine extérieure) de son état d'énergie. Par conséquent, il faut idéalement renoncer à toute mesure, et donc aussi à la représentation spatio-temporelle. Réciproquement, si on veut localiser le système dans l'espace-temps, il faut l'observer par une mesure et, idéalement, il faut donc renoncer à la description causale de ce système. Ainsi, alors que les deux descriptions sont possibles conjointement en mécanique classique, il n'en va plus de même en mécanique quantique où « le postulat quantique nous oblige à renoncer à une description à la fois causale et spatio-temporelle » [Bohr 1929, 51]. Par ailleurs, on ne peut se passer d'aucune des deux descriptions, qui sont nécessaires pour épuiser l'ensemble des informations disponibles sur un système. C'est pourquoi il faut considérer qu'elles sont à la fois incompatibles et complémentaires :

> dans la théorie quantique, un élément tout à fait nouveau, incontrôlable, surgit à chaque observation par suite de l'interaction finie avec l'instrument de mesure. [...] [L]a mesure des coordonnées de position d'une particule [...] entraîne toujours une rupture complète dans la description causale de son comportement dynamique ; de même, la connaissance de son impulsion n'est obtenue qu'au prix d'une lacune dans sa description spatio-temporelle. C'est précisément cet état de choses qui traduit nettement le caractère complémentaire de la description quantique des phénomènes atomiques. [Bohr 1929, 64]

Dans la pratique, les contextes expérimentaux ne réalisent qu'imparfaitement les conditions idéales de l'une ou de l'autre des descriptions, et on peut tendre plutôt vers les unes ou plutôt vers les autres, mais pas vers les deux à la fois. C'est comme cela qu'il faut comprendre les relations de Heisenberg selon Bohr : elles donnent la mesure de l'incompatibilité irréductible des deux descriptions et des contextes expérimentaux qui leur sont associés. Les grandeurs d'énergie et d'impulsion sont associées à la description causale, celles de position et de temps à la description spatio-temporelle. Plus on s'approche des conditions qui permettent de déterminer les premières, plus on s'éloigne de celles qui permettent de déterminer les secondes, et réciproquement. Les relations de Heisenberg donnent la valeur numérique du jeu qui existe forcément entre les possibilités de détermination des grandeurs conjuguées :

> Il existe une relation réciproque générale entre les incertitudes minimales avec lesquelles les vecteurs d'énergie-impulsion et d'espace-temps associés aux « individus » [c'est-à-dire aux systèmes] peuvent être *respectivement définis*. Cette relation peut être considérée comme une expression symbolique très simple de la nature complémentaire de la description spatio-temporelle et du principe de causalité. [Bohr 1929, 57, nous soulignons]

N'est-il pas possible, toutefois, de surmonter cette incompatibilité en faisant se succéder les contextes expérimentaux ? Si les deux descriptions d'un même système quantique ne sont pas possibles au même moment, pourquoi ne pas les établir successivement, puis les considérer comme valables conjointement pour un seul et même objet ? Si on pouvait considérer les grandeurs physiques comme indépendantes des contextes expérimentaux qui leur donnent sens et les attribuer au seul système quantique considéré, on pourrait conserver ce qu'une description nous a permis d'obtenir (par exemple l'impulsion) et ajouter ce que l'autre apporte (la position). Mais c'est précisément ce que nous ne pouvons faire en raison de la contextualité des phénomènes quantiques : si on change de contexte, on ne peut plus parler des grandeurs qui lui étaient associées. Les grandeurs conjuguées sont donc irrémédiablement incompatibles en raison de la contextualité [Bohr 1991, 207–208].

Sur la base des analyses précédentes, il apparaît que la position de Bohr peut difficilement être accusée de subjectivisme. D'une part, il considère que les relations de Heisenberg portent sur la possibilité de définir les grandeurs conjuguées, et non pas seulement sur la possibilité de les mesurer. D'autre part, la notion de trajectoire disparaît dans les analyses de Bohr : les grandeurs de position et d'impulsion étant associées à des contextes expérimentaux incompatibles, il n'y a pas de contexte dans lequel cette notion trouverait un sens et pourrait être définie. À aucun moment, Bohr n'envisage de considérer que les relations de Heisenberg mesureraient l'imprécision avec laquelle on pourrait connaître la trajectoire des électrons ou des photons (voir en particulier [Bohr 1929, 51] et [Bohr 1991, 209]). Il n'est donc pas question ici des limites de la connaissance humaine et Bohr n'a pas adopté l'interprétation que Popper appelait « subjective » des relations de Heisenberg. De façon plus générale, toute l'analyse de Bohr repose sur le postulat quantique et ses conséquences sur l'acte de mesure, à savoir l'échange incontrôlable d'énergie et la contextualité. Or, tous ces processus sont supposés se dérouler au sein de la matière, entre systèmes physiques, et ils sont indépendants du sujet humain, de sa conscience, ou de sa connaissance. Ce sont des processus qui incluent tout le contexte expérimental, mais qui demeurent purement physiques.

L'accusation de subjectivisme, enfin, n'est pas non plus recevable pour ce qui concerne l'« effondrement du paquet d'ondes ». Pour Bohr, la fonction Ψ est un outil prédictif et ne reflète aucune réalité physique. Il n'y a donc pas lieu de dire que le sujet provoquerait un quelconque processus physique lors de la mesure. Bohr le dit explicitement au Ve Congrès Solvay de 1927, à propos de l'échange entre Dirac et Heisenberg sur la question de savoir si, lors de la réduction du paquet d'ondes, on a affaire à un choix opéré par la nature (Dirac) ou par l'observateur (Heisenberg). Bohr écrit :

> ces terminologies paraissent l'une et l'autre bien douteuses, car il n'est guère raisonnable d'attribuer à la nature une volonté au sens habituel et, d'autre part, *l'observateur ne peut avoir aucune influence sur les événements qui peuvent apparaître dans les conditions qu'il a préparées.* [Bohr 1949, 224–225, nous soulignons]

Le seul rôle que Bohr fait jouer au sujet concerne la question du langage. Bohr considère en effet que les concepts et le langage de la physique classique, bien qu'ils soient inadaptés pour décrire les phénomènes quantiques en raison du postulat quantique, demeurent indispensables pour décrire nos expériences :

> *D'aussi loin que les phénomènes puissent transcender le domaine des explications de la physique classique, la description de tous les résultats d'expérience doit être exprimée en termes classiques.* La raison en est simple : par le mot d'« expérience », nous nous référons à une situation où nous pouvons dire à d'autres hommes

> ce que nous avons fait et ce que nous avons appris ; il en résulte que la description du dispositif expérimental et des résultats des observations doit être exprimée en un langage dénué d'ambiguïté, se servant convenablement de la terminologie de la physique classique. [Bohr 1949, 207][12]

Pour Bohr, le langage de la physique classique est nécessaire parce qu'il permet le type d'objectivité requise par la science et la communication entre scientifiques. En raison du fait qu'on ne peut plus faire abstraction du contexte, le langage quantique n'est pas du tout adéquat pour parler des expériences physiques. En revanche, au niveau macroscopique, le quantum d'action est négligeable : les interactions entre systèmes macroscopiques ne sont pas soumises à l'indivisibilité du postulat quantique et on peut les décrire indépendamment du contexte. Pour décrire ce qu'on a fait pour préparer l'expérience et pour obtenir les résultats de mesure, on pourra donc utiliser le langage de la physique classique, dit Bohr. Comme on le voit, les analyses qu'il mène sur le langage et la communication entre sujets sont guidées par l'exigence d'objectivité[13].

Par rapport à la question de la constitution de l'objet scientifique, la nouveauté selon Bohr est que le phénomène quantique inclut l'appareillage : si l'on veut maintenir la référence à un objet, il faut le construire à partir du tout constitué du système et des appareils de mesure. Bohr déplace donc la frontière de l'objet, en y incluant l'appareillage, mais il ne la déplace pas jusqu'à inclure le sujet au sens traditionnel. En un sens, on peut dire qu'il inclut un sujet purement physique, constitué des appareils de mesure, mais pas le sujet humain[14]. C'est en ce sens qu'il faut comprendre l'utilisation que fait Bohr des termes « subjectif » et « subjectivité » : ces termes renvoient aux conditions physiques d'observation des phénomènes, et non pas à la subjectivité humaine (ses sentiments, ses passions, ou sa conscience). Ainsi, explique Bohr, la théorie de la relativité a amené à un réexamen de la question de la subjectivité à travers la question de la simultanéité : à quelles conditions pouvons-nous dire que deux événements ont lieu au même moment ? Il ne s'agit pas du tout de verser dans la psychologie, ni d'analyser les contenus de conscience d'un sujet humain [Bohr 1929, 91–92], mais seulement de réfléchir aux conditions physiques et techniques dans lesquelles nous pouvons faire des observations.

Ainsi, Bohr ne s'en tient pas à l'objet classique, conçu indépendamment de l'appareillage, mais il ne renonce pas à l'objectivité : il se contente de définir une nouvelle forme d'objectivité, en y incluant la mention du contexte expérimental, tout en s'interdisant d'y inclure aussi le sujet humain. Cette nouvelle objectivité est ainsi pleinement solidaire de la thèse de la contex-

12. Souligné par Bohr. Voir aussi [Bohr 1929, 89].

13. Voir par exemple lorsque Bohr précise qu'il développe ses analyses « sans avoir, bien entendu, l'intention d'introduire une quelconque mystique inconciliable avec l'esprit scientifique » [Bohr 1929, 109].

14. C'est un point qu'avait déjà souligné [Feyerabend 1969].

tualité. Or, Popper se trouve dans l'impossibilité de discuter la proposition de Bohr en matière d'objectivité, puisque la contextualité fait défaut dans sa restitution de la pensée de Bohr : de ce fait, Popper le présente comme s'il renonçait à toute forme d'objectivité[15], alors qu'il ne renonce qu'à une forme particulière de l'objectivité. De nouveau, c'est la difficulté à restituer la thèse de la contextualité qui conduit Popper à formuler son accusation de subjectivisme et à passer à côté d'un véritable examen critique des thèses de son adversaire.

4 L'article EPR et la contextualité

Le fait que Popper n'ait pas saisi cet aspect de la pensée de Bohr est confirmé par l'analyse de [Einstein, Podolsky *et al.* 1935][16] et de la manière dont Popper comprend le débat entre Einstein et Bohr. L'article EPR est un article particulièrement riche et la restitution que nous en faisons ici est très sélective[17]. Le raisonnement développé dans l'article est fondé sur ce que les auteurs appellent le « critère de réalité » :

> si, sans perturber le système en aucune façon, nous pouvons prédire avec certitude (c'est-à-dire avec une probabilité égale à 1) la valeur d'une grandeur physique, alors il existe un élément de la réalité physique correspondant à cette grandeur physique. [Einstein, Podolsky *et al.* 1935, 225]

Ce critère énonce ainsi deux conditions distinctes : une condition de prédiction certaine et une condition d'absence de perturbation.

Le critère de réalité est ensuite appliqué à la situation suivante : supposons que deux systèmes (notés I et II), initialement séparés et indépendants l'un de l'autre, interagissent entre les temps $t = 0$ et $t = T$, de sorte que l'état du système global soit intriqué pour ce qui concerne les grandeurs de position et de quantité de mouvement. Le caractère intriqué implique ceci : si l'on fait une mesure de la position sur le système I, alors on peut prédire avec une entière certitude le résultat d'une mesure de position sur le système II. Inversement, si l'on fait une mesure de la quantité de mouvement sur le système I, alors on peut prévoir avec une entière certitude le résultat d'une mesure de quantité de mouvement sur le système II.

---

15. Parfois, les formulations de Popper distinguent la conscience et les appareils de mesure, voir notamment [Popper 1982, 42, 124]. Mais Popper considère qu'il s'agit fondamentalement d'une seule et même doctrine [Popper 1982, 119], et cela ne change pas son accusation de subjectivisme.

16. Nous utiliserons l'appellation courante pour cet article : « l'article EPR ».

17. Une abondante littérature est consacrée à cet article. Parmi d'autres références, on pourra lire [D'Espagnat 1994, chap. 9], [Bitbol 1996, section 3.2], [Bächtold 2008, chap. 3] et [Fine 2020].

L'intérêt de l'état intriqué est qu'il semble remplir les deux conditions du critère de réalité. D'une part, la condition portant sur la prédiction certaine est remplie par simple application des propriétés de l'intrication. D'autre part, on ne fait aucune mesure sur le système II : tout est déduit de mesures qui peuvent être faites sur le système I. Par conséquent, pour que la condition sur l'absence de perturbation ne puisse pas s'appliquer, il faudrait supposer que la mesure sur le système I perturbe instantanément à distance le système II. Or, les systèmes I et II peuvent être très éloignés l'un de l'autre et, en principe, la prédiction peut suivre immédiatement la mesure. Toute action perturbatrice liée à la mesure devrait donc se propager instantanément jusqu'au système II. D'après les auteurs, il est raisonnable de supposer qu'une telle action à distance n'a pas lieu.

Finalement, écrivent-ils, on peut appliquer le critère de réalité au système II en lui attribuant une position, et on peut aussi l'appliquer au même système II en lui attribuant une quantité de mouvement. Ainsi, il faut conclure que, pour le même système, il existe deux éléments de la réalité physique correspondant l'un à la position, l'autre à la quantité de mouvement. Or, la mécanique quantique ne donne pas accès à une description conjointe de ces deux grandeurs. Par conséquent, elle est incomplète : elle ne décrit pas de manière exhaustive la réalité physique.

Pour Popper, il est difficile d'échapper à l'argumentation des auteurs et leur conclusion est parfaitement exacte :

> le soi-disant paradoxe d'Einstein, Podolsky et Rosen [...] n'est pas un paradoxe, mais un argument valide, car il établit simplement ceci que nous devons attribuer aux particules une position et une quantité de mouvement précises. [Popper 1982, 64]

Il lui semble que l'article EPR met aux prises Einstein, le réalisme, le principe de l'action locale, et la thèse de l'incomplétude de la mécanique quantique d'un côté, et Bohr, le subjectivisme, l'action à distance, et la thèse selon laquelle la mécanique quantique est la théorie ultime, de l'autre. Popper considère ainsi que le mieux que Bohr pourrait faire pour éviter la conclusion de l'article EPR, serait de renoncer à l'action à distance.

Pourtant, ce n'est pas comme cela que Bohr répond à Einstein. D'une part, il écarte explicitement toute possibilité d'une action à distance qui perturberait le système II en raison des mesures sur le système I : « il est vrai que dans les mesures considérées, toute interaction mécanique directe du système et des dispositifs de mesure est exclue » [Bohr 1935*b*, 65][18]. D'autre part, il ne conteste pas non plus le critère de réalité en tant que tel.

Ce que Bohr conteste, c'est qu'on puisse appliquer le critère de réalité *conjointement* à la position et à la quantité de mouvement. Pour pouvoir parler de la position du système II, il faut qu'il y ait un appareil qui mesure

18. Suite à l'article EPR, Bohr ne parlera plus de « perturbation » lors de la mesure. Sur ce point, voir [Bitbol 1996, 249–256].

la position du système I. Mais dans cette situation expérimentale, on ne peut pas mesurer en même temps la quantité de mouvement de I, et on ne peut donc pas non plus parler de la quantité de mouvement de II. Bien sûr, il en va de même si on mesure la quantité de mouvement de I : on ne peut plus parler de la position de II. Par conséquent, en raison de la contextualité et de ce qu'elle implique, on ne peut pas parler conjointement de prédictions certaines concernant *à la fois* la position et la quantité de mouvement :

> Évidemment, il n'est pas question dans un tel cas d'une perturbation mécanique du système étudié durant le dernier stade critique du processus de mesure. Mais, même à ce stade, la question essentielle est celle d'*une influence sur les conditions mêmes qui définissent les types possibles de prédictions relatives au comportement futur du système.* Comme ces conditions constituent un élément inhérent à la description de tout phénomène auquel le terme « réalité physique » peut être attaché à juste titre, nous voyons que l'argumentation des auteurs cités ne leur donne pas le droit de conclure que la description par la mécanique quantique est essentiellement incomplète. [Bohr 1935*a*, 702]

Comme nous l'avons dit précédemment, la restitution faite par Popper de la réponse de Bohr confirme les difficultés qu'il a à restituer la thèse de la contextualité. Dans la section 17 de [Popper 1982], Popper propose une analyse détaillée de l'article EPR et de la réponse de Bohr, dont il dit qu'elle n'est pas claire et qu'il n'est pas sûr de l'avoir comprise. Popper commence par reprendre l'affirmation de Bohr selon laquelle les conditions pour faire des prédictions sur la position et celles pour faire des prédictions sur la quantité de mouvement sont mutuellement exclusives. Il restitue aussi l'étape suivante du raisonnement de Bohr, à savoir qu'on peut donc appliquer le critère de réalité successivement, mais pas simultanément. Formellement, la restitution que donne Popper est donc exacte. Mais, curieusement, Popper ne prend pas au sérieux la conclusion de Bohr, à savoir qu'on ne peut pas parler de la vitesse et de la quantité de mouvement comme de grandeurs physiques présentes *simultanément* au sein de la réalité physique :

> la suggestion selon laquelle il est dénué de sens de parler de la position et de la quantité de mouvement à moins que nous puissions mettre la particule en rapport avec le système de coordonnées correspondant [soit à la position, soit à la quantité de mouvement] est aussi gratuite que l'assertion selon laquelle il est dépourvu de sens de dire d'un homme qu'il est riche à moins qu'il ne paye l'impôt sur le revenu. [Popper 1982, 149]

Le fait de payer l'impôt sur le revenu *révèle* qu'un homme est riche, mais *ne constitue pas* sa richesse. Il en va de même, selon Popper, de la mesure de la position : elle révèle la position de la particule, mais ne participe pas à la constitution de cette position. Or, c'est précisément ce que Bohr conteste, au travers de la contextualité : l'acte de mesure est une condition du phénomène.

Ainsi, Popper ne prend pas au sérieux l'idée que la mesure puisse être autre chose qu'une simple mise en évidence d'une grandeur physique qui lui préexiste. Toute affirmation contraire lui semble impensable :

> La discussion [entre Einstein et Bohr] portait principalement sur le simple point selon lequel si je peux librement décider – et si je peux mettre à exécution avec succès ma décision *sans interférer avec vous* – que je souhaite mesurer votre taille et votre poids, il est alors déraisonnable de dire que nous n'avez pas, dans le même temps, à la fois une taille et un poids, mais que vous adoptez l'un ou l'autre en vous adaptant au stimulus de la mesure. [Popper 1982, 149]

« Gratuite », « déraisonnable » : Popper en vient à ne voir là qu'une façon « hautement scolastique » de « défendre une position intenable » [Popper 1982, 149]. Cette thèse de la contextualité lui paraît à ce point inacceptable qu'il a du mal à l'attribuer à Bohr :

> je n'affirme pas du tout que c'est ce que [Bohr] voulait dire. Ma critique [...] n'est par conséquent pas dirigée contre Bohr, mais seulement contre ma propre version de sa réponse à Einstein, Podolsky et Rosen. [Popper 1982, 148]

Dans les comptes-rendus qu'il fera ultérieurement de la discussion entre Bohr et Einstein, Popper finira même par omettre cette thèse de Bohr qu'il juge tellement invraisemblable (par exemple dans la préface de [Popper 1982]). De même, lorsqu'il restitue les expériences de [Aspect, Grangier *et al.* 1982], et même s'il concède qu'elles ont été une déception pour lui [voir Redhead 1995], Popper reste fidèle à la lecture qu'il a toujours eue de l'article EPR. Le résultat de ces expériences est une violation des inégalités de Bell, ce qui est conforme aux prédictions quantiques et au point de vue de Bohr, mais contraire aux prédictions auxquelles conduit le point de vue d'Einstein. Pourtant, Popper multiplie les tentatives pour amoindrir leur portée et sauver le point de vue d'Einstein. Il y voit ainsi une remise en cause du principe de l'action locale et du réalisme, mais à aucun moment il n'envisage que ces résultats soient une corroboration du point de vue de Bohr.

Il apparaît finalement que l'article EPR pousse Bohr et Popper dans leurs retranchements. D'un côté, la réponse de Bohr tient tout entière dans la thèse de la contextualité, qui est le dernier rempart contre les arguments d'Einstein et qui apparaît comme étant la clé de voûte de sa pensée. De l'autre, la réponse de Bohr se limitant à réaffirmer la thèse de la contextualité, Popper se retrouve bien en peine pour la restituer, ce qu'il finit par reconnaître. L'article EPR apparaît ainsi comme une confirmation à la fois du rôle central joué par la contextualité dans la pensée de Bohr et des difficultés de Popper à restituer cette dernière[19].

5 Conclusion

L'objectif de notre article était de montrer que Popper ne restitue pas fidèlement la position de Bohr, en omettant systématiquement la thèse de la contextualité, et de mettre en évidence que cette omission a pour conséquence les accusations de subjectivisme que Popper soutient à l'encontre de Bohr. Sur cette base, d'autres interrogations peuvent être menées, concernant la question du réalisme : quelles modifications la thèse de la contextualité introduit-elle dans le réalisme en général ? Ces modifications sont-elles incompatibles avec le réalisme de Popper ? Ou bien y a-t-il une manière de les concilier, comme le suggère [Howard 2012] ? Ce sont des questions qui permettraient d'aller au-delà de la seule restitution par l'un des thèses de l'autre, et d'examiner sur le fond l'opposition entre Bohr et Popper, questions que le cadre de notre étude n'a pas permis d'aborder.

Remerciements

Pour cet article, nous avons bénéficié des remarques constructives de deux rapporteurs anonymes et nous leur adressons nos remerciements les plus chaleureux.

Bibliographie

Aspect, Alain, Grangier, Philippe, *et al.* [1982], Experimental realization of Einstein-Podolsky-Rosen-Bohm Gedankenexperiment : A new violation

19. De notre point de vue, [Howard 2012] ne tire pas bien les leçons de l'article EPR quant à la discussion par Popper des thèses de Bohr. D'une part, bien que publié en 2012, [Howard 2012] a été initialement écrit en 1981 et a été à peine modifié ensuite par l'auteur. De ce fait, il occulte [Popper 1982], alors même qu'il s'agit d'un ouvrage majeur entièrement consacré à la mécanique quantique, et il ne peut pas tirer profit des parties de cet ouvrage consacrées à l'article EPR. Il ne peut ainsi pas analyser les passages où Popper reconnaît qu'il a des difficultés à saisir la réponse de Bohr, ni sa manière (problématique) de restituer le débat et les implications de l'article EPR, comme nous avons cherché à le faire ici. D'autre part, l'article d'Howard ne prend pas au sérieux la réponse de Bohr à l'article EPR [voir Howard 2012, 48] et ne montre pas que l'article EPR fait apparaître la contextualité comme étant un élément central de la pensée de Bohr. Pour ces deux raisons, et en dépit de son intérêt par ailleurs, [Howard 2012] ne met pas en évidence que la thèse de la contextualité est la source d'une difficulté systématique de Popper à restituer les thèses de Bohr.

of Bell's inequalities, *Physical Review Letters*, 49, 91–94, doi : 10.1103/PhysRevLett.49.91.

BÄCHTOLD, Manuel [2008], *L'Interprétation de la mécanique quantique. Une approche pragmatiste*, Vision des sciences, Paris : Hermann.

BITBOL, Michel [1996], *Mécanique quantique. Une introduction philosophique*, Paris : Flammarion.

BOHR, Niels [1929], *La Théorie atomique et la description des phénomènes*, Paris : Gauthier-Villars, *Atomteori og Naturbeskrivelse*, Copenhague : L. Bogtrykkeri, 1932. Trad. fr. par A. Legros et L. Rosenfeld (à partir de la version allemande du texte), rééd. Sceaux : Éditions Jacques Gabay, 1993. La pagination de nos citations correspond à l'édition française.

—— [1935*a*], Can quantum-mechanical description of physical reality be considered complete ?, *Phys. Rev.*, 48, 696–702, doi : 10.1103/PhysRev.48.696, trad. fr. dans [Bohr 1991]. La pagination de nos citations correspond à la traduction française.

—— [1935*b*], Quantum mechanics and physical reality, *Nature*, 136(3428), 65–65, doi : 10.1038/136065a0, trad. fr. dans [Bohr 1991]. La pagination de nos citations correspond à la traduction française.

—— [1949], Discussions with Einstein on epistemological problems in atomic physics, in : *Albert Einstein : Philosopher-Scientist*, edited by P. Schilpp, Cambridge : Cambridge University Press, 202–241, trad.fr. dans [Bohr 1991] ; la pagination de nos citations correspond à la traduction française.

—— [1991], *Physique atomique et connaissance humaine*, Folio, Paris : Gallimard, trad. fr., introd. et annot. par C. Chevalley.

BORN, Max [1949], *Natural Philosophy of Cause and Change*, Oxford : Clarendon Press.

CHEVALLEY, Catherine [1991], *Physique atomique et connaissance humaine*, Paris : Gallimard, chap. Introduction : le dessin et la couleur, 17–140.

D'ESPAGNAT, Bernard [1994], *Le Réel voilé ; analyse des concepts quantiques*, Paris : Fayard.

EINSTEIN, Albert, PODOLSKY, Boris, *et al.* [1935], Can quantum-mechanical description of physical reality be considered complete ?, *Phys. Rev.*, 47, 777–780, doi : 10.1103/PhysRev.47.777, repris dans Einstein, A., 1989, *Œuvres choisies*, 5 vol., éd. par F. Balibar, O. Darrigol & B. Jech , Paris : Seuil. La pagination de nos citations correspond à l'édition française.

FAYE, Jan [1991], *Niels Bohr : His Heritage and Legacy. An Anti-Realist View of Quantum Mechanics*, Dordrecht : Kluwer.

FEYERABEND, Paul K. [1969], On a recent critique of complementarity : Part II, *Philosophy of Science*, 36(1), 82–105, doi : 10.1086/288238.

FINE, Arthur [2020], The Einstein-Podolsky-Rosen Argument in quantum theory, in : *The Stanford Encyclopedia of Philosophy*, edited by E. N. Zalta, Metaphysics Research Lab, Stanford University, Summer 2020 edn., URL https://plato.stanford.edu/archives/sum2020/entries/qt-epr/.

HEISENBERG, Werner [1927], Über den anschaulichen Inhalt der quantentheoretischen Kinematik und Mechanik, *Zeitschrift für Physik*, 43(3), 172–198, doi : 10.1007/BF01397280.

HOWARD, Don [2004], Who invented the "Copenhagen Interpretation"? A Study in mythology, *Philosophy of Science*, 71(5), 669–682, doi : 10.1086/425941.

—— [2012], Popper and Bohr on realism in quantum mechanics, *Quanta*, 1(1), 33–57, doi : 10.12743/quanta.v1i1.9.

LÉVY-LEBLOND, Jean-Marc & BALIBAR, Françoise [1998], Answer to question #62. When did the indeterminacy principle become the uncertainty principle?, *American Journal of Physics*, 66(4), 279–280, doi : 10.1119/1.18873.

PAULI, Wolfgang [1954], Wahrscheinlichkeit und Physik, *Dialectica*, 8(2), 112–124, doi : 10.1111/j.1746-8361.1954.tb01125.x.

PERES, Asher [2002], Karl Popper and the Copenhagen interpretation, *Studies in History and Philosophy of Science Part B*, 33(1), 23–34, doi : 10.1016/S1355-2198(01)00034-X.

POINAT, Sébastien [2014], *Mécanique quantique : du formalisme mathématique au concept philosophique*, Visions des sciences, Paris : Hermann, préface par J. Benoist.

POPPER, Karl [1934], *Logik der Forschung*, Vienne : Springer, trad. fr. par N. Thyssen-Rutten & P. Devaux, *La Logique de la découverte scientifique*, Paris : Payot, 1973 (avec les appendices).

—— [1982], *The Postscript to The Logic of Scientific Discovery, III*, Londres : Hutchinson and Company, trad. fr. par E. Malolo Dissakè, *La Théorie quantique et le schisme en physique*, Paris : Hermann, 1996.

—— [1990], *A World of Propensities*, Bristol : Thoemass Antiquarian Books, trad. fr. par A. Boyer, *Un univers de propensions*, Combas : L'Éclat.

REDHEAD, Michael [1995], Popper and the quantum theory, in : *Karl Popper : Philosophy and Problems*, edited by A. O'Hear, Cambridge : Cambridge University Press, 163–176.

SHIELDS, William [2012], A historical survey of Sir Karl Popper's contribution to quantum mechanics, *Quanta*, 1(1), 1–12, doi : 10.12743/quanta.v1i1.4.

VON NEUMAN, John [1955], *Mathematical Foundations of Quantum Mechanics*, Princeton : Princeton University Press.

Adresses des auteurs

Enrico Berti

Padoue – Italie
enrico.berti@unipd.it

Viktor Blåsjö

Mathematical Institute
Utrecht University
P.O. Box 80010
3508 TA Utrecht – The Netherlands
v.n.e.blasjo@uu.nl

Jean Christianidis

University of Athens
Department of History and Philosophy of Science
University Campus
15771, Athens – Greece
ichrist@phs.uoa.gr

Sébastien Gandon

Centre Philosophies et Rationalités (PHIER)
Maison des sciences de l'homme
4, rue Ledru
63057 Clermont-Ferrand Cedex 1 – France
sebastien.gandon@uca.fr

François Loget

Université de Limoges – INSPE
Campus Condorcet
209, Boulevard Vanteaux
87036 Limoges – France
francois.loget@unilim.fr

Gianluca Longa

Centre Philosophies et Rationalités (PHIER)
Maison des sciences de l'homme
4, rue Ledru
63057 Clermont-Ferrand Cedex 1 – France
gianluca.longa@uca.fr

Marco Panza

IHPST
13, rue du Four
75006, Paris – France
marco.panza@univ-paris1.fr

Ken Saito

Hokkaido – Japan
ksaito@joy.hi-ho.ne.jp

Sébastien Poinat

Université Côte d'Azur
Centre de Recherches en Histoire des Idées (CRHI)
ESPE de l'Académie de Nice
89, ave George V 06046 Nice Cedex 1 – France
Sebastien.POINAT@univ-cotedazur.fr

ABONNEMENT

Philosophia Scientiæ

Travaux d'histoire des sciences et de philosophie

Revue périodique publiée par les

Archives Henri-Poincaré

Philosophie et Recherches sur les Sciences et les Technologies

UMR 7117 CNRS – Université de Lorraine – Université de Strasbourg

Je m'abonne à *Philosophia Scientiæ*

à partir du volume : ....

Nom : ....

Prénom : ....

Institut ou bibliothèque : ....

Adresse : ....

Code postal : .... Ville : ....

Règlement joint à la commande à l'ordre des Éditions Kimé.

Date : ....

Signature : ....

Prix du numéro 24 €

L'abonnement annuel couvre 3 numéros

Tarif France 65 €

Tarif étranger 70 €

Pour vous abonner remplissez ce bulletin et renvoyez-le à l'adresse suivante :

ÉDITIONS KIMÉ
2, Impasse des Peintres
75002 Paris

Achevé d'imprimer en octobre 2021 par

Créaprojet

N° d'impression : 161160

Imprimé en France